UNDERSTANDING MODERN GOVERNMENT

The Rise and Decline of the
American Political Economy

UNDERSTANDING MODERN GOVERNMENT
The Rise and Decline of the
American Political Economy

Edward S. Greenberg

University of Colorado at Boulder

JOHN WILEY & SONS

New York   Chichester   Brisbane   Toronto

Library of Congress Cataloging in Publication Data:

Greenberg, Edward S   1942–
   Understanding modern government.

   Includes index.
   1. Business and politics–United States.
2. Industry and state–United States. I. Title.

JK467.G735   322'.3'0973   78-10104
ISBN 0-471-02913-0 pbk.
ISBN 0-471-32487-6

Printed in the United States of America

10 9 8 7 6 5 4 3 2 1

PREFACE

Intention and execution do not consistently coincide, an observation that is particularly appropriate in the case of the present work. What began as a simple effort to prepare a revised edition of *Serving the Few: Corporate Capitalism and The Bias of Government Policy,* primarily by updating materials, ended as a closely related yet vastly different book. *Serving the Few* represented an attempt to describe the many ways in which government spending, taxing, and regulatory activities contribute to inequality and, consequently, made government a powerful force for the maintenance of a social class system mainly derived from the operations of a capitalist market economy. I remain convinced that *Serving the Few* helped its readers better understand the reality of modern government by closely describing the implications of a wide range of governmental policies. However, it remained description and not explanation and, from my point of view, inherently limited and unsatisfactory.

As I grappled with the problem of how to best revise the earlier work, I found my attention continually drawn to those bits and pieces of explanation that existed in scattered and embryonic form in *Serving the Few.* As I began to rethink, to expand, and to integrate these fragments, I came to the perhaps presumptuous conclusion that it was necessary and possible to formulate an overall, theoretically convincing explanation for the development of what I have called the modern positive state, as well as reasoned judgments about its future. What I wanted to explain, first to myself and then to my readers, is why modern government does what it does. How is it that government acts as the main prop to corporate capitalism and its most powerful elements and not, as is conventionally argued by neoconservatives, as the helpmate of the weakest and worst-off elements of our population? What developments in capitalism as a system of production and exchange have been most responsible for the molding of the contours of government policy in general, and what do such developments portend for the future? It is to these and closely related questions that I found myself drawn, and as I devoted my attention to them, what gradually emerged, much to my surprise (and to that of my editor at John Wiley, I must ruefully admit), was a new work, closely and intimately related to *Serving the Few,* but of a different character. In effect, the present work might best be seen as an explanatory sequel to *Serving the Few,* or better still, as the second half of a hithertofore incomplete two part book. I have found the necessity of including a great deal of material from *Serving the Few* unavoidable, nevertheless, this work moves well beyond the earlier one in a theoretical sense. Whether the resulting explanatory product proves to be convincing is another matter entirely, a judgment that I leave to the reader.

The sources of stimulation for any scholarly endeavor are always sufficiently subtle, complex, and wide ranging, that I hesitate to attempt to acknowledge all of my debts in this brief space. Nevertheless, and entirely mindful of the pitfalls involved, I would like to acknowledge the influence of the work of Perry Anderson, Gabriel Kolko, Ernst Mandel, Nicos Poulantzas, and Emmanuel Wallerstein; the many stimulating exchanges with members of the "Friday Group" at the University of Colorado (particularly Martha Gimenez and Tom Mayer); and the casual yet provocative methodological remarks made by Professor Joel Samoff of the University of Michigan at an APSA panel several years ago. Needless to say, none of these people can be held even remotely responsible for what follows.

Finally, I would like to thank Jean Umbreit for her many hours of typing from nearly illegible handwritten sheets. This is by no means the first time she has rendered such an important service, and I venture the hope it will not be the last.

Boulder, Colorado   EDWARD S. GREENBERG
August 1978

CONTENTS

1. On the Troublesome Problems of Size and Bias in Modern
   Government: Some Popular Explanations   1

2. Toward a Theoretical Understanding of the Modern State   29

3. On the Construction of the Modern Positive State: Part 1   47

4. On the Construction of the Modern Positive State: Part 2   70

5. The Structure of Mature Capitalism   92

6. The Modern Positive State   126

7. The Promise and the Threat of Late Capitalism   159

   Index   191

UNDERSTANDING MODERN GOVERNMENT
The Rise and Decline of the American Political Economy

1
ON THE TROUBLESOME PROBLEMS OF SIZE AND BIAS IN MODERN GOVERNMENT: SOME POPULAR EXPLANATIONS

Americans no longer seem able to make much sense of their government. In the view of many, government seems to have literally run amok. Complaints about a wide range of government programs, procedures, policies, and abuses are today commonplace and reflect a generally declining sense of confidence in government and in public officials. The litany of complaints—about government size, cost, inefficiency, bias, intrusion on rights, and the like—come from a surprisingly wide range of opinion and find articulation in everyday conversation as well as in reasoned argumentation from representatives of the political Left and political Right. For the most part, however, these complaints remain fragmented, intellectually undeveloped, unarticulated with each other, and devoid of convincing theoretical content. While the multitude of governmental activities and policies that have given rise to these complaints have been extensively documented and described, they have hardly begun to be adequately explained in a fashion that is both theoretically convincing and popularly comprehensible. Any such explanation, in our view, would have to be able to link ongoing government activities with a theoretical understanding of the genesis and development of modern government as well as with the ability to chart likely future developments. This book attempts to reach such a theoretical understanding of modern government in the United States, a theoretical understanding that, we would argue, is only possible by grounding governmental and political processes within the context of an understanding of

American capitalism, especially its laws of motion and transformations. We shall turn to the explication of the elements of such a theoretical framework in the next chapter. For now, however, let us focus on the most persistent of the generally heard complaints about modern government in the United States—namely, its size, growth, and cost—and describe the most widely voiced explanations for these developments. Here and in the remainder of this book, we shall try to demonstrate the degree to which conventional explanations are limited, unconvincing, and theoretically deficient, and therefore inadequate as a guide for the American people as they try to come to grips with their own political situation and, perhaps, to change it.

ON GOVERNMENT SIZE AND GROWTH

Government in the United States has grown so enormously and transformed its activities to such an extent over the past several decades that it is barely recognizable to many Americans. It has become for many citizens the object of concern and even alarm, for the process of growth and transformation seems to them destined to continue unabated into the foreseeable future. George Wallace, in his characteristically blunt fashion, has perhaps best articulated the feelings of his compatriots in the following pithy remarks made to delegates at the 1976 Democratic Convention: "The monster bureaucracy is driving people in this country nuts. It should get off their backs and out of their pocketbooks."

Very much the same mood was evident at the Republican Convention. Note the preamble to the 1976 Republican platform.

> The Democratic platform repeats the same thing on every page— more government, more spending, more inflation. Compare. The Republican platform says exactly the opposite—less government, less spending, less inflation. In other words, we want you to retain more of your own money, money that represents the worth of your labors, to use as you see fit for the necessities and conveniences of life.

Hardly stirring words, they closely articulate the popular fears of government expansion. The same theme was posed more dramatically by Senator Howard Baker in his keynote address to that same convention.

> The issue this year isn't virtue. It isn't love or patriotism or compassion. These are the common concerns of all of us, regardless of party. Rather, the issue is "How much government is too much

government? How many laws are too many laws? How much taxa-tion is too much taxation? How much coercion is too much co-ercion?"

One might certainly argue that such perspectives have long been the domain of the Republican party and its right wing, and that such senti-ments do not reflect new developments of any consequence. Yet, there appears to be increasing evidence that the fears expressed by these tradi-tional foes of "big government" have become the common parlance of a large majority of the American people. One can see this development affirmed, for instance, in the expression of popular attitudes tapped by the ubiquitous opinion polls of Gallup or Harris. Or one might find it in the popularity of such "anti-big-government" Democratic politicians as Jimmy Carter[1] and California Governor Jerry Brown, both of whom built their election campaigns around "anti-Washington" and "government can't do everything" themes. Indeed, during the 1976 campaign, it behooved most politicians to don anti-Washington camouflage no matter what other political coloration they might be wearing for that season. One senses, then, a new popular resonance with those fears so long articulated by such free-market theorists as Ayn Rand, Milton Friedman, Frederick Hayek, and James Buchanan, thinkers long convinced that the growth of govern-ment means the end of the free market, the imposition of mass conform-ity, the decline of individualism, the loss of creativity and the growth of the stranglehold of mindless bureaucracy; in short, the loss of freedom and the beginning of that journey on the road to serfdom.[2]

The Size of the Federal Government

In fact, the popular mood is a response to a very real development—name-ly, the enormous, nay explosive growth of governmental activities over the past handful of decades. Adam Smith, John Locke, Thomas Jefferson, Herbert Spencer and other antistatists of the past three centuries would no doubt be horrified by developments if they could visit the contemporary American republic. Instead of the passive agency they had envisioned, they would see a government that has become an active, potent engine of society that touches on almost every facet of the lives of Americans. They would see a modern "positive state"[3] that regulates business and the economy in general; that provides welfare payments to the poor and dis-abled; that regulates labor-management relations; that distributes monthly payments to the elderly; that owns vast quantities of land, equipment, and

Table 1-1 Governmental Expenditures in the United States, Federal, State, and Local (rounded off in billions)

1932	12
1940	20
1950	70
1960	151
1970	333
1974	480
1975	557

Source: U.S. Bureau of the Census, *Statistical Abstracts of the United States* (Washington, D. C.: U.S. Government Printing Office, 1971 and 1977).

Table 1-2 Government Employment in the United States (all governments)

	Government Labor Force (in thousands)	Ratio of Government Workers to Persons in Population
1870	265	1:150
1900	1,401	1:54
1920	2,920	1:36
1940	4,902	1:27
1949	7,559	1:20
1952	10,697	1:15
1972	16,052	1:13

Source: Roger Freeman, *The Growth of American Government* (Stanford: Hoover Institution Press, 1975), p. 203.

plants; that helps educate the nation's children; that regulates communications and commerce; that undertakes vast explorations in outerspace and under the seas; and that takes for public use a healthy portion of every working American's paycheck. What they would see in all of these diverse governmental activities, mostly products of this century, is nothing less than a revolution in the tasks, goals, and functions of the American state.

One may gain a better sense of these vast changes by looking at a number of simple indicators of growth in governmental activities. Take the matter of government expenditures, for instance. Table 1-1 indicates nothing less than a fortyfold increase in government expenditures since 1932!

Another useful indicator of the expansion of the public sector is the increase in the number of people employed by all levels of government in the United States (Table 1-2. The figures would be more startling, one

Table 1-3   Debt Outstanding by all Levels of
Government (in $ billions)

1950	281
1955	319
1960	356
1965	417
1970	514
1974	693
1975	765

Source: *Statistical Abstracts of the United States*
(Washington, D.C.: U.S. Government Printing Office, 1977).

should note, were we to add to the totals those persons who, while not
directly employed by government, are largely dependent upon government
expenditures. The defense industry, of course, is the most obvious sector
of the economy where this is the case.

As one might easily guess, the vast increases in program indicated by
the figures on employment and expenditure has been accompanied by a
multiplication of governmental debt (see Table 1-3), a development viewed
with growing uneasiness by most Americans.

The Tradition of Limited Government
Much of the uneasiness about the growth in both the size and function
of government in the United States can be traced to the contradiction that
these developments represent in relation to traditional and familiar American notions about the proper role of government in a democratic society.
For at least the first century of its existence as a nation, the United
States was dominated by a view of government activities derived primarily
from the laissez-faire tradition in political economy. Although the theory
was often violated in practice by government in the United States, most
Americans tended to hold to the position that the state "governs best that
governs least." Government was distrusted by a people that had recently
thrown off the shackles of the English monarchy and its centrally directed
mercantilist economic system. Government was, to most Americans, a
necessary evil, good only for insurance against external threats to nation-
hood and internal threats to property and, as a necessary evil, its duties
were perceived to be extremely narrow and circumscribed. To do more,
to turn the reins of government over to idealists so as to alter the social

order for the common good, was seen as nothing less than an invitation to the subversion of liberty. While government was seen as necessary for the preservation of a social order in which people were free to pursue their self-interest, it was perceived at the same time as a threat to the practice of that very freedom, and not to be trusted. The concrete manifestations of this point of view were seen most clearly in the Declaration of Independence, the Articles of Confederation, the strictures on state executives, and the provisions for the separation of powers in the Constitution of 1789. The notion that government should be the tool by which society ministers to the needs of the less fortunate or regulates economic life was foreign to the thinking of the period.[4] In short, the proper stance of the state was seen as passive and limited. This strongly felt attitude was buttressed, no doubt, by the fact that America in the late eighteenth and early nineteenth centuries was characterized by small-scale agriculture, widespread property ownership, and the absence, relative to the modern era, of severe and widespread maldistributions in wealth and income.[5] In short, laissez-faire theory was buttressed by its consistency with the conditions of American life, conditions that hardly called for a positive, interventionist national government.[6]

This antistatist point of view had many roots, being the amalgamation of several seventeenth- and eighteenth-century streams of thought. One stream was the Protestant Reformation which signalled not only a split with the universal Catholic church, but a renewed emphasis on the individual and individualism. The main impact of the Reformation (and America was largely populated in its early days by Protestant participants and victims of the religious struggles of that age) was to emphasize the possibility, indeed the necessity, of individual salvation and regeneration. While it is not at all clear that the leading figures of the Reformation held to such an intention, the ultimate result of the break from Catholic order, community, and hierarchy was the questioning of all order, legitimacy, and hierarchy in the name of individual search, salvation, and fulfillment. In its most extreme form, as formulated by Thoreau, this individualism came close to its logical antistatist conclusion, anarchism.

Another antistatist stream derived from natural law theory, a world view that dominated eighteenth-century political thought. It stressed the existence of a natural order in the world that transcended, in both moral and scientific terms, [artificially constructed] government, and that natural order served, consequently, as a moral and scientific limitation upon its activity. The widely read works of the English philosopher John Locke encouraged American leaders to believe that governments were institutions with limited areas of legitimate activity, activity that could not intrude upon the rights held by people derived from natural law. In fact, Locke and the early leaders of the American republic believed that the only legitimate activity of government was to secure and protect those rights, and that any government that transgressed these limits had forfeited its right to command the obedience and allegiance of its citizens. This line of thinking is seen most clearly, of course, in the Declaration of Independence with its statement of the theory ("all men are endowed by their creator with unalienable rights," and "governments are instituted among men, deriving their just powers from the consent of the governed—that whenever any form of government becomes destructive of these ends, it is the right of the people to abolish it . . . .") and its cataloging of the repeated violation of natural rights by the English monarch.

Perhaps the most important impetus to antistatism came, however, from the economic interests and demands of the newly emerging commercial middle class in the late feudal period. These interests and demands were expressed most articulately by the French physiocrats and the Scottish parson, Adam Smith,[7] who directed their criticisms against *mercantilism* (the dominant economic organization of western European nations), an economic system that sought for each nation the maximum accumulation of gold and, to that end, attempted to control all aspects of economic activity, particularly commerce. This tight reign on commercial activities by the sovereign was rightly seen as a fetter upon the activities of a new and increasingly powerful class of merchants, financiers, and industrialists—a class that Karl Marx later came to call the bourgeoisie. In the name of this emerging class, the physiocrats and Adam Smith called for the end of mercantile restrictions and for the institution of a policy of free and unrestrained trade. They based their proposals on what they described as a natural law of economic life whereby the common good was secured through a system in which each person pursued his or her own selfish interest. Each person, according to Smith, was "led by an invisible hand to promote an end (the common good) which was no part of his intention."

Most important, since there exists a natural law of economic life in this view, intervention by the state could only serve to interfere with the wondorous workings of nature. As paradoxical as it might seem to the mercantilists, Smith and his contemporaries contended that the wealth of nations was increased to the extent that the state left the commercial system free to pursue its own logic. The intervention of monarchs to expand national wealth only served to interfere with the intended goal. Armed with such a theory about the relationship of state and economy, the emerging capitalist class gained intellectual and even moral legitimacy for its self-interested struggles and freed itself for the task of capital accumulation and expansion.

With the development of these lines of economic thought, an important addition had been made to the laissez-faire notion of government. Government had long been seen by proponents of this view as inherently coercive, and it followed that human freedom was enhanced to the extent that government removed itself from the field, merged into the background, and acted as guarantor of the larger game but not as an active participant. What the laissez-faire economic theorists added to this notion was the argument that freedom in the economic sphere, the removal of government from economic policy making, was sound and rational social policy, as well. Freedom and rationality were both served, therefore, by a minimalist government.

Seventeenth- and eighteenth-century political thought in the West, especially in England, came to be dominated by natural law theory, *laissez-faire,* and Protestant individualism. The English who populated the New World came armed with such an antistate perspective that was only enhanced and concretized by the conditions of the new society.

In America, at the end of the eighteenth century, the view of the state as destined to be a passive, limited, and circumscribed one swept aside all other contenders. As early as 1800, laissez-faire antistatism had become an article of faith,[8] even approaching official ideology, an ideology so powerful that, despite exceptions to the contrary (e.g., internal improvements and the Louisiana purchase), the federal government remained small, passive, and relatively noninterventionist. The laissez-faire theory of the state, then, has both normative and empirical aspects. That is, it expressed how the commercial class thought ideal governments ought to act, and it also very closely described the level of activities of the federal government from about 1789 to 1860.

Interestingly enough, the most extreme statement of this perspective of the state in America came at that moment in history when the industrial revolution was generating the very conditions that would require governments to behave in radically different ways. At the moment in American history when antistatism enjoyed its highest acclaim, forces were at work to make the theory seemingly obsolete.

The most influential and popular antistatist of the period (roughly in the 1880s) was the Englishman Herbert Spencer who merged traditional laissez-faire economic doctrine with the new Darwinian biology, a synthesis that came to be called Social Darwinism.[9] To Spencer, science had discovered that the natural law of social life was that of competition generated from self-interest; out of such a struggle, the best and fittest elements of society triumphed, and the lazy, the feebleminded, and the criminal fell by the wayside. Although superficially a cruel and harsh system, to Spencer and his compatriots it was the only way that society, like nature, assured itself of the continued production of the fit (the talented, the ambitious and the meritorious), and of the gradual but inexorable disappearance of the unfit.

To Spencer and other Social Darwinists, unfettered competition and the survival of the fittest were the laws of nature, and it behooved statesmen to refrain from any interference in social and economic life. At best, any state intervention to soften or deflect the laws of nature could only fail; at worst such interference was both arrogant and dangerous. They vigorously opposed "poor laws" (what we now call welfare), because such laws interfered with the natural processes by which society purifies itself. Many even opposed public health measures for the same reason. The sociologist William Graham Sumner summarized his views about the proper functions of government with the following inelegant yet cogent observation.

> *Here we are then once again back at the old doctrine*—Laissez-Faire. *Let us translate it into blunt English, and it will read, mind your own business. It is nothing but the doctrine of liberty. Let every man be happy in his own way.*[10]

This traditional view of the necessity of limited government remains surprisingly vigorous. While the United States is no longer a society of small-scale agriculture, widespread property ownership, and minimal stratification so conducive to an inactive, passive state (but is, in fact, a nation of industrial employment, giant corporations, teeming cities, and class inequality), the laissez-faire conception of government remains one of the stock beliefs of Americans. Even while government looks decreasingly less like the ideal, the ideal is continuously reaffirmed. One must be struck, for instance, by the free-market rhetoric of American politicians, Republican and Democrat; by the articulation of the small government

ideal in popular culture; by the expressed fears of a powerful government
from all points of the political spectrum; and by the honored position of
free-market intellectuals.

Perhaps the best known modern statement of the free-market/limited
government ideal is that of Nobel prize winning economist Milton Friedman. The theme of his enormously popular *Capitalism and Freedom* is the
necessary relationship between a free-market economy, a strictly delimited
and decentralized government, and the attainment of human freedom.
Note the following position:

> *Viewed as a means to the end of political freedom, economic arrange-
> ments are important because of their effect on the concentration or
> dispersion of power. The kind of economic organization that pro-
> vides economic freedom directly, namely, competitive capitalism,
> also promotes political freedom because it separates economic power
> from political power and in this way enables the one to offset the
> other.*
>
> *Historical evidence speaks with a single voice on the relation be-
> tween political freedom and a free market. I know of no example in
> time or place of a society that has been marked by a large measure
> of political freedom, and that has not also used something compar-
> able to a free market to organize the bulk of economic activity.*[11]

In Friedman's view, government retains an important role in keeping the
competitive market place and its twin, the competitive society, from falling into an anarchistic disorder harmful to the rights and liberties of all,
but the role is a strictly delimited one.

> *A government which maintained law and order, defined property
> rights, served as a means whereby we could modify property rights
> and other rules of the economic game, adjudicated disputes about
> the interpretation of the rules, enforced contracts, promoted com-
> petition, provided a monetary framework, engaged in activities to
> counter technical monopolies and to overcome neighborhood effects
> widely regarded as sufficiently important to justify government in-
> tervention, and which supplemented private charity and the private
> family in protecting the irresponsible, whether madman or child—
> such a government would clearly have important functions to per-
> form. The consistent liberal is not an anarchist.*
>
> *Yet it is also true that such a government would have clearly lim-
> ited functions and would refrain from a host of activities that are
> now undertaken by federal and state governments in the United
> States, and their counterparts in other Western countries.*[12]

Such sentiments find continued and recurrent resonance among many Americans, including many of those who do not necessarily define themselves as conservatives. Indeed, while not as articulately expressed, views like those of Friedman form the bedrock of the ideological equipment of most Americans, and one of the starting points for popular notions about the proper role of government.

ON GOVERNMENT BIAS

Complaints about the operations of modern government in the United States are not confined to those which focus on its impressive growth in size and reach, however, though these complaints remain the most popular and widely articulated. A secondary though increasingly evident theme heard in recent years speaks to the existence of a persistent structural bias in governmental programs towards the needs and interests of the well-to-do and the privileged in American life. Behind the universalistic, nationalistic, and egalitarian rhetoric that accompanies almost every program, one finds a more sobering reality in which the vast financial, legal, and personnel resources of government are fairly consistently used to bolster the position of those persons and institutions already predominant in the private economy.

We know, for instance, that the primary dollar flow from the enormously swollen national defense budgets are directed primarily to the coffers of a relative handful of giant corporations and defense contractors, while federal subsidies flow to a wide range of industries, ranging from ship building to the aerospace industry. Federal regulatory commissions, instituted to protect the public interest against abuses from powerful and concentrated business enterprises (Interstate Commerce Commission, Federal Trade Commission, Civil Aeronautics Board, Federal Communications Commission, etc.) today almost universally serve to protect and advance the interests of the very groups they are charged to regulate. Despite a handful of housing programs directed toward the needs of the poor, the overwhelming effect of federal policy (mortgage and interest deductions on federal income taxes, as well as FHA lending practices) has been to subsidize the housing of middle- and upper-income groups. As to the progressive income tax, most people are now generally aware that its progressive character is seriously undermined by the barrage of tax breaks favorable to those wealthy in property—capital gains, income-splitting, tax-free bonds, interest payment deductions, accelerated depreciation allowances, and a host of others.

Unfortunately, these listings could be almost infinitely expanded. We are beginning to become aware of the fact, for instance, that the Social Security System, the pride of the New Deal and of reform liberalism, is in its overall effect one of the most regressive programs in the entire federal arsenal. Most importantly, its financing is built upon a taxing system that taxes a low wage earner at higher effective rates (taxation as a percentage of income) than that for the high wage earner. Agricultural subsidy programs of the federal government flow disproportionately to the largest farmers in the United States and help speed the process by which smaller farmers are driven off the land. Enormous increases in federal health care spending over the past decade, mainly through medicare and medicaid, while not doing much in the way of improving the health of the American people, has done admirably well in improving the financial health of doctors, hospitals, drug companies, and medical equipment manufacturers. The list could go on, ad infinitum, ad nauseam, but the point remains, we believe, unarguable. Its programs make the federal government one of the principal instrumentalities for the maintenance and stabilization of the entire system of inequality derived from the normal operations of the market economy.[13]

While this enumeration certainly does not exhaust the list of popular complaints, it should serve to establish the existence of a growing popular concern that government is increasingly unable to accomplish decent and humane outcomes with its swollen budgets and employment roles. The federal government seems neither efficient nor just. It cannot seem to satisfy the very expectations which called forth its heightened activity in the first place. Paradoxically, with enhanced size, penetration, and impact, government has experienced a simultaneous loss of respect and a decline in its legitimate authority. Corporate and financial leaders decry its inability to control inflation or establish an environment conducive to adequate capital accumulation. Labor leaders decry its inability to foster an economy that is capable of providing employment for all Americans. The poor and dissident scoff at its presentations to justice, and point to its class biases. And almost all elements of American society protest at the high costs of this decreasingly effective machinery.

ALTERNATIVE EXPLANATIONS
How have we arrived at such a state of affairs? How is it that in a society historically committed to a limited and relatively passive government, we have witnessed, primarily over the past one-hundred years, the rise of what some have called a new *Leviathan,* a government active and influential in

practically every sphere of social life? How is it that this Leviathan seems so helpless and inefficient before the tasks set for it? We believe that there is a way to explain these developments in a theoretically sophisticated, logically consistent, and empirically veriable manner, and in the next chapter we shall discuss the structure of such an explanation. However, it is important that we attempt, in as fair a manner as possible, to sketch out for the reader the most popular and influential alternative explanations for the rise, development, and ongoing operations of modern government in the United States. We do so not only so that the reader might sense the range of views that are available with respect to these problems, but also so that the reader might begin to grasp the extent to which each of these familiar views remains, despite an occasional glimmer of enlightenment, seriously wanting. Such an understanding will then serve to open the way toward a serious consideration of an alternative and unfamiliar perspective.

FREE-MARKET CONSERVATISM

We shall begin our consideration of alternative views on the growth and purpose of the positive state with that of free-market conservatism, a view that is at once the most popular and the most confused. In fact, while this aggregation of complaints, explanations, and nostrums seems loosely articulated and out of touch with larger developments in the social order, it retains, nevertheless, a significant following, articulates the deeply felt disquietude of many Americans, and points to a number of very real and important developments in modern American life, and is therefore worthy of further consideration.

The modern free-market conservatives are direct descendents, or perhaps, the historic residue, of the deeply ingrained American laissez-faire tradition. As we pointed out earlier, the proper function of government, in this view, is that of protector of individual rights, enforcer of the rules of the free market, and guarantor of public order. Since there is perceived to be a natural harmony and self-regulatory nature to market society, government tasks in the just society are to be strictly limited, lest rights be violated and irrationality and inefficiency be introduced into economic relations. By being held to such views, yet faced with the enormous expansion of government activities in the United States, and bereft of a theory that ties developments in the organization of capitalism to developments in state activities, free-market conservatives have been reduced to a desperate helter-skelter search for wrongdoers.

To Milton Friedman, Frederich Hayek, and James Buchanan, the root of our troubles can be traced to the strange reform-liberal notion popular among intellectuals, reformers, and government officials, that government might be an instrument for the alleviation of social distress and conflict, that it might be an instrument for social betterment. In the words of James Buchanan,

> *Burgeoning budgets are an outgrowth of the American liberal tradition which assigns to government the instrumental role in creating the "good society." The arrogance of the administrative and, particularly, the judicial elite in changing basic law by fiat arises from the same source. If the "good society" can first be defined, and, second, produced by governmental action, then men finding themselves in positions of discretionary power, whether in legislative, executive, or judicial roles, are placed under some moral obligation to move society toward the defined ideal.*[14]

While almost certainly a view held by well-intentioned people, the notion that government might play such a role flies squarely in the face of the assumptions of the free-market and the free-society, and thereby prepares the ground not only for the growth of government but for its correlate, the erosion of freedom and the growth of tyranny. As Hayek once put it, since tyranny is the inevitable result of any "deliberate organization of the labors of society for a definite social goal,"[15] any effort to push the activities of government beyond the minimum, even well-intentioned ones, prepares the ground for totalitarianism.

The origins of the notion that government might be more than minimalist in its activities are unclear. To some free-market conservatives the notion is quite simply the product of a combination of muddled thinking and bleeding hearts. To others, it is the product of the otherwise admirable American "can do" mentality. That is, when faced with a problem, Americans are likely to turn toward whatever works, to seek pragmatic solutions, and to ignore or consciously reject consistent theory or principle. To other free-market conservatives, the belief in the efficacy of governmental action in the social and economic spheres is primarily derived from the appeal that socialism has always held for intellectuals (for whatever reasons), and the revulsion most of them have felt for the materialism of capitalist society. Milton Friedman perhaps best summarizes the position of those who see modern government as the outcome of some curious combination of muddled thinking, misplaced aspirations, and socialist appeal.

In the 1920's and the 1930's, intellectuals in the United States were overwhelmingly persuaded that capitalism was a defective system inhibiting economic well-being and thereby freedom, and that the hope for the future lay in a greater measure of deliberate control by political authorities over economic affairs. The conversion of the intellectuals was not achieved by the example of any actual collectivist society, though it undoubtedly was much hastened by the establishment of a communist society in Russia and the glowing hopes placed in it. The conversion of the intellectuals was achieved by a comparison between the existing state of affairs, with all its injustices and defects, and a hypothetical state of affairs as it might be. The actual was compared with the ideal.[16]

To James Buchanan, an exponential expansion of government is all but inevitable in a democracy.[17] All of the major constituent elements of a democratic regime, in his view, point in a unidimensional direction toward such an expansion. He points out, for instance, that politicians are almost universally in favor of such trends, and he proposes a number of reasons why this might be so. From a psychological viewpoint, he argues that political life probably tends to attract people who like to make decisions that affect others, people who seek a larger stage on which to display their personal attributes. Instituting programs with a personal imprint is one of the best ways to play out such a drama. Furthermore, the objective self-interest of politicians points in the same direction, since election and reelection are heavily dependent upon the continued support of various interest groups, all of whom, at one time or another, seek government favors, preferences, and program support. Thus, those people and groups that politicians are most likely to hear from tend to favor expansion of government activities, not in the abstract but for some particularistic motive. As Buchanan so cogently puts the matter, "few natural anarchists or libertarians frequent capital cloakrooms."[18] The rational politician, it follows, does well to be responsive to these diverse, particularistic aspirations and tends to sponsor further expansion of state activities. Finally, to the extent that corruption is a lamentable but ever present feature of American political life, Buchanan adds that an expanded governmental budget leaves considerable leeway and opportunity for graft.

Once programs become operational, moreover, it is in the self-interest of bureaucrats to seek expansion of their agency program. Bureaucratic advancement, salary, working conditions, and morale are all tied to agency budget expansion. As Buchanan puts it, there is simply "little or no potential reward to the government employee who proposes to reduce or limit his own agency or bureau. Institutionally, the individual bureaucrat is motivated toward aggrandizement of his own agency."[19] The situation is made even more damaging, from his view, because as government employment increases, coterminous with program and budget increase, government employees become an ever more powerful voting bloc. They represent today a formidable and implacable foe of the concept of limited government.

Much of this has been made possible, from Buchanan's point of view, by the active derelection of constitutional duty by the federal judiciary. Rather than being the main protectors and guarantors of the basic structure of inviolable individual rights as they are charged to be by the constitutional tradition, federal judges have become not only a rubber stamp for Congressional and Executive program initiatives, but also active participants in the alteration of the structure of rights and the rewriting, without consent, of the American constitutional contract. He calls, in the end, for a reaffirmation of duty by members of the judiciary and a resurrection of their practice, long ignored, of placing limits upon government activity.

The free-market conservatives present a full if diverse cast of candidates for the villains of this piece, yet their main salvo, surprisingly, is reserved for the American people and their practice of democratic politics. The theme that runs throughout all of the writing of the free-market conservatives, wherever else they may disagree, is that the American people have come to expect too much and that they impose these expectations on government by virtue of the opportunity afforded by the democratic processes.

Whether free-market conservatives speak of "democracy unchained,"[20] "system overload,"[21] or the "democratic distemper,"[22] the mission of people who are committed to the preservation of freedom is to place limits upon the aspirations and expectations of the American people and to control in a variety of ways their willingness and ability to be active democratic participants. As neoconservative Sam Huntington so bluntly puts matters,[23]

> *Al Smith once remarked that "the only cure for the evils of democracy is more democracy." Our analysis suggests that applying that cure at the present time could well be adding fuel to the flames. Instead, some of the problems of governance in the United States today stem from an excess of democracy .... Needed, instead, is greater degree of moderation in democracy ... the effective opera-*

tion of a democratic political system usually requires some measure of apathy and noninvolvement on the part of some individuals and groups. In the past, every democratic society has had a marginal population, of greater or lesser size, which has not actively participated in politics. In itself, this marginality on the part of some groups is inherently undemocratic, but it has also been one of the factors which has enabled democracy to function effectively. Marginal social groups, as in the case of the blacks, are now becoming full participants in the political system. Yet the danger of overloading the political system with demands which extend its functions and undermine its authority still remains. Less marginality on the part of some groups thus needs to be replaced by more self-restraint on the part of all groups.

In the final analysis, the free-market conservative position is unsatisfying and unconvincing. While they react to some very real developments in modern life, their position is composed of little more than a wild flailing about after every conceivable villanous influence—human nature, democratic life, venal politicians, fuzzy-headed intellectuals, spoiled American citizens—and poignant reminiscences about and aspirations for a free-market society that never existed except in the imagination.[24] Given this unconnected mishmash of explanations, a failure to specify the nature of the relationships between the various elements, and the failure to connect the developments in governmental activity (which it deplores) to structural changes in American economic and social life, the free-market conservative stance remains theoretically underdeveloped, even childish. The reader, of course, ought not to be satisfied with such a minimal response on our part. We believe that the limitations of the free-market perspective, especially its inability to explain structural bias in government policy, will become more obvious in the course of this volume as we attempt to construct a convincing alternative explanation of modern government and its activities.

REFORM LIBERALISM

The main countervailing view to that of the free-market conservatives is what has been called *reform liberalism*. Unlike the position of the free-market conservatives, however, this perspective remains somewhat underdeveloped because of the absence of a set of founding thinkers—there being no equivalents to John Locke, Adam Smith, or even Herbert Spencer and Milton Friedman. This view, rather, has emerged over a long period out of the actual practices of government without being given sharp focus and definition anywhere along the line. Nevertheless, this view, or at least the bits and pieces that comprise this view, have been and remain popular and influential, and in the actual practice of American government since the 1930s, have been decisive. We shall attempt, having made these caveats, to construct a relatively coherent and concise description of the claims made by reform liberals out of these scattered bits of theory and practice.[25]

According to reform liberals, the best way to appreciate the basic meaning of the activities of the modern positive state is to see government as the instrument through which the whole community provides for its needs. Though imperfect, to be sure, government is the means by which the general welfare is served, by which the whole people provide themselves with the services unavailable to them through individual action, and by which they attempt to alleviate that set of problems always endemic to group life.

It has long been recognized (except, perhaps, by the free-market conservatives), that unregulated market economies are problematic for those who live and work within them. That is to say, the operations of an unrestricted market almost invariably produce a set of outcomes that are damaging to the bulk of the population and are subject to correction by reasonable people. Reform liberals usually point to four principal difficulties that require state action.[26] First is the problem of the abuse of property rights, the malicious or careless use of property which adversely affects others who cannot reasonably be expected to protect themselves. In response to this set of problems, reformers have counterposed statutes dealing with child labor, environmental pollution, public health, and hours and conditions of work, first, for women, and then for the remainder of the labor force. Second is the problem of the production of casualties of the industrial order, the vast numbers of people who, no longer useful to that order (the unskilled or the elderly), are discarded and left without resources. To this, reformers have counterposed old-age insurance, unemployment insurance, vocational education and retraining, and the like. Third, is the problem of cyclical fluctuation, the wild yet predictable swings that market society takes between periods of inflation and unemployment. To this, reformers have counterposed Keynesian fiscal and monetary policies,[27] and, occasionally, wage and price controls. The fourth and final problem is the concentration of capital, the ironic and all but inevitable outcome of free-market operations. In response to this problem, reformers have counterposed inconsistent yet well-meaning sets of policies ranging from trust-busting to government oversight and have asked for more regulation of large corporations.

To reform liberals, the modern state represents a middle road between the anarchy, waste, and destructiveness of unrestricted market society and the tyranny and unfreedom of totalitarian ones. In their view, the modern state is a device by which most of the cruelties of the market system are tempered while private property and liberty are conserved. It is the device by which capitalist economies are humanized and softened, and thus preserved. Thus, most reform liberals see the history of the twentieth-century capitalist nations as one in which the hardships of the poor have been lessened; in which the position of the worker has steadily improved; in which progressive tax systems have helped to redistribute wealth and income significantly; and where collective needs such as public health, education, and transportation have been provided for the general population. To be sure, few see the provisions of the positive state as perfect or complete. Most acknowledge that much remains to be done to improve the condition of the more disadvantaged sectors of the population. Indeed, many have even incorporated elements of the popular complaints about government abuses and inefficiencies and called for more careful regulation of government activities. None, however, doubt the basic commitment of western governments to the task of social betterment or the possibility that they may eventually accomplish their laudable goals.

Basically, the modern state, being the only institution in society without interests of its own, is seen as a mediator between classes, an unbiased entity that acts in the best interests of society as a whole. In particular, reform liberals argue, the positive state (composed in the United States of a myriad of programs from the Progressives, the New Deal, the Fair Deal, the New Frontier, and the Great Society) is the means by which the community deals with the harsh by-products of the industrial system, controls unchecked privilege, guarantees full employment, cares for the aged and disabled, supports the disadvantaged, and guarantees opportunity for minority group citizens.

In the United States, much of the groundwork for reform liberal measures was prepared by a branch of the Protestant church, proponents of what was commonly called "the *Social Gospel.*" While the Protestant church in America largely supported the strictures of the laissez-faire system, these "Social Christians," influential because of their education, their class position, and their wealth, attacked the roots of the laissez-faire system. In particular, they attacked competition, individualism, and self-interest as morally and ethically wayward, and called for a new society of cooperation, sharing, and self-sacrifice. In their broad-ranging and persistent attacks on the moral foundations of the laissez-faire system, these church leaders helped to prepare society for the period of reform that was to explode on the American scene after 1900.[28]

With the same sentiments as the church leaders, but with different methodologies and analytic tools, social scientists like Richard Ely, Henry Carter Adams, and John R. Commons also attacked laissez faire, arguing that conditions in laissez-faire society made the full development of individuals impossible. In calling for union-management collective bargaining, unemployment insurance, planning, social services and the like, these economists argued that the state would help both to institute Christian principles into society and to steer clear of the threat of socialism. The change from laissez-faire attitudes was perhaps most cogently expressed by Henry Carter Adams:

> *We do not need a new world or a new man . . . but we do need a new society and a state whose power will be superior to that of any combination of selfish individuals, and whose duties will be commensurate with human wants. That not the best government which governs* least, *but which governs the most wisely.*[29]

The political theory of the reform liberal perspective is more difficult to pin down, mainly because there are two major strands of thought. One of the strands emphasizes that the positive state is the product principally of the concern of political leadership for the welfare of citizens suffering under the blows of industrial advance, and points prominently to the compassion of national leaders like Robert LaFollette, Woodrow Wilson, Franklin Roosevelt, Robert Wagner, John Kennedy, and Lyndon Johnson. The other strand tends to emphasize the vote and democratic mass politics as the decisive ingredient in the construction of the positive state, arguing that "a democracy usually gets . . . the kind of government it wants."[30] In sum, while its major speakers are in general agreement about what the positive state looks like, agreement about the origins and driving political force of the positive state remains elusive.[31]

To reiterate the essence of their shared view, reform liberal theorists see the positive state as the unselfish instrument of the common welfare; as a system of government with a heart, if you will, designed to alleviate the suffering and hardship caused by industrial, commercial, and technological advances and changes. Although acknowledging that the system of services and benefits remains incomplete, they claim that the inexorable movement of public policy is toward the fulfillment of these laudable goals. They believe that challenge of public policy is to complete the merging of welfare aspirations and accomplishments, a process already well on the way to fruition, despite the existence of occasionally serious yet soluable problems.

PLURALISM

While the reform liberal and free-market conservative perspectives speak with reasonable assuredness to the issue of growth in governmental size, neither one is able, within the theoretical boundaries of its analysis, to adequately explain the persistent structural bias of government policy toward the most privileged and advantaged sectors of the American population. In fact, under the terms of each, one would expect to see the converse. Free-market conservatives, for instance, interpret the rise of large-scale government as the result, among other things, of popular pressures for government services, of the attractions of socialism for intellectuals and some politicians, and of a hostility to the free use of property. The expected outcome of such a confluence of forces would be for public policy to generally favor the *least* well-off members of society. While free-market conservatives believe this to be the case,[32] the empirical evidence, of course, points to the opposite conclusion: favoritism for the wealthy.[33] From the reform liberal perspective, with its view of government as the main healer of the social order and as the institutional expression of society's concern for those left out, harmed, or incapacitated by the operations of the market system, one would also expect public policy to favor the less fortunate rather than the converse. Both views, then, help to explain some aspects of the growth of modern government but remain utterly unable to shed light on the directions, commitments, and effects of overall government policy.

There remains another perspective, however, that is better able to speak to this issue, though it is also, we shall argue, inadequate as a general theory of modern government. We are referring to the perspective of the policy process favored by most practicing political scientists, namely *pluralism.*

As surprising as it may seem, in pluralist theory very little attention is explicitly paid to the role and function of modern governments. This is not to suggest, however, that pluralist social theorists lack a theory of the state. Quite to the contrary, although largely unstated, unacknowledged, and perhaps even unrecognized by some, a definite perspective of the state lies embedded in pluralism.[34] Some readers, in fact, may be made slightly uneasy by a discussion of theories of the state, primarily because the recent domination of western political thought by pluralism has largely eliminated the subject of the state from modern political discourse.

While the roots of the pluralist persepctive lie in the early American Republic, particularly in the work of James Madison in *The Federalist Papers,* the detailed construction of the theory that has come to dominate modern political science is primarily the work of two contemporary scholars, David Truman and Robert Dahl.[35] Although other scholars have contributed to this tradition, their work is largely built upon the impressive base laid by Truman and Dahl. What follows, then, is a synthesis of their points of view about politics and the state.

As James Madison pointed out in Federalist #10, any large, diverse society is characterized by many factions or groups. The phenomenon of group proliferation, as Truman ably demonstrates, is greatly enhanced and accelerated as society becomes more industrialized, urbanized, and populated by successive waves of immigrants.[36] In the contemporary United States, society is so complex that it fosters many groups, each with a distinct set of interests and goals. Indeed, Truman contends that it makes little sense to think of political society as a collection of isolated citizens, for empirically, like-minded individuals tend to gather together into groups to seek the fulfillment of their goals.

Since no modern society has as yet conquered the problem of scarcity, and since no society is able to satisfy the desires of all its population, groups contend for the available social benefits. It is in the struggle and interaction of these groups for scarce resources, both material and nonmaterial, that we see the essence of politics. In fact, according to Truman, politics is simply this group struggle. The state is embroiled in this struggle in essentially two ways: it is a collective body with the power to make binding decisions about the distribution of many social values. It consequently becomes the primary target for contending groups. Moreover, it is itself composed of many groups interacting with each other and with nongovernmental groups.

This picture of the state as a fragmented, internally competitive institution (or more correctly, a set of institutions) is a central feature of pluralist thinking.[37] It is readily apparent that if the state itself is fragmented, power is not concentrated anywhere. On most issues, the state tends to be, from the pluralist perspective, highly complex, fragmented, multidecisional, and multipower centered. The implications here are significant. Most important, since power is dispersed, not only in the state but in society in general (given its group nature), the danger of oppression and tyranny is greatly reduced, if not eliminated. As Robert Dahl states:

> *Because one center of power is set against another, power itself will be tamed, civilized, and limited to decent human purposes, while coercion, the most evil form of power, will be reduced to a minimum.*[38]

Furthermore, since the state is multifaceted and multipower centered, it tends to be porous and open to the variety of groups that exist in society. Governments in the United States, being so complex and internally contentious, are permeable and accessible. Pluralists claim that such permeability means, ultimately, that any legitimate social group can make its interests and opinions felt at some point in the decision-making process. No legitimate group can long be kept out of the decision-making process on major public policies, if it desires a part, and if it is capable of generating sufficient resources to sustain a bargaining position.

It would follow that given a society characterized by many groups holding different interests and goals, by dispersed power in both society and state, and by an open, permeable governmental apparatus, public policy must be the result of a complex process of bargaining and negotiation. There being no power sufficiently dominant to impose its will, policy tends to be the outcome of the combined power of temporary, bargained, majority coalitions. There are two important consequences of this imperative of policy formation. First, it ensures that public policy is *democratic,* since all interested groups are free to participate in the bargaining process at some point. Second, it implies that public policy, that which government does, is essentially the product of the perpetual contention and bargaining between groups. Government policy is a reflection of the balance of group forces at any given time in history.

This brings us to the pluralist theory of the state. That is, other than a general interest in preserving the basic ground rules of the bargaining process, the state has no *inherent* interests of its own. The state is nothing more than a neutral sounding board for the total society; it does not favor inherently any particular group or class. Its activities are simply the bargained outcomes of the political struggle. This does not mean that the state is at all times neutral—at any particular moment it favors the dom-

inant coalition—but it will be so in the long run, since the political process
and access to bargaining resources are open to all.

While this line of reasoning represents a distinct advance over free-
market conservatism and reform liberalism in its ability to explain bias in
government policy—policy being the outcome of majority group coalitions
in which the rich and powerful usually play a central role—it does so only
in the short run. In the long run, as we have pointed out, this perspective
leads to the expectation that public policy biases will tend to even out, to
favor no particular section of society, rich or poor, over another. Pluralism
remains deficient, then, as a theory to explain the general drift of modern
government and the social impact of its policies.

UNDERSTANDING MODERN GOVERNMENT AND ITS PURPOSES

In this chapter we have attempted to highlight some of the most puzzling
aspects of contemporary government in the United States, to raise for
consideration some of the issues that are troubling many Americans. This
contradiction between the traditional American ideal—a government both
limited and fair—and the contemporary reality—a government both imposing and biased—begs for an explanation. What are we to make of the
appearance of such a government within the bosom of a society holding a
divergent ideal of the proper role of government? How do we explain the
appearance of a government whose size, reach, penetration and impact go
far beyond the wildest imaginings of the founders of the American Republic? It is the purpose of this book to explore these questions and to
present a coherent and theoretically persuasive explanation for these
developments.

Our view will clash sharply with the explanations most familiar to
Americans, but we believe that the theoretical explanation presented in
these pages will be persuasive nonetheless. We are of the opinion that the
generally confused and contradictory explanations that dominate public
discussion and debate about the purposes and implications of modern
government are generally misdirected and misleading, and in the chapters
that follow, we hope to present a more logically convincing and politically
useful theoretical explanation, one that is capable of explaining both the
growth in government size and the direction of its commitments. What we
shall attempt to do, in sum, is to illuminate more accurately the meaning
of this revolution in state activities; to explain *what* government does with
this vast treasury and legion of employees, and *why* it does what it does.

It is our view that the perspectives presented in this chapter, namely free-market conservatism, reform liberalism, and pluralism, all of which in a rather confused and often contradictory manner get jumbled together in popular explanations of government, are seriously deficient as guides to understanding. Each, of course, has its legions of supporters and proponents, a phenomenon probably derived from the partial truths they each embody. Nevertheless, partial truths remain partial truths. We would argue that each of the perspectives suffers from a number of logical inconsistencies and explanatory deficiencies, as we have already pointed out. Their most serious shortcomings, however, relate to their curious ahistorical character and theoretical narrowness of vision. What is needed in coming to grips with modern government, in our view, is a perspective that takes as its points of departure both the richness, flux, and contradiction of historical change, and the interrelatedness of economic, social and political forces. We turn in the next chapter to the formulation of a theoretical perspective that fulfills these requirements. The remainder of the book is a test, in effect, of the extent to which this alternative theoretical perspective works; that is to say, a test of its ability to make the development and operation of the contemporary American state fully comprehensible.

NOTES

[1] During the 1976 Democratic convention platform meetings, Jimmy Carter's domestic issues advisor, Stuart Eisenstad, led a successful move to substitute the words "public service" for the words "governmental service" in that section of the platform committing the party "to making the U.S. Postal Service function properly as an essential governmental service." In support of this change, Eisenstad stated that Mr. Carter was not in favor of the creation of another government agency. See *Congressional Quarterly,* June 19, 1976, p. 1852.

[2] The loss of freedom is the central theme of Milton Friedman's perennially popular *Capitalism and Freedom* (Chicago: University of Chicago Press, 1962), while *The Road to Serfdom* is the title of Frederick Hayek's very influential polemic (Chicago: University of Chicago Press, 1944).

[3] "Positive state" is the general term we shall use to indicate the tendency of all modern capitalist governments to be active and interventionist to one degree or another, rather than inactive and passive. We use it in preference to the term "welfare state" which has too many emotional implications and is theoretically vague and undeveloped.

[4] There are some notable exceptions to this general point of view, the most prominent being that of Alexander Hamilton who proposed a commonwealth based on and directed by a partnership of government and industry.

[5] This holds true, however, only if one ignores the painful fact that a healthy proportion of the American population lived as slaves. These people not only owned no property, but also did not even own their own bodies.

[6] For a discussion of this point, see Sidney Fine, *Laissez-Faire and the General Welfare State* (Ann Arbor: University of Michigan Press, 1966). Much of what follows is based on this stimulating volume.

[7] On this point see two excellent books by C. B. MacPherson, *The Political Theory of Possessive Individualism* (Oxford: Clarendon Press, 1962) and *The Real World of Democracy* (Oxford: Clarendon Press, 1966).

[8] This is shown by the defeat of Hamilton's party, the Federalists, in the election of 1800.

[9] Again, much of the following discussion is based on Fine, *Laissez-Faire*.

[10] William Graham Sumner, *What Social Classes Owe to Each Other* (New York: Hayser and Brothers, 1883), p. 120.

[11] Friedman, *Capitalism and Freedom*, p. 9.

[12] Ibid., pp. 34, 35.

[13] For a complete discussion of these issues as well as extensive source references see Edward S. Greenberg, *Serving the Few: Corporate Capitalism and the Bias of Government Policy* (New York: John Wiley, 1974). Also see Edward S. Greenberg, *The American Political System: A Radical Analysis* (Cambridge: Winthrop, 1977).

[14] James M. Buchanan, *The Limits of Liberty: Between Anarchy and Leviathan* (Chicago: University of Chicago Press, 1975), p. 164.

[15] Frederich A. Hayek, *The Road to Serfdom* (Chicago: University of Chicago Press, 1944), p. 56.

[16] Friedman, *Capitalism and Freedom*, p. 196.

[17] See Buchanan's discussion in Chapter 9, "The Threat of Leviathan," in *The Limits of Liberty*.

[18] Ibid., p. 157.

[19] Ibid., p. 161.

[20] Ibid.

[21] See the discussion of the concept in Michel Crozier, "Western Europe," in Michel Crozier, Samuel P. Huntington, and Joji Watanuki, *The Crisis of Democracy: Report on the Governability of Democracies to the Trilateral Commission* (New York: New York University Press, 1975).

[22] Samuel Huntington, in *The Crisis of Democracy,* pp. 102–106. We shall have more to say about Huntington's views and their relationship to the crisis of the modern state in the final chapter.

[23] Ibid., p. 113. Professor Huntington seems to delight in making such provocative observations. He once praised the American saturation bombing of the South Vietnamese peasentry as a positive device for the urbanization and thus the modernization of that tragic country.

[24] For a summary of the history of the active state during theoretically laissez-faire periods, see Carter Goodrich, *The Government and the Economy* (Indianapolis: Bobbs-Merrill, 1967) and Alan Wolfe, *The Limits of Legitimacy: Political Contradictions of Contemporary Capitalism*) New York: Free Press, 1977), Chapter 1.

[25] This construction relies on the following works: Robert Eyestone, *Political Economy* (Chicago: Markham, 1972); Joyce M. Mitchell and William C. Mitchell, *Political Analysis and Public Policy* (Chicago: Rand-McNally, 1969); Paul Samuelson, *Economics* (New York: McGraw-Hill, 1970); Andrew Shonfield, *Modern Capitalism* (London: Oxford University Press, 1969); Clair Wilcox, *Towards Social Welfare* (Homewood, Illinois: R. D. Irwin, 1965); Harold Wilensky and Charles Lebeaux, *Industrial Society and Social Welfare* (New York: Free Press, 1965); and Harold Wilensky, *The Welfare State and Equality* (Berkeley: University of California Press, 1974). Again, the description that follows may not accord perfectly with the views of any of the above scholars, but we do hope that it *agrees substantially* with all of them.

[26] See Tilton and Furniss, *The Case for the Welfare State,* for discussion of these points.

[27] A subject to which we shall turn in a later chapter.

[28] For this story see Fine, *Laissez-Faire.*

[29] Ibid., p. 208.

[30] Samuelson, *Economics,* p. 143.

[31] The most myopic view is that of Harold Wilensky who sees the positive state as the natural and inevitable outcome of economic growth and demographic change. See Wilensky, *The Welfare State and Equality.*

[32] Note that free-market conservatives persistently criticize welfare cheats, food stamp hippies, and other "unworthy" recipients of government largesse.

[33] Refer again to Greenberg's, *Serving the Few* and *The American Political System.*

[34] This general insight is best expressed in Ralph Miliband, *The State in Capitalist Society* (New York: Basic Books, 1969).

[35] Both inspired by the work of Arthur Bentley, *The Process of Government* (Chicago: University of Chicago Press, 1908).

[36] David Truman, *The Governmental Process* (New York: Alfred Knopf, 1951), Chapter 1.

[37] See Robert Dahl, *A Preface to Democratic Theory* (Chicago: University of Chicago Press, 1956); Dahl, *Pluralist Democracy in the United States* (Chicago: Rand-McNally, 1967); Dahl, *Who Governs?* (New Haven: Yale University Press, 1961); Nelson Polsby, *Community Power and Political Theory* (New Haven: Yale University Press, 1967); Truman, *The Governmental Process.*

[38] Dahl, *Pluralist Democracy,* p. 10.

2
TOWARD A THEORETICAL UNDERSTANDING OF THE MODERN STATE

The central question to which this volume is addressed is how government in the United States came to look the way it does. We want to try to explain in a manner that is both intellectually satisfying and readily comprehensible how and why the federal government grew to such an imposing scale and came to use its complex and powerful machinery in such a systematically biased manner. In the previous chapter, we briefly reviewed two familiar ways of looking at these phenomena (free-market conservatism and reform liberalism), and one which, while not as familiar to the general population, remains the dominant view among practicing political scientists (pluralism), and found all of them wanting. None of the three views is capable, we would submit, in taking us very close to an understanding of modern government.

What is needed is a theory that can, within its framework, allow for the incorporation of the richness and complexity of social interactions in general, as well as for the dynamics of historical development. We need a theory that is capable of encompassing the rich panopoly of forces—economic, social, political, and cultural—that interact over time and produce institutional change and transformation. We need a theory that is, in some sense, as complex, as interactive, as global as historical development itself. We believe that only Marxist social theory is capable of fulfilling these requirements, and as such, offers us the best single set of tools for understanding the genesis, development, and ongoing practices of modern government.

We shall call this specific set of intellectual tools the *Marxist theory of the state,* and in the remaining pages of this chapter, we shall attempt to describe this theory in a way that is analytically useful. We will then turn, in the chapters that follow, to the actual use of this theory on the materials of historical and contemporary government, and attempt to demonstrate how it, in relationship to alternative theories, gives us the best handle for understanding the development of American public policy during the course of the twentieth century.

Now there exists no scientific way, given the state of the art and the nature of the issues, to either absolutely "prove" or "disprove" the validity of the theoretical perspective we shall present or, for that matter, any other theoretical perspective. All one can reasonably hope is that our analysis helps the reader to more easily grasp the complexities of the modern state, the implications of its activities, the dynamics of its development, and the possible future direction of its activities. It will be entirely up to the reader to judge the degree to which the use of this theory helps make the American "positive state" a more understandable set of social institutions by organizing complex materials in theoretically and experientially convincing ways, by making sense of observed empirical materials, and by accounting for seemingly anomalous, unconnected, and diverse phenomena. With that said, let us turn to the explication of the Marxist theory of the state.

THE STATE AND CAPITALISM

If to pluralists the American state is a democratic instrument responsive to the desires of organized, active groups from all strata of society; and if to reform liberals it is the instrument for the social betterment of the entire community; and if to free-market conservatives it is an instrument run amok serving no useful purpose; to Marxists the state is simply that instrument by which the interests of a single class—the owners of the productive apparatus of society—are advanced and protected. It is the instrument by which those who own the basic means of material production ensure their continued dominance of the totality of society. It is the means by which dominant economic actors protect their position against real or potential threats, whether threats to their position emanate from downtrodden classes or from impersonal economic forces. As Marx and his life-long friend and collaborator Frederick Engels so powerfully put the matter in their 1848 political tract *The Communist Manifesto,* "the executive of the modern state is but a committee for managing the common affairs of the whole bourgeoisie."

This remains, of course, an overly simplified statement of Marx's view, one that requires theoretical and historical elaboration and careful qualification. Most important, a full understanding and appreciation of the rather bold position staked out above is only possible within the context of an understanding of the broader Marxist theoretical territory within which this theory of the state is imbedded. The theory of government or of the state is, in fact, but a particular instance of a larger social theory and without an appreciation of these deep interconnections, the Marxist theory of the state is contextually isolated and, therefore, meaningless.

The Mode of Production

The starting point for an understanding of Marxian theory is the concept of the *mode of production*. While Marx never explicitly defined the term, being as he was hostile to static concepts and committed to the evolution of an understanding of complex relationships only through equally complex forms of historical and dialectical analysis, we might loosely define mode of production for ourselves as a "way of life," or "way of working and producing."[1] In any and all societies, people work together to produce the food, clothing, shelter, and amusement they require for their survival by bringing socially evolved and elaborated tools, techniques, and skills to bear on basic raw materials. Since all human production is in some sense social, that is to say, not carried out in total isolation, people find themselves imbedded in sets of complex yet regular interactions and interrelationships with other people. In other words, the exercise of human capacities and capabilities takes place in socially organized and recognizable ways. The combination of these *forces of production* (tools, raw materials, products) and *relation of production* (the characteristic sets of social relations) are the component elements of the mode of production, or the general "way of life" of any particular society. As Marx put it,

> *In the social production of their existence, men inevitably enter into different relations, which are independent of their will, namely relations of production appropriate to a given stage of their material forces of production. The* totality *of these relations of production constitute the economic structure of society (from* Critique of Political Economy*)*[2]

We must add that the ways in which people produce the goods and services they require as well as the ways in which they relate to each other in the process of these activities are never solely habitual and static, but are ever changing in response to the reflective thought and conscious activity of human beings who continually create new tools, processes of production, abilities, forms of social relations and new expectations and needs.[3] As such, the mode of production is itself never static, but ever changing and evolving into different forms.

The concept of the mode of production should not be taken then as a simple economic category, as it is by almost all conventional interpretors of Marx, but as a more global notion. It is a concept which denotes a complex totality comprised of what is normally thought of as separate and distinct phenomena, namely the economic, the social, the political, and even the ideological, although it is a totality "dominated" (though not absolutely determined) in the last instance by the economic."[4]

To Marx, this totality of productive forces is the central mechanism by which society is molded. The particular form that labor and production take in a society gives a particular form to the society in general. Thus, hunting and gathering societies differ from agricultural societies, or from large-scale industrial societies in all of their aspects, economic and non-economic. In fact, Marx argues that the best manner by which to distinguish between societies or between different historical epochs is by their characteristic and dominant forms of labor and production. Now with the exception of early forms of primitive communism to which Marx and Engels often refer, within each historical epoch and within each mode of production, the basic instruments and means by which the material environment is produced is controlled not by the total society, but by a section of it. In all of these situations, a few people own the means of production, and the remainder of the population does not. Thus, in the classical period, only part of the community owned slaves. In the feudal period, only a section of the total population owned land. In the period of capitalism, only a relative handful of people own the factories, the machinery, the tools, and investment resources, while the remainder must sell their labor for wages and salaries. It is in the differentiation between those who own the basic means of production and those who do not that Marx finds class division. In each mode of production, two classes are antagonistically related to each other; the one that owns and the one that does not own the means through which goods are produced, and no less important, through which labor becomes creative and fulfilling.

In all modes of production, the relationship of these classes are unequal and exploitative because that class that owns the basic means of material production takes for itself that part of the socially produced surplus not necessary for the survival of the other class, that portion of the social surplus termed *surplus value* by Marx. Indeed, it is the specific form of surplus value extraction which is the lynchpin of class relations, both the mechanism and the operational indicator of the specific form that the confrontation of social classes take in any particular society. In fact, one important Marxist economist has argued that the key to the analysis of any society is an understanding of how surplus value is produced, appropriated, and used.[5] Thus, surplus value becomes the lens by which class society is brought into focus, the skeleton of the mode of production.

The Capitalist Mode of Production

The *capitalist* mode of production, that mode of production prevailing in the United States, the western nation states, and much of the remainder of the world, differs from other modes of production both in its exaggeration and heightening of those characteristics common to all modes of production and in its expression of certain unique characteristics. Class relations, to take a case in point, are both more universal and hidden in capitalism. That is to say, unlike earlier modes in which class relations failed to touch whole sectors of social life (there being many large-scale pockets outside of classical and feudal social relations), the historical tendency of capitalism is the perpetual expansion into all of the interstices of the social order, and into all corners of the globe, concentrating the means of production into fewer hands, and separating the direct producers from the means of material production. Yet these class relations remain relatively opaque because the superior position of the owning class is only rarely visible as naked coercion. Domination is maintained, rather, through the seemingly natural and inevitable processes of the marketplace and the wage relation, the hidden bases of surplus value extraction and exploitation.

The capitalist mode of production is also unique to the extent that it is characterized by the universality of the commodity form of production, a commodity being that which is sold in the marketplace with the goal of realizing a profit. The universality of the commodity form, the fact that literally *everything* is for sale in capitalist society, marks a new stage in the human story. For the first time in human history labor power is itself for sale. For that portion of the population without ownership rights to the means of production, survival is dependent upon the sale of labor. Should there be no buyer for that labor power, either because of the oversupply of labor in general, or because of the possession of a no longer valued skill, labor is simply discarded and left to its own devices.

Finally, the capitalist mode of production is unique in the extent to which it is driven by the search for *exchange value* in contradistinction to *use value*. That is to say, the engine for capitalist production and social relations is not the rational calculation and assessment of social needs, but the drive for profitability in the market. The implications of such an organization of productive life is profound for it results in a social machine that is without a rational steering mechanism, one that is driven not only on both sides of the road but onto the shoulders and roadside ditches as well. This anarchy of production, this obsessive pursuit of market profitability by separate and competitive economic units, contrary to Adam Smith's conforting disclaimers, most often leads to generalized social irrationality—waste, alternating periods of over- and underproduction, unemployment, increased concentration of ownership, and the creation of scarcity.[6]

THE THEORY OF THE STATE: A FIRST APPROXIMATION
All historical modes of production, then, have been class societies in which only one section of the population controls the means and purposes of production and organizes the labor power of the vast majority of the remainder. At the center of all class societies there is a basic antagonism or tension. Whether people are conscious of its existence or not, it is this inescapable antagonism that makes "class struggle" the central dynamic in the mode of production.

The expression in structural terms of this antagonism under normal conditions is one of domination and subordination, the owners of the means or production being generally dominant over the whole of society. This domination takes three forms: economic, ideological, and political.[7] Economic domination is the most logical and apparent form by which ownership provides benefits for those that own. In any society, according to Marx, the primary fruits of production flow to those who own productive resources. In feudal society, the predominant part of social wealth flowed to those owing the land, and in capitalist societies, benefits flow primarily to those who own the means of capitalist production (e.g. factories, tools, and investment capital). Since ownership allows owners to control what shall be produced, how things shall be produced, to what ends they shall be produced, and how the benefits of that production shall be distributed, then one would expect to find in modern capitalist nations severe and persistent inequalities in the distribution of wealth and other social benefits with the distribution divided primarily along the lines of owners or nonowners.

The assertion that ownership confers certain not inconsiderable benefits to those who own is not, one would think, terribly controversial. Marx extends the argument, however, by pointing out that the class that owns the means of material production also sees that its own ideas, perspectives, and biases are translated into the dominant modes of thought for the entire society. As Marx and Engels put it in *The German Ideology,*

> *The ideas of the ruling class are in every epoch the ruling ideas . . .*
> *the class which is the ruling material force in society is at the same*
> *time its ruling intellectual force . . . .*[8]

Through its control of the media and educational institutions but, most important, through its control of the forms by which people labor and earn their living, the dominant class finds its ideas permeating the social order. In feudal society, for example, ideas conducive to the stability of the feudal order—such as the sanctity of land, of the serf-landlord relationship, and of mutual loyalties—dominated social thought. In capitalist societies, ideas requisite to the maintenance of capitalist economic arrangements dominate social thought: the rights of private property, competition, free enterprise, consumption, and individualism. In short, the supremacy of a social group through ownership becomes expressed also in the ideological sphere. In any stable society in which one group becomes dominant "one concept of reality is diffused throughout society in all its institutional and private manifestations, informing with its spirit all tastes, morality, customs, religious and political principles, and all social relations, particularly in their intellectual and moral connotation."[9] In all class societies, the principle ideology acts to legitimize the domination of a particular class, and to produce forms of behavior in the remainder of society conducive to the continued operations of the productive enterprise in its ongoing form.

Finally, and especially because of its domination of economic life and of the reigning ideology, the class that owns the means of production in any society also dominates the total governmental apparatus, or the state. Thus, in the classical period the state was the organizational expression of the need of slave owners to hold down slaves; while in the modern period, representative government is the instrument of the exploitation of wage labor by capital.[10] Under capitalism, the state is necessary to the owning class because by itself this class cannot, because of limitations of time, skills, and resources, fulfill all of the tasks necessary to maintain its own domination. This class, to the extent that such functions are not carried out already by the normal operations of material production and by the socializing power of the prevailing ideology, requires agents (1) to help maintain the division of classes; (2) to coopt, deflect, or crush threats to prevailing property relations; and (3) to regulate social and economic life to protect the distribution of benefits and advantages that flow to them from the processes of production. To Marx, in short, the state is an organ of class domination, an organ of oppression of one class by another. "It is always the direct relation between the masters of the conditions of production and the direct producers which reveals the innermost secret, the hidden foundation of the entire social edifice . . . and of the political form of the relation between sovereignty and independence; in short, of the particular form of the state."[11] It follows that the state will always exist as an oppressive force so long as class society persists.

Marx summarizes the interrelationships among production, class relations, and the state in the following way: "The bourgeoisie pay their state well and make the nation pay for it in order to be able without danger to pay poorly."[12] The state is, then, both the expression of the basic tension in the social relations of production derived from class division, and the instrument necessary to ease that tension and to prevent the full expression of the class struggle. The state becomes a principal instrument in the protection and reproduction of the overall system, the general provider of the conditions for continued production.[13] The state is, thus, an aspect of class relations—an aspect, however, which serves to mask and disguise the reality of class antagonism. Though it is at all times either the direct instrument of the economically dominant class or the protector of class society in general, the state is a political institution that masks this domination by speaking in universal and general terms and by speaking for and acting in the name of the "general interest" of the whole society and all of its classes. The state is the instrument of a particular class parading around, as it were, under the banner of universality.[14] While the state might take many forms in the capitalist mode of production, from monarchy, to fascism, to representative democracy, the latter remains the most effective class form because it most easily masks the true functions and purposes of the state behind an illusionary democracy.

THE THEORY OF THE STATE: SPECIFICATIONS AND QUALIFICATIONS

In the above discussion of the Marxist theory of government, we have made what we believe to be a simplified, straightforward, and parsimonious presentation, as all working models must be. However, such an undertaking is costly in terms of the loss of complexity, richness, and nuance found in the original work. This general problem of models is a particular problem with regard to the Marxist one since the general tendency among social scientists and political commentators has been (either because of misreadings of his work or because of deliberate distortions) to see Marx's work as overly deterministic, closed, and final; as offering a theoretical analysis which constructs almost mathematical relationships between economy, society, and state. Nothing could be further from the example of Marx's own work, work in which he insisted upon close examination of particular societies set in particular historical situations. Marx, to be sure, conceptualized general historical laws and tendencies but insisted that real societies were historically specific entities that varied within these general laws according to their own unique circumstances. Thus in *The Eighteenth Brumaire of Louis Napoleon* he analyzed a situation where the state, embodied in the personal dictatorship of Louis Napoleon, found itself relatively independent of any particular class because of the deterioration of the power of one class (the bourgeoisie) and the immaturity of the other class (the proletariat).

While the Marxian tradition takes the general relationship between class and state as given, the particular form of state activity is wholly dependent upon particular historical settings and circumstances, variations in the mode of production, and the particular constellation of class forces. While Marx expressed the general tendency for the state to act as the instrument of the dominant class, he held open for analysis the manner and form such domination would take. It is incumbent upon us, then, not to rest with Marx's general law of state function but to examine particular states in particular historical periods. Thus, the forms of class domination through the state might differ among various capitalist countries, or between two periods of development within the same country (e.g., the United States in 1887 as compared with the United States in 1973). Or the forms of state action may differ when government enjoys widespread legitimacy compared to a period when such legitimacy is absent. The point remains that each particular situation must be examined, although the variations take place within more general tendencies.

We must always be attuned, then, when using this theoretical perspective, to the variations, contradictions, and alterations which occur within the more generalized operation of the "laws of motion" of the capitalist mode of production. We must constantly work back and forth between the general and the particular, between the general theory and the manifestations and alteration of the theory in practice. As one scholar has put it, the Marxist theory of the state ". . . applies to normal times and conditions in roughly the same way as Euclidean geometry applies to normal space."[15] In the remainder of this chapter we shall specify in greater detail the specific caveats and variations in the general theory which make that theory more understandable, and serviceable as an instrument for coming to terms with the American state and public policy. It forms the basis, in fact, for the remainder of this volume.

Variations in the Mode of Production

We have argued that the capitalist mode of production is one characterized by a class system based on the ownership of the means of material production, the universalization of the commodity form (especially, the transformation of labor into a commodity), and the direction of material life towards exchange relationships. However, within these very generalized descriptive characteristics, wide variations in the particular forms and dynamics of the mode of production are possible, and these variations affect all of the complex sets of relationships found within the social order, especially those connected to state activities.

To take some of the more important variations as cases in point, all of which will be analyzed in greater detail in subsequent chapters, we may note the following. The capitalist mode of production may vary widely with respect to the degree of concentration of its economic units and the degree to which coordination between them is possible. The comparison between laissez-faire capitalism and *monopoly* or *corporate* capitalism is perhaps most relevant here. While each shares the basic elements of the capitalist mode, their particular characteristics, processes, and problems are sufficiently different to call forth different state activity. The capitalist mode of production may also vary in the specific forms by which surplus value is extracted from the working class. *Direct extraction* is accomplished, for instance, by such procedures as increasing the pace of work of each worker, lengthening the work day, tightening labor discipline, and so on. *Indirect extraction* is accomplished primarily by increasing the productivity of each unit of labor through qualitative improvements in health, education, skill, machinery, or other infrastructure. Again each form of extraction requires qualitatively different types of governmental support. Capitalism may also find itself either in "long wave" periods of accumulation and growth, or of disaccumulation and decline.[16] The point to be made is that the capitalist mode of production has its own history; it itself experiences change, variation, and alteration, and the particular activities of the state respond in kind. State activities in different phases of this history will show strikingly different forms, yet each is designed so that it might better serve its overall class functions. What we find then, as paradoxical as it may seem, is variation within unity, and particularization within the universal, and we must be continually attuned to this complexity.

The Capitalist Mode of Production as a World System

By its very nature, capitalism has never been confined within national boundaries, but it has consistently expanded its operations when and wherever the ambitions of individual capitalists or firms have pushed it. The relentless search for exchange value—for markets, raw materials, and cheap sources of labor power—has pushed capitalism into the far corners of the world. As Marx and Engels put it in *The Communist Manifesto,*

> *The need of a constantly expanding market for its products chases the bourgeoisie over the whole surface of the globe. It must nestle everywhere, establish connections everywhere.*

There are several important matters to keep firmly in mind with respect to this world system. Just as the capitalist mode of production is based in general on the division of labor, so to is the world system based upon a division of labor. However, the world system is composed of a division of labor between whole societies, each of which performs specific economic roles within an interdependent network of economic exchange. More importantly, the capitalist world system has been historically divided into *core states* (economically dominant and basically exploitive), *periphery states* (suppliers of cheap raw materials and labor, economically dependent and backward), and, as some have suggested, *semiperiphery states* (partly exploited, partly exploiter) "linked to each other by capitalist relations of exchange and dominated by the capitalist world market."[17]

While each of these types is interrelated within an overall system of capitalism, the particular state forms and activities of a society will vary depending on the structural location of that society in the world system. Moreover, the relationships are never static, and it is possible for a society to gradually find its position in the world system altered. This has, for instance, certainly been the case for the United States which has found itself during its 200-year history transformed from periphery, to semiperiphery, to the dominant core state in the world capitalist system. Such fundamental alterations in position tend to call forth vastly different sets of system needs and requirements for the attention of government, and in coming to terms with such requirements, the very forms of state structure and process are themselves changed. What all of this suggests is that any analysis of the genesis of the modern American state must not only come to grips with the internal dynamics of the capitalist mode of production within the boundaries of the United States, but must also place that analysis within the context of America's changing position in the world capitalist system as a whole.

Class Struggle

In Marxist theory, class struggle is the connecting link between economics and politics, the basis for what used to be called political economy. That is to say, class struggle is both the structural framework of all productive activity in capitalism, and the division which calls forth government and shapes the bulk of its activities. As we have suggested above, no comprehension of the form, operation, and purposes of the capitalist state is possible without a comprehension of the system of class relations and the nature of their connections to political life. Such a task is rarely a simple matter, for the state is not merely a class instrument but is itself a product of class struggle. Furthermore, the state must always carry out certain necessary social functions, that is, functions that any and all societies must have fulfilled, so that every action may not be traced to class designs and purpose. Let us examine some of these issues, so that we may be sensitive to the complexity of the relations of class and state.

First, the capitalist state always has a dual character. On the one hand it exists, as we have already suggested, as the direct instrument of the dominant class. It is a reflection in a concentrated and distilled form of the needs of an economically dominant class faced with the continual problem of advancing the process of capital accumulation and the pacification of the subordinate class. State activities in these realms have ranged from the provision of subsidies, to the ideological defense of property, to overseas expansion, to strikebreaking. On the other hand, the state also performs certain socially necessary functions, functions all societies are forced to perform simply because of inescapable collective needs. One might include in this socially necessary category such activities as sanitation, public health, disaster relief, and defense.

While all of these activities have a seemingly nonclass character, it is vital that we understand that in class societies even socially necessary activities take place within the context of a class system and are distorted by it. To take an example, it has been pointed out that city-wide sanitation historically became a reality only when it was demonstrated to members of the dominant class that disease originating in urban slums could not be confined to that place of darkness, but was a threat to them and their families as well.[18] Much the same can be said for urban improvements:

> *Note the practice, which has now become general, of making breaches in the working class quarters of our big cities, particularly in those which are centrally situated, irrespective of whether this practice is occasioned by considerations of public health and beautification or by traffic requirements, such as the laying down of railways, streets, etc. No matter how different the reasons may be, the result is everywhere the same: the most scandalous alleys and lanes disappear to the accompaniment of lavish self-glorification by the bourgeoisie on account of this tremendous success, but—they appear again at once somewhere else, and often in the immediate neighborhood.* [19]

Though the above observation by Engels referred to late nineteenth-century Paris, it is not very far from the mark in characterizing contemporary American urban renewal.

What the state does in these areas is again put quite forcefully by Draper who has observed that "the state really does have nonclass tasks and it carries them out. But it carries them out inevitably in class distorted ways, for class ends, with class consequences."[20] This is invariably the case because socially necessary tasks are carried out through political institutions that arise out of class society and conflict.

We must, therefore, be sensitive to the wide variety of tasks performed by capitalist governments and to the multiple origins of these tasks, and not allow ourselves to remain satisfied with "simple" class explanations. While class remains determinative, it often exercises its influence by circuitous routes. There are many other complexities involved in studies of the class state and these are derived from class struggle itself. By its very nature, class struggle is never static but reflects a reality that is always in tension, conflict, change, and flux. Society is never composed simply of two internally unified and opposed classes, but rather of classes which not only vary over time in the degree to which their opposition to each other is manifested, but which vary internally as well. In the long run, the specific nature of government activities is affected by the nature of the class struggle at any historical conjuncture.

The working class, for instance, will show wide variations over time in the degree to which it is organized and suffused with an understanding of its position in society vis-à-vis capital. This will greatly affect not only the degree to which serious conflict takes place in the social order but also the ability of the capitalist class to extract surplus value. The dominant class also varies in its cohesiveness and consciousness as a class over time, and this, in turn, affects the ability of this class to give direction to governmental activities, to place the stamp of its interests upon the state. In fact, the dominant class seems to be inherently torn by a tension between its unitary class interests against the subordinate class, taken as a whole, and its multitude of competing interests as capitalists against other capitalists.

Government policy is never a simple reflection of class interests, then, but the result of a complex class struggle which has both *inter*class and *intra*class components, all of which are subject to movement and change. To reiterate a point made earlier, the state is not merely a class instrument, though many of its activities can be so explained, but rather the product of class struggle. What this suggests is that an understanding of contemporary government activity cannot rest with any precise formula but must be the end product of an exploration that takes classes and class struggle as the starting point and traces out connections to political life and specific state actions.

A LOOK AHEAD

We have hopefully moved a considerable distance in this chapter away from the notion that Marxist theory in general and the Marxist theory of the state in particular can be summarized in simple formulas. It has been our goal to demonstrate the nature of the complex interactions involved in any understanding of the capitalist state. Specifically, we have argued that an understanding of the form, origin, processes, and purposes of modern government in the United States requires nothing less than an analysis of a multitude of changes; specifically in its mode of production, in the position of the United States in the world capitalist system, and in the specific nature of the continuing class struggle. In the remainder of this volume we shall be guided by these three imperatives as we attempt to explain the American state as a set of institutions whose functions and purposes are defined by the specific tensions, problems, contradictions, and constraints of the capitalist system as a whole. Out of these broad imperatives, and only out of these broad imperatives, can we delineate the genesis of specific governmental policies.

The reader should note that this approach takes as its point of departure the requirements of the system as a whole, and not, as is currently fashionable in popular sociology, the tracing out of the influence of specific economic elites who sit in the chairs of government. In the Marxist formulation we have set out in this chapter there is no requirement that the *capitalist class* be the *ruling class,* that its members fill the key positions of the governmental apparatus. All that the Marxist formulation posits is the class nature of the state in its purposes and effects. Thus it is interesting but beside the point whether cabinet members, presidents, or prime ministers were born into the capitalist class.[21] As Nicos Poulantzas has put this issue,

> *The relation between the bourgeois class and the state is an* objective relation. *This means that if the* function *of the state in a determinate social formation and the* interests *of the dominant class in this formation coincide, it is by reason of the system itself: the direct participation of members of the ruling class in the state apparatus is not the* cause *but the* effect, *and moreover a chance and contingent one, of this objective coincidence.*[22]

Another caveat is in order at this point. There is a tendency in most discussions of the modern state, whether Marxist or non-Marxist, to see the state as omnipotent, skillfully able to handle the problems presented by capitalist development. What we shall find in the chapters that follow, however, is that governmental attempts to deal with the contradictions and tensions of the developing capitalist mode of production in the United States have been halting, partial, and only temporarily successful, and have often themselves been contradictory and problematic. That is to say, government has usually responded to problems on an ad hoc basis rather than rationally anticipating them, and the temporarily successful solutions have themselves, more often than not, created additional problems as serious as those they were designed to treat.[23]

We hope to demonstrate in the chapters that follow that as imperfect and as incomplete as it might be, the Marxist theory of the state comes closest to helping us make sense of the multitude of activities to which government devotes its vast reservoirs of wealth, resources, skills, and coercive power in the United States, how it got to be that way, and where it might be going in the future. None of the other perspectives we have examined—

reform liberalism, free-market conservatism, or pluralism—comes close in the degree of its explanatory power, though each occasionally stumbles upon a truth. The reader is not asked, of course, to accept such a bold assertion on its face, but rather to carefully examine with us the evolution of U.S. government policy *concretely*. Our primary focus will be on the description of government policy, the discovery of the sources of policy, the motivation of the policy makers, and, finally, some notion of the impact of these policies on American society.

We hope, in the process, to contribute to an understanding of how and why government in the United States has come to act in the ways that it does; of how and why it came to be transformed from a relatively passive instrument into an active, interventionist one.

NOTES

[1] See James O'Connor, "Productive and Unproductive Labor," *Politics and Society,* Vol. 5, No. 3 (1975), p. 297.

[2] "Economic" should not be taken in the narrow sense of its contemporary usage but in its broader sense as the material basis of all social existence.

[3] See a discussion of this point in James O'Connor, *The Corporations and the State* (New Yorker: Harper & Row, 1974), Chapter 1, "Capitalism."

[4] For the concept of "dominated in the last instance," see the work of the French Marxist Louis Althuser and his followers: *Pour Marx* (Paris: Maspero, 1969); *Reading Capital* (New York: Pantheon, 1970); also see Nicos Poulantzas, *Political Power and Social Classes* (London: New Left Books, 1973).

[5] O'Connor, *The Corporations and the State,* Chapter 2, "The Theory of Surplus Value."

[6] For a general discussion of the multiple forms of this irrationality see Edward S. Greenberg, *The American Political System: A Radical Approach* (Cambridge: Winthrop, 1977), Chapter 3.

[7] Much of the following is based on Wlodzimierz Weslowski, "Marx's Theory of Class Domination," in Nicholas Lobkowicz, ed., *Marx and the Western World* (Notre Dame, Ind.,: University of Notre Dame Press, 1967).

[8] *The German Ideology* (New York: International Publishers, 1947), p. 64.

[9] Gywn A. Williams, "The Concept of Egemonia in the Thought of Antonio Gramsci: Some Notes on Interpretation," *Journal of the History of Ideas,* Vol. 21 (1960), p. 587.

[10] Robert C. Tucker, "Marx as a Political Theorist," in Lobkowicz, *Marx and the Western World.*

[11] Karl Marx, *Capital,* Vol. III (London: Lawrence and Wishart, 1970).

[12] Marx and Engels, *The German Ideology* (Moscow: Progress Publishers, 1964), p. 216.

[13] The state is, thus, more than mere superstructure, more than a derivative and secondary institution, but an integral part of production itself. For discussion of this point see Ernest Mandel, *Late Capitalism* (London: New Left Books, 1975), Chapter 15.

[14] On this point see Shlomo Avineri, *The Social and Political Thought of Karl Marx* (Cambridge: Cambridge University Press, 1971); Hal Draper, *Karl Marx's Theory of Revolution: State and Bureaucracy* (New York: Monthly Review Press, 1977); Bertall Ollman, *Alienation: Marx's Concept of Man in Capitalist Society* (Cambridge: Cambridge University Press, 1971); and Alan Wolfe, "New Directions in the Marxist Theory of Politics," *Politics and Society,* Vol. 4, No. 2 (1974).

[15] Draper, *Karl Marx's Theory of Revolution,* p. 387.

[16] For discussion of "long waves" in capitalism see Mandel, *Late Capitalism.*

[17] Emmanuel Wallerstein, *The Modern World Systems* (New York: Academic Press, 1974). Also see Mandel, *Late Capitalism.*

[18] Draper, *Karl Marx's Theory of Revolution,* p. 260.

[19] Frederick Engels, "The Housing Question," in Marx and Engels, *Selected Works in Three Volumes* (Moscow: Progress Publishers, 1969-70), Vol. 2, p. 350.

[20] Draper, *Karl Marx's Theory of Revolution,* p. 260.

[21] Pluralist attacks on so-called "elite theory" suffer from an incorrect interpretation of the radical position precisely at this point. Pluralists seem to think that if one can demonstrate the non-upper-class origins of political decision makers then one has eliminated the possibility of a ruling class. For useful discussions of the ruling-class concept see Ralph Miliband,

State in Capitalist Society (New York: Basic Books, 1969); and David Nichols, "Ruling Class as a Scientific Concept," *Review of Radical Political Economics,* Vol. 4, No. 5 (Fall 1972), pp. 35-70.

[22] Poulantzas, *Political Power and Social Classes,* p. 245.

[23] This theme is examined in Gabriel Kolko, *Main Currents in American History* (New York: Harper & Row, 1976); Claus Offe, "Advanced Capitalism and the Welfare State," *Politics and Society,* Vol. 2 (Summer 1972); and Alan Wolfe, *The Limits of Legitimacy: Political Contradictions of Contemporary Capitalism* (New York: Free Press, 1977).

3
ON THE CONSTRUCTION OF THE MODERN POSITIVE STATE: PART 1

The incubating period for the growth of modern government in the United States was the approximately five or six decades that stretch from the late nineteenth century to the beginning of the Second World War, a period generally referred to as "the Age of Reform."[1] In this period when the United States became transformed from a decentralized, rural society to an urban-industrial society, a series of reform movements—populism, progressivism, and New Deal liberalism—helped to irrevocably change the state from a relatively passive to a relatively active institution. In particular, and for the first time during this period, government assumed responsibility for the regulation of the corporation and the economy and for the alleviation of some of the difficulties and hardships of the victims of the new industrial order. To reform liberals, this period generally represents the beginning stages of an evolutionary process in which the American people fashioned their government into an instrument for the humanization of capitalism. To free-market conservatives, on the other hand, this period can only be construed as the beginning of the tragic retreat from the market economy, and the attendant decline of individual freedom.

Neither view, in our opinion, makes much sense of the period, for when all is said and done, the results of the Age of Reform seem less than the rhetoric of the supporters and detractors of reform suggest. Despite government regulation and intervention, giant industrial, commercial, and financial institutions continue to sit astride and to dominate the economy, and to shape the general contours of American life. They do so not only unhindered by the state, but also often with its active support. Moreover, the benevolent impact of state activities on the life conditions of the non-affluent and the nonwhite have been minimal at best, and at worst, have actively contributed to their subordinate position. The Age of Reform, in short, has not significantly bettered the lot of people in the lower reaches of society, nor has it adversely affected those at or near the top of society. This is not to suggest, however, that major institutional reforms did not take place. The American state was certainly a far different creature in 1939 than it was in 1890. Observers have certainly not exaggerated, then, the scope of the transformation. What has been generally misunderstood, however, are its origins, directions, and implications. Part of that misunderstanding is derived from the conventional wisdom that progressivism and New Deal liberalism were the products almost entirely of grass-roots movements.[2] What has not been fully appreciated is the extent to which the most advanced sector of the business community set the boundaries of political debate during this period, defined the alternatives, and, in many cases, was itself the initiator and formulator of reform measures. Seen from this perspective, the Age of Reform was primarily an effort by leading members of the business community to bring order, stability, and predictability to the competitive chaos of the emerging industrial order, to incorporate labor into the business system through conservative unionism, and to prevent social revolution through the distribution of minimal relief benefits to the poor. The Age of Reform was essentially a series of reforms designed to ensure the dominance and profitability of large-scale capital and to blunt movements for radical alternatives to the status quo.

An additional and more important source of misunderstanding about the nature of the reform era is traceable to a general tendency among social scientists and historians to ignore structural change in the capitalist system, and the general sets of needs and requirements for state intervention called forth by such change. As we suggested in the last chapter, it is our view that one can only understand the overall shape of the state by reference to the capitalist mode of production, the world position of American capitalism, and the particular nature of the class struggle. It follows, that to understand dramatic transformations in the nature, scope, and scale of government activity, one needs to look to transformation in these three basic determinants of the capitalist state.

It shall be our position in this chapter that the period commonly designated the Age of Reform is best understood as a transition period between the disappearance of simple market society and the maturation of what we shall call monopoly capitalism, a period in which government was gradually fashioned into the instrument of coordination and management for this new form of concentrated capitalism. It was during the Age of Reform, to be more specific, that the giant corporation rose to predominance in the economy, that a large if diverse industrial proletariat first made its appearance and came to maturation, and the United States moved from a semiperiphery state to a central or core position in the world capitalist economy. Reform during these years represented the wide, complex, and often contradictory range of governmental responses to these enormous changes in American life. This chapter and the next one will try to explain how the American state transformed the particulars of its day-to-day activities, yet remained wedded to its historic mission of guaranteeing the processes of capitalist accumulation and regulating the potentially explosive relations between classes.

THE STATE AND THE PRECORPORATE ECONOMY
Prior to that powerful combination of elements which, when brought together in the later third of the nineteenth century, provide the decisive elements in the emergence of the modern corporate economy (namely, the industrial revolution and the innovations in centralized business organization), the United States was essentially a nation of relatively isolated, island communities where economic, social, and political relationships were informal and parochial.[3] During the early and middle decades of the nineteenth century, the United States was a nation comprised of people engaged in small-scale agriculture, artisanship, and commerce, a nation with relatively small cities and few sizable industrial enterprises. It was a nation, as well, with widespread property ownership and a small, widely scattered, and unorganized working class.[4] Communications were local or regional and unevenly developed as were markets for agricultural, artisan, and industrial products. The primitive transportation systems failed to effectively link diverse local communities into regularized national networks. Economic direction was primarily determined by a multitude of diverse entrepreneurs and consumers, and not by devices of government decision makers or major business firms. Society and economy were essentially self-regulating and self-directed. In short we find in this period an economy and society that comes as close to the free-market ideal as we are likely to find in American history.

To say that, of course, is not to say that the state was totally inactive in this setting. We should not expect otherwise, for proponents of laissez-faire theory, (from John Locke to Milton Friedman) have never pretended to favor anarchy as the appropriate model for free-market captialism. Instead, they have proposed what has been commonly called a *minimal* state.[5] That is to say, they have argued for the necessity of a state system capable of creating and sustaining the conditions necessary for the operation of a self-regulatory capitalist society. Paradoxically, this has often meant periods of rather vigorous activity by the minimalist state, particularly to the extent that it acted, in Ernest Mandel's words, as "the midwife of the capitalist mode of production."[6] This seeming paradox was particularly the case in Europe where the establishment of laissez-faire capitalism required the active intervention of the state to destroy those feudal and traditional practices inimical to the spread and free operation of the capitalist market. Most importantly in this respect, government became an active instrument in almost all of the European nation states for the destruction of the complex institutions and practices which stood in the way of transforming land and labor into commodities. These institutions and practices included the guild system, the traditional rights to the use of "common" lands, and the traditional obligations for the mutual care and sustenance of all communal members.[7] The state intervened, as paradoxically as it may seem, to create the ground for an inactive state. In the United States, where feudal society did not sit astride the road to capitalist development as it did in Europe, government during the laissez-faire period was, nevertheless, surprisingly active, though never as active as in the European states. The federal government during the early and middle decades of the nineteenth century was engaged in building roads and canals, removing Indian populations from potentially exploitable lands, conducting internal and external wars, and annexing territories through purchase and force.

In free-market capitalist systems, the main social steering mechanism, that is, the main instrument for the direction of society in general, remains the market. The role of the state in such systems is nothing less than that of the main creator of the framework for the operation of market society, and the institution responsible for the maintenance of the conditions necessary for market operation, continuation, and adaptation. In the main, this means that the *minimal* state in liberal-capitalist societies, and the United States is no exception in this respect, has historically engaged in: (1) the establishment of the legal framework of market society (a system of civil law involving the sanctity of contract and the primacy of property); (2) the provision of mechanisms for financial transactions (direct or indirect provision of a system of currency, credit, and banking); (3) the preservation of order (police, militia, army, courts, etc.); (4) the protection of domestic industry (tariffs, customs service); and (5) the provision of direct subsidization (aid to the railroads is the most obvious example— fully one-fourth of all the land in Minnesota and Washington was given to private railroad companies.)[8]

We find, then, that the *minimal* state is not a *non*state, but a quite active one. Nevertheless, and relatively speaking, the scale, scope, and penetration of governmental activity during the early and midnineteenth century remained not only limited, but constantly subject to diminution rather than expansion. In effect, all of the available evidence seems to suggest that governmental intervention into the economic and civil society were likely to be less extensive in the years just prior to the Civil War than in the first several decades of the century.[9]

We thus have the rather curious picture, both in the United States and in Europe where it was much more pronounced, for the capitalist class to require far greater state support and action at the beginning of liberal-capitalist society, when it was necessary to establish the conditions for its survival, than later when that system was in full and vigorous operation. Once liberal capitalism had triumphed, in other words, there remained less need for an active and supportive government. Once the framework for market activities was created, government could retire to the sidelines to be called upon only when needed in difficult times. We find in the United States, for instance, that the rhetoric of the free market reached its most blatant and pronounced form only after the strength of the free-market economy, with much government assistance, reached its zenith in the years after the Civil War, at the very moment when, in one of history's recurrent jokes, the conditions that would lead to the destruction of the laissez-faire economy were beginning to make their presence felt.

THE RISE OF A NEW ECONOMY
In the last third of the nineteenth century, out of the very midst of laissez-faire society arose a powerful force created by the confluence of the Civil War, the Industrial Revolution, and new forms of business organization which all but destroyed laissez-faire society. By the year 1900 America was no longer a nation, by and large, of relatively isolated island communities with nonindustrial, nonurban economic, social, and political relationships.[10] Railroads connected the rar reaches of the nation and tied small local communities to regional and national markets. Cities on the American continent grew more rapidly than ever, spurred by the industrial

machine and stocked by massive European migration. Business discovered a variety of arrangements to aid expansion, consolidation, and extra-regional influence—the holding company, the trust, and the corporation. Communications became national in scope, as did banking and finance. The three decades after the end of the Civil War also saw the rise of mechanized farming, crop specialization, and the first serious manifestations of maldistributions of wealth in the agriculture sector. In addition, the expansion of standardized methods of manufacturing, increased specialization, and the emergence of factory labor as the most pervasive form of work occurred during this period.

In only three decades, the nature of the American economy and society underwent revolutionary and chaotic change. By the end of the century, America was well on its way to becoming a nation of industry, large cities, interconnected economies, and large-scale business enterprise. It is in the attempt by various groups to deal with this revolutionary and chaotic change, to make sense of it and to gain control of it, that we can best trace the roots of the Age of Reform.

The immediate response made by affected groups to the chaos of the industrial revolution was to organize, to attempt to deal collectively with problems for which individuals were ill-equipped to cope. This period saw many of these collective efforts to bring order to particular environments: the farm cooperative movement, agricultural commodity organizations, organizations of distributors (in groceries, hardware, and farm equipment), and the creation of professional societies (doctors, lawyers, and teachers). No group, however, was as successful as large-scale business enterprise in organizing, rationalizing, or, in fact, in stimulating state intervention in its own interests.

The Rise of the Corporation

The history of the corporation is the history of the efforts of the capitalist class to transcend the strictures of the free market, to invent devices by which the control production, create stable markets, set prices, and ultimately, to ensure profitability and growth. Such a history may be seen in the initial growth of corporations, in the seemingly inexorable processes of concentration of economic and social power in the corporate sector of the economy, in the processes of intercorporate cooperation, and in the contemporary political activities of their owners and managers.

As we suggested above, the creation and growth of giant companies is traceable to both the industrial revolution (with its new sources of power, advances in transportation, and other technological innovations), and certain legal innovations in business organization. These developments provided both the means and the necessity for concentrated growth. That is to say, new technological developments like the steam engine, electrical power, the conveyor belt, better forms of steel, and the like, all provided the means to gather together enormous numbers of men, women, and children for purposes of industrial production. Furthermore, most of the new technologies, steel-making being a case in point, required large-scale fixed plant and equipment, and hithertofore unimagined amounts of capital. Unlike earlier technologies, significant and ever increasing barriers to entry kept the pool of potential industrial entrepreneurs minimal. The period of the industrial revolution in all of the western nations, therefore, is a history of the rapid concentration of industrial enterprise.[11]

Size, expansion, and concentration, however, also posed problems for business. On the one hand, business empires tended to grow beyond the immediate control of their owners; far-flung operations were desperately held in hand through the managerial, technical, and financial tools appropriate to a small company. The results were often chaotic and expensive.[12] Another and far more serious problem was the inability of traditionally powerful companies to maintain their market positions in an economy where market potential had expanded from 25 million persons in 1850 to 100 million in 1900, where new technologies were being rapidly introduced, and where an ample supply of investment capital, both domestic and foreign, was available. The result of this uncontrolled economy for many large firms was unaccustomed and fierce competition, and economic decline. As business historian Thomas Cochran put it:

> *Rapidly expanding markets and resources led to the breakdown of local or regional efforts at cooperation and hence to a period of intense, harsh competition, in which businessmen suffered from high risks and uncertainties even though they commanded the social, intellectual, and economic resources of the nation.*[13]

For the largest firms in each economic sector, this competition represented tangible threats to their very survival. As their ability to control the business environment declined, certain business leaders began to search for methods by which to reintroduce stability and assured profitability through interbusiness cooperation. While some of the earlier local and regional models were resurrected for a national scale, a series of important legal innovations proved more decisive.

The goal of all these efforts was to establish whatever cooperative agreements were required for control of production, limitation of competition, and the assurance of adequate and stable prices. The nature of the problem business leaders faced is suggested by the case of the oil industry. Within a year of the establishment of the Pennsylvania Rock Oil Company in 1859, the first major oil company in the United States, *seventy-seven* competitors entered the field and forced prices for refined oil to fall from $20 barrel in 1859 to $.10 in 1861.[14] In order to avoid potentially disastrous developments in this and other economic sectors, business leaders attempted a number of intriguing schemes, for example, gentlemen's agreements on pricing and marketing. However, when these agreements proved to be broken too easily, business leaders turned to more formal arrangements, for example, price-regulation associations (oil), selling pools (meat packing), or syndicates with the power to fine violators of agreements. An important innovation was the creation of the *trust,* a form of business in which formally separate companies were wedded together by entrusting their shares to an institution charged with regulating their common affairs, in trade for share certificates in the trust itself. Under the direction of John D. Rockefeller, the first monopoly trust was created out of the chaos of the oil industry. By 1884, Standard Oil refined fully 90 percent of all American petroleum products.[15] The *holding company,* particularly popular in the utility industry, was a device for the control and coordination of formally separate companies through various financial mechanisms in which only limited capital was required for bringing together a vast number of companies.

The most important legal breakthrough occurred, however, in 1889 when the state of New Jersey transformed the traditional law of incorporation by allowing corporations to own stock of other companies. With this innovation, and Delaware's rescinding all requirements for corporate residency for incorporation in that state, the business world was swept by a wave of direct mergers, mergers which represented not only the end of all pretense about the separate existence of cooperating companies, but also a convenient way around the laws related to restraint of trade. Not unexpectedly, since these mergers required enormous amounts of investment capital, banks and other sources of finance capital became central to the entire merger process. The first billion dollar corporation, for instance, the U.S. Steel Corporation, was promoted, organized, and financed by J.P. Morgan and his associates. Bankers like Morgan, in fact, were the key actors in the great merger movements of 1896-1904.[16] With the emergence of these giant corporations and financial institutions around the turn of the century, the American economy was beginning to assume the form that is characteristic of our own today.

The giant corporation, then, can best be seen as the end point in a process of development in which leaders of the largest business enterprises sought to reassert or to gain control over the marketplace, to check vicious and unbridled competition, and to guarantee market shares and profitability. It was only after this new form of business was unable to guarantee the anticipated stability and predictability for large firms with enormous fixed capital assets that business leaders turned to the state to provide the necessary conditions for continued growth and survival.

The Corporations and the Social Order

Such a momentous transformation squeezed into so short a span of time is never without its disruptions. Such was the case with respect to the rising industrial giants and their effects on American life. Agriculture, perhaps surprisingly, was deeply affected by these events. Development in the industrial sector, for instance, spurred farm mechanization, concentration of farm ownership, and higher agricultural productivity. While one might think this a process all to the good, it contributed not only to the mass migration of surplus agricultural population to the fast growing urban centers of the North and East, but to recurrent periods of falling prices and agricultural depression brought on by overproduction.[17] Further economic uncertainty was added by the capital requirements of large-scale mechanized farming and the consequent reliance on credit institutions. When these developments were added to the effects of rail transit into farm areas—railroads were known then for their policies of kickbacks, rebates, and favoritism toward industrial giants as against agriculture—the mixture proved to be volatile. American agricultural regions, especially in upper midwestern and the southern areas, experienced a recurrent series of farm protest movements toward the end of the nineteenth century, the most important being the populist movement. This movement, which directed its wrath against oligopolistic institutions in industry, commerce, and finance, was sufficiently powerful to help nominate William Jennings Bryan as the Democratic party candidate in 1896, to capture a number of governorships and state legislatures by 1900, and to provide the muscle for a series of national and state-level reforms, the most important being the *Sherman Anti-Trust Act* and the *Interstate Commerce Act*.

For the first time in American history in the late nineteenth century, the growth and concentration of industrial enterprise led to the appearance of a class of proletarian labor. This history is an old and familiar one. The new industrial giants, whether in steelmaking, textiles, railroad construction, or mining, required a work force of a size never before imagined. Agents of the industrial giants scoured worldwide to recruit labor for the mills, mines, and foundries of America, often exaggerating, as one might expect, the benefits awaiting each recruit. Multiple streams of immigrants converged upon American industrial enterprises from all points of the globe, and from every corner of the social structure, driven by both misery and a sense of opportunity. Immigrants arrived from southern and eastern Europe forced out by land consolidation and famine, as well as by political and religious persecution. Blacks came from the South, driven out by the terrible poverty and hunger caused by sharecropping, farm consolidation and mechanization as well as outright oppression. Farmers came from all over America forced from the land by the processes of land concentration and the capitalization of agriculture. Former artisans and small business people came to large industries when they were unable to compete with the new giants of industry and commerce.

Nonunionized, internally divided by ethnic, racial, and religious differences, and often faced by a capitalist class determined to squeeze and extract every last ounce of surplus value from its work force. the lot of this new class was dismal. Little thought was given to safety in American industry, and death and mayhem were commonplace. Poor ventilation, unshielded noise, abundant dirt, and insufficient lighting were normal working conditions. Hours were long, often twelve to fourteen hours a day, seven days a week for a labor force which included a very high proportion of children. Pay, needless to say, was at all times insufficient to minimal needs and subject to arbitrary cuts when management thought it necessary for reasons of economy or labor discipline.

The miserable lot of this new industrial army was expressed in anti-capital outbreaks throughout the latter part of the nineteenth century, outbreaks which invariably brought fierce countermeasures. In the Schuylkill County coal region of Pennsylvania where 566 miners had been killed within a span of only seven years, where men worked in semidarkness and in knee-deep water, where pay was always inadequate, and where an incipient miners union was destroyed by company thugs, vigilante committees of local businessmen and hired Pinkertons, Irish miners organized as the Molly Maguires conducted a rear-guard, guerrilla battle of terror against the mining companies in the 1870s. In 1877, in response to arbitrary wage cuts, railroad workers organized their first nationwide strike and paralyzed the national transportation system for two weeks. The 1886 national strike for the eight-hour day mobilized hundreds of thousands of workers, and resulted in widespread violence and mayhem as capital called forth its usual antilabor combination of business-sponsored vigilante groups, hired private armies, state and federal troops, and the courts. Armed confrontation between labor and capital was the outcome of Andrew Carnegie's desire to break the largely ineffectual Amalgamated Association of Iron and Steel Workers at his steel mill in Homestead, Pennsylvania, in 1892. In response to paycuts at a time when railroad companies were announcing substantial profits, 150,000 railroad workers under the direction of Eugene Debs left their jobs in the 1894 Pullman strike. Once they convinced President Cleveland that anarchy threatened the nation, railroad owners were able to count on federal troops to break the strike. Labor wars were a continual feature, as well, in the mining life of the Rockies as the names Ludlow, Cripple Creek, and Coeur d'Alene recount.[18] Further examples could be added, of course, but it would simply reinforce the point already made: developments in the capitalist mode of production were creating a situation in which capital and labor faced each across a deep divide. Building a bridge over this divide would be one of the great tasks on the future agenda of American government.

The State in the Late Nineteenth Century

During this time when capital became concentrated into giant corporations and financial institutions, and when agrarian and labor rebellion were commonplace because of the disruptive impact of that process, government assumed a fairly traditional role. By and large, it remained the principal guarantor of the capitalist class as enforcer of the civil law of contract and property, as ultimate strikebreaker in its use of the military, and as subsidizer of industrial development. Nevertheless, the main impetus to and direction of the major transformations occurring in economic life, namely rapid economic development and the concentration of capital, came not from the state but from private entrepreneurial sources, both domestic and foreign. In this process, government kept its distance. In its relationship to capital, the state played little more than its traditional "night watchman" or "policeman" role articulated in laissez-faire theory. In effect, the state had not yet caught up to developments in the mode of production that were rapidly moving the economy away from any approximation to the free market. It would soon have to learn to cope with the implications of corporate size and concentration, as well as the problems of interclass tension and conflict. The full development of government regulatory and support services would have to wait for another day. The first halting steps in that direction would be taken during the first two decades of the twentieth century.

THE PROGRESSIVE MOVEMENT

The reader will recall the point we have made several times in this chapter: namely, the evolution of the corporate form of business enterprise represented an attempt by business leadership to bring order and stability into their economic affairs. As powerful as it was as an economic organization, however, the corporation was unable by itself to bring about the desired order and stability. It seems that by 1900 the principal problem worrying the business community was not the threat of monopoly, but the threat of excess competition and a consequent decline in profits.[19] The failure of executives in the steel industry, for instance, to enforce the informal "gentlemen's agreement" on prices established at the initiative of Eldridge Gary of U.S. Steel led to an intense period of competition between steel firms and to serious declines in profits. The competition was so fierce that steel prices did not return to their 1902 level until 1916. In the oil industry, increasing competition in this period led to the steady and substantial decline of the position of Standard Oil (Standard's share of the oil market fell from 90 percent in 1900 to 50 percent in 1921).[20] Similar situations of intense competition and falling profits were characteristic of the automobile, agricultural machinery, telephones, copper, and meat packing industries. Most importantly, in the midst of these events voluntary cooperative efforts on the part of the largest firms in each industry to control competition and to maintain prices failed. Given this failure, and having no desire to see continued price competition and instability within their industries, the largest firms turned to the government for help, and their successful efforts in legislation represent, in fact, the heart of the progressive achievement.

The Meat Inspection Act (1905) is an interesting example of this process, especially because it is customarily interpreted as a great victory of the grass-roots population over the large meat trusts. There is no gainsaying public attention and feeling about this legislation. The public demand for government regulation of the meat-packing industry was stimulated, of course, by the powerful book *The Jungle,* written by the young socialist reporter Upton Sinclair, a book that exposed filth, disease, and oppressive working conditions in the packing industry. Most historians focus on the public reaction to this book in explaining the origins of government regulation, and largely ignore the two-decade effort by the largest packers for such state intervention. In fact, the industry sought state intervention and regulation in order to increase meat sales in European markets. The largest firms found that the severe competition ᛒy hundreds of small packers in the industry not only hurt profits, but the lack of sanitary standards in these small enterprises, and the absence of government inspection machinery led to serious declines in the quality of American meats. The declines were so serious, in fact, that various meats were banned from Italy in 1879, from France in 1881, from Germany in 1883, and from England in 1888. Faced with a crisis of this magnitude, the large packers, led by Armour, lobbied for federal inspection and certification of meats. The public support generated by *The Jungle* served primarily to give democratic legitimacy to a form of government intervention favored by the large firms. Rather than being in strong opposition to regulation, the large packers were in full support. As A. Swift and Company put it, "It is a wise law. Its enforcement must be universal and uniform."[21] Not coincidentally, the major meat industries hoped that the smaller firms would be unable to meet federal standards and would be forced to drop out of the competitive race.

Similar observations can be made about the Pure Food and Drug Act (1906). As with the Meat Inspection Act, the major impetus behind the drive to regulate the food and drug industries came from the largest firms within each industry, each of whom had a strong desire to control competition, to gain legitimacy for their product, and to hinder what they considered unscrupulous smaller competitors. The campaign for regulation, in fact, was led by the National Board of Trade, the Wholesale Grocers' Association, the Retail Grocers' Association, and the National Association of Manufacturers.[22] We do not infer that large firms manipulated the public or influenced the state to move in directions not desired by most of its citizens; we do suggest, however, that the progressive movement cannot be seen solely as a movement of the public against corporations. It was not a movement that can be explained as a state response to public sentiment to control, regulate, and even humble the giant corporations. It was, rather, a successful effort by large enterprises to enlist the aid of the state in creating situations of ordered stability, with the full support and concurrence of the public. When we turn to some of the other landmark legislation of the progressive era, the Federal Reserve Act and the Federal

Trade Commission, we see the even more prominent role played by giant corporations and financial institutions.

The Federal Reserve Act (1914) is judged as one of the great pieces of reform legislation not only for the progressive era but for the entire period of American reform. It is granted such esteem because it is conventionally perceived as a measure by which the nation's banking and financial institutions were placed under public regulation, control, and scrutiny. In reality, however, the act was similar in origin and purpose to previously discussed measures; namely, an effort by large firms to enlist the assistance of the state in stabilizing the environment of a particular industry after the failure of voluntary cooperative efforts.[23] The passage of the act in 1914 came after two decades of patient efforts by large bankers for regulation. As James A. Forgan, the leading Chicago banker of his day, recounted: "From the time I came to Chicago in 1892 the necessity of new banking and currenty legislation was appreciated by most bankers. . . ."[24] In fact, from as early as 1893, when the American Bankers' Association called for banking legislation, scores of regulatory schemes were introduced in Congress that were conceived, written, and endorsed by the nation's leading bankers. Impetus was added to this effort by the financial panic of 1907. While the resulting depression was relatively short-lived, the failure of banks to tame the panic until it was almost too late frightened both financial and government officials, and renewed efforts were made to secure banking regulation.

The main problems from the point of view of the banking community were the inelasticity of the supply of currency, the absence of adequate reserve funds, and the chaotic instability of the proliferating smaller banks. Representatives of the American Bankers' Association testified before Congress that it would support any measure that would lead to elasticity and cooperation in money reserve management. The demands for federal currency legislation and regional reserve systems were publicly advocated by leading bankers, including J. P. Morgan. When the bill was finally drafted, it was the legislative committee of the American Bankers' Association, in conjunction with Congressman Carter Glass, that was most responsible for its provisions.

The Federal Reserve Act was the first major step toward the regulation and stabilization of the general economy, a process that was not completed until the Employment Act of 1946. The measure created an instrument for regulating one important aspect of the economy. The central function of the Federal Reserve system, which is in effect a bank for bankers, was and remains one of regulating the flow of money and credit in the economy. The system does this by indirect determination of interest rates, by its transactions in government bonds (called "open-market operations") and by altering the interest rates on loans by the Federal Reserve to member banks. Through these devices, the banker-backed Federal Reserve Act added a significant element of control to the economy: reducing money during times of inflation and expanding the supply to counter economic downturns. It would take the Great Depression and World War II to convince economic and political leaders, however, that the "monetary" controls of the Federal Reserve were not sufficient for the requirements of a modern capitalist system.

Perhaps the most symbolically important legislative measure of the progressive era was the Federal Trade Commission Act (1914) which created the Federal Trade Commission (FTC) to regulate corporations. It is important because it helped to create the impression that the progressives in general and Woodrow Wilson in particular were anti-big business. Nothing, however, could be further from the truth. As with the other measures under review, it is now clear that the FTC was the creation of many of the major corporations and, in this case, their organizational manifestation, the National Civic Federation (NCF).[25]

The major impetus to corporate efforts to regulate itself through the state was the general ambiguity in the meaning of the Sherman Anti-Trust Act. This act made illegal all combinations in restraint of trade, a phraseology sufficiently vague that it failed to halt the massive wave of corporate mergers and consolidations between 1897 and 1904. The courts, consistent with English and American common law precedents, generally interpreted the act to mean that combinations in restraint of trade were allowable so long as they were not unreasonable. Under the common law, efforts to maintain prices, to prevent ruinous competition, and to restrict production were legal as long as other parties were theoretically free to enter the competition. As long as no attempt was made to prevent competition, monopoly was also allowable under the common law. There remained however, considerable uncertainty among business leaders as to the long-term willingness of the courts to tie the Sherman Act closely to the common law. Business was made especially uncomfortable by the Supreme Court's decision in the Trans-Missouri case (1897), a decision that made no distinction between reasonable and unreasonable restraint.

Besides their already described distaste for cutthroat competition, price cuts, and diminishing profits, and their search for methods to guarantee stable growth and guaranteed profits to the largest firms, business leaders also came to realize that federal regulation would preempt and transcend efforts by many of the states to regulate corporations. Both the lack of uniformity between states and the tendency for some states to take far more hostile action against corporations convinced leading elements of the business class to turn to Washington.[26]

The principal force behind the establishment of the FTC was the National Civic Federation, an organization formed by some of the nation's most influential business leaders in 1900 to orient government policy in directions favorable to business. Composed of leading businessmen like Mark Hanna, August Belmont, and J. P. Morgan, influential academics like John R. Commons and Richard Ely, and labor leaders Samuel Gompers and John Mitchell, the NCF was an organization devoted to the construction of the positive state. It advocated national regulation of the economy, labor-management peace through collective bargaining, and the provision of social welfare services, like unemployment insurance and workmen's compensation. It was at the initiative of the NCF that a national conference was held in 1907 for the express purpose of urging Congress to revise the Sherman Act so that it would approximate common law interpretations of restraint of trade. For that reason, it made the first step toward the Federal Trade Commission legislation. Their subsequent lobbying efforts were so successful that congressional leaders asked the NCF to put their ideas into the form of a legislative proposal, a task that they completed in 1908.[27] Although the bill was not passed by Congress, most probably because of the intense opposition of small- and middle-sized businesses, it served as the model for later legislation.

The National Civic Federation continued to press for federal regulation, and moved in 1909 under the direction of its president, Seth Low, to draft a revised piece of model legislation. The federation's principal public relations victory was its national poll of 30,000 businessmen that showed overwhelming majorities in favor of federal incorporations, federal licensing, and an interstate trade commission along the lines of the Interstate Commerce Commission. By 1913, the model legislation was submitted to Congress, where in 1914 a bill was passed that approximated almost sentence by sentence the NCF proposal.

Rather than a measure proclaiming the anti-big business bias of the Wilson administration, the Federal Trade Commission Act represented a major accomplishment for big business. Most important, it tied the Sherman Act to the common law tradition and made allowances for "reasonable" restraints, prohibited certain practices of "unfair" competition (thus, lessening competition), and had the effect of allowing trade associations to set prices within their industries. The act also provided for the gathering of business information and for the incorporation of uniform procedures of accounting and reporting, thereby furthering the processes of planning, rationality, and control in the corporate economy. Finally, the legislation served an important protective function for big business, because while it in reality gave governmental legitimacy to business efforts to regulate itself, it looked as if the anticorporation sentiments of many Americans were heeded by government. The act thus served to protect the corporations against potentially more radical threats to corporate prerogatives and profits at the state level.

Local Political Reform

At the same time business was beginning its first halting steps toward a government-sponsored cooperative capitalism at the national level, and motivated by many of the same aspirations, business groups launched a series of reforms designed to make politics, particularly local politics, more "business-like."[28] What this meant, of course, was a politics committed to business ends and run either directly by business or particularly sensitive to its interests. The reform movement took the form of "cleaning up" politics. The reality was an effort to deflate the power of working class and ethnic groups in the political process.

The particulars of this movement varied, but all of them were directed toward the destruction of the urban machine and the system of coalition, ward politics at its base. In the classic urban machine, the political leader, usually the elected mayor, traded a variety of favors, benefits, concessions, and the like in return for the votes of working-class and immigrant populations organized on a ward basis. The machine also traded favors like city services and police protection with local businesses in return for their financial support. While such a complicated system of favor trading and petty corruption was sufficient for and even beneficial to small businesses, it seemed to the leaders of the largest and most important firms to be not only too inefficient, wasteful, and uncertain, but to grant to lower class and potentially radical populations a degree of political influence that was not warranted.

The attack on machine-ward politics took many forms, but the most important innovations remained the substitution of a professional city manager for an elected mayor, the expansion of civil service designation at the expense of a political appointment process, citywide elections as opposed to ward elections, and the substitution of nonpartisan elections for the party system. Perhaps even more important was the near universal imposition of strict registration requirements for electoral participation. While all of these reforms hold a hallowed place for most Americans today, they were all designed and were largely successful in enhancing the power of business over local government and seriously diminishing that of the growing working class. That the entire process was not as mysterious as it seems to us today is suggested by the fact that these political reforms were actively sponsored and supported by local business groups and opposed by working class, immigrant, and labor groups. It is significant, in fact, that in almost every case these reforms were imposed on municipalities by state legislatures and not voluntary introduced by municipal voters.

The effects were very much as anticipated. What is most striking about the impact of these reforms was the general decrease in voter turnout in all elections and the growth in class differentials in electoral participation. These methods, then, in the opinion of one of the leading students of American elections, were the means "by which a large and possibly dangerous mass electorate could be brought to heel and subjected to management and control within the political system appropriate to capitalist democracy."[29]

THE MEANING OF PROGRESSIVE REFORM

In politics, as in life, things are often not what they seem. The distinctive image of progressive reform in American history textbooks is its anticorporation stance yet, as we have demonstrated, much of the landmark legislation of the period not only served to assist the corporation, but was, in fact, conceived, formulated, and drafted by business leaders. Much of the confusion about this matter can be traced to the considerable and important legislative activity at the state level aimed at curbing certain corporate abuses like child labor, political and commercial corruption, and unsafe products. Additional confusion is contributed by that legislation at the national level which, while serving corporate ends, also had net advantages for the general public, namely, meat, food, and drug inspections. Most importantly, however, most people fail to distinguish between pre- and post-1900 reform. The first period was concomitant with the rise to business ascendency of the trusts in the last fifteen years of the nineteenth century. The emerging giant corporations were then enjoying rapid consolidation, market domination, and escalating profits. Their very success as business enterprises, however, adversely affected the interests of small businesses, farmers, and small-town residents, and ruffled the moral sensibilities of many churchmen and advocates of laissez faire. As a result, this period was consistent with the textbook characterization of progressivism: grass roots hostility to the "trusts," demand for legislative reform of business practices, and corporate resistance to government interference.

As Gabriel Kolko so brilliantly points out, however, the economic situation of the giant corporations and financial institutions changed drastically after 1900, when they found themselves faced with increased competition, loss of market control, and declining profits. In the midst of this crisis, especially after the failure of giant firms to stabilize the economy through private efforts, the most sophisticated leaders of corporate enterprise turned to the federal government to perform the stabilizing role they could not accomplish for themselves.

There is no denying the very real and intensely felt anticorporation sentiments among many Americans, particularly farmers. What is ironic is that business leadership was able to funnel this sentiment, generated during the first reform period, into directions favorable to itself during the second period. Indeed, the sentiment helped to provide the energy and democratic legitimacy for many reforms long sought by business leaders. In fact, the purportedly anticorporation progressive era did not adversely affect the position of big business. At the termination of progressive reform during World War I, the position of the giant corporation and financial institution was more entrenched and stable than it had been in decades. This occurred because business was able to divert popular desires for reform into favorable channels and because business itself was the driving force behind much of the landmark progressive legislation. In progressivism, we see one of the first and most successful examples in which the leading and most sophisticated elements of the business class used the state apparatus to meet certain needs that it was unable to meet through voluntary cooperative efforts.

The early decades of this century were witness, then, to a fundamental change in political philosophy among an important segment of the business class, primarily the leaders of the largest firms. For most of the eighteenth and nineteenth centuries, the ideas of laissez-faire economics held sway among business leaders. In their fight against mercantilist restrictions on entreprenuerial activity, business leaders evolved and supported social theories that emphasized the benefits of the minimal state and of vigorous competition between economic units. Laissez-faire theory reached the height of its influence in the latter half of the nineteenth century when, gaining the scientific legitimacy of its ties to Darwinian biology, it extolled the business leader as contributor to the general welfare and as the "fittist" survivor of life's struggles.

However, the emerging industrial revolution, the growth of giant enterprises, and the nationalization of economic life called for new ways of comprehending social reality and new guidelines for political and social action. Out of these needs arose a new social theory of cooperation and regulation. While medium and small businesses continued, in general, to believe the maxims of laissez-faire economics, Protestant clergy of the "social gospel," economists like Richard Ely, E.R.A. Seligman, and Henry Carter Adams, and social theorists like Lester Ward, William James, John R. Commons, and John Dewey all helped lead a frontal assault on laissez faire in the name of a new, cooperative society in which the state would play a prominent role.[30] While each viewed the American condition from a different perspective, all of them came to advocate a society in which the state would be utilized for the solution of common problems, for provisions of health and safety, for the amelioration of the harsh by-products of the industrial order, and for the regulation of the economy in the name of security. All argued that in the complex interdependent world of large-scale industry, urbanization, communication, and transportation, the state could not retain the passive role defined for it under laissez-faire, and that the state was the only entity capable of providing the necessary coordination, guidance, and rationalization.

These theorists of the general welfare state, as they are designated by Sidney Fine, believed that in an urban-industrial society, the ends of nineteenth-century liberalism (freedom and individualism) could only be preserved through positive state action, that, as paradoxical as it might seem, laissez faire ends were not attainable by laissez-faire means. As Woodrow Wilson put it in a 1912 campaign speech describing *The New Freedom*,

> *I feel confident that if Jefferson were living in our day he would see what we see: that the individual is caught in a great confused nexus of all sorts of complicated circumstances, and that to let him alone is to leave him helpless as against the obstacles with which he has to contend; and that, therefore, law in our day must come to the assistance of the individual. . . . freedom today is something more than being let alone. The program of government of freedom must in these days be positive, not negative merely.[31]*

These theorists were not advocating socialism, however. While attempting to alleviate the harsh qualities of laissez-faire society, they were vitally concerned with the preservation of the private property system. They wished to avoid the extremes of both socialism and laissez faire, and to stimulate enough positive state action, through essential reforms and improvements in social justice, to preserve and strengthen the free enterprise system. In the words of the most prominent social gospeler of his day, Washington Gladden, "New occasions bring new duties; the functions of the state must be broadened to meet the exigencies of our expanding civilization. We may go far beyond Mr. Spencer's limits and yet stop a great way this side of socialism."[32]

It was within the context of this new vision of the relationship of state, society, and economy that the reforms of the progressive era took shape. The completion of the vision and of the construction of the main outlines of the new welfare state (in Fine's terminology) or positive state (our terminology) would have to wait for the Great Depression and the New Deal.

NOTES

[1] See Eric Goldman *Rendezvous with Destiny* (New York: Knopf, 1952) and Richard Hofstader, *The Age of Reform* (New York: Knopf, 1952).

[2] For a strong articulation of this view see Arthur M. Schlesinger, Jr., *The Age of Jackson* (Boston: Little, Brown, 1946), p. 505.

[3] Robert H. Wiebe, *The Search for Order: 1877-1920* (New York: Hill and Wang, 1967).

[4] These descriptions hold true, however, only if one ignores for the moment the pre-Civil War slave economy of the south.

[5] See Robert Nozick, *Anarchy, State, and Utopia* (New York: Basic Books, 1974) for a leading philosophic defense of the minimal state.

[6] Ernest Mandel, *Late Capitalism* (London: New Left Books, 1975), p. 477.

[7] See Karl Polanyi, *The Great Transformation* (Boston: Beacon Press, 1957) for this history.

[8] For a review of the literature on the early American state see Alan Wolfe, *The Limits of Legitimacy* (New York: Free Press, 1977), Chapter 1.

[9] For this history see Sidney Fine, *Laissez-Faire and the General Welfare*

State (Ann Arbor: University of Michigan Press, 1956) and Wolfe, *The Limits of Legitimacy.*

[10] For a description of this transformation see Samuel P. Hays, *The Response to Industrialization* (Chicago: University of Chicago Press, 1957) and Weibe, *The Search for Order.*

[11] Ernest Mandel, *Marxist Economic Theory* (New York: Monthly Review Press, 1962), Chapter 12.

[12] See Thomas C. Cochran, *Business in American Life: A History* (New York: McGraw-Hill, 1972).

[13] Ibid., p. 145.

[14] Mandel, *Marxist Economic Theory,* p. 400.

[15] Ibid., p. 401.

[16] Ibid., p. 406.

[17] In western Kansas in 1893, for instance, farm income fell 59 percent. See Gabriel Kolko, *Main Currents in American History* (New York: Harper & Row, 1976), p. 25.

[18] A useful introduction to this history may be found in Sidney Lens, *The Labor Wars* (Garden City, N.Y.: Anchor Books, 1973).

[19] For the principal documentation of this point see Gabriel Kolko, *The Triumph of Conservatism: A Reinterpretation of American History 1900–1916* (Chicago: Quadrangel, 1967). Much of the following discussion is based on Kolko's landmark scholarship.

[20] Ibid., p. 40.

[21] Quoted in ibid., p. 107.

[22] Ibid., p. 109.

[23] The discussion is based on ibid.

[24] Ibid., p. 146.

[25] Most of the following is based on James Weinstein, *The Corporate Ideal in the Liberal State; 1900–1918* (Boston: Beacon Press, 1968).

[26] Kolko, *The Triumph of Conservatism.*

[27]The drafting committee included, among others, E. G. Gary of U.S. Steel; Samuel Mathes, prominent investment banker; and August Belmont and George Perkins of J. P. Morgan and Company. The actual bill was written by attorneys for J. P. Morgan. See G. William Domhoff, *The Higher Circles: The Governing Class in America* (New York: Random House, Vintage Press, 1971).

[28]The remainder of this section is based on Walter Dean Burnham, *Critical Elections and the Mainsprings of American Politics* (New York: W. W. Norton, 1970) and Samuel P. Hays, "The Politics of Reform in Municipal Government in the Progressive Era," *Pacific Northwest Quarterly*, Vol. 55 (October 1964).

[29]Burnham, *Critical Elections and the Mainsprings of American Politics*, p. 90.

[30]For the outstanding discussion of this revolution in social theory see Fine, *Laissez-faire*.

[31]Cited in ibid., p. 383.

[32]Ibid., p. 186.

4
ON THE CONSTRUCTION OF THE MODERN POSITIVE STATE: PART 2

Making sense of the New Deal response to the Great Depression of the 1930s, without a doubt the most severe crisis of capitalist accumulation and class relations in our history, is not an easy task, for feelings about it remain so strong. To many conservatives, it represents the single most important step toward socialism in the United States. To reform liberals the New Deal is the watershed period in recent American history—a period that represents proof of the commitment of the state to social justice. A close reading of New Deal history suggests, however, that both views are essentially misplaced. It is our contention that the New Deal may be best understood as a series of attempts to save capitalism by further regulating and rationalizing the economy, by bringing important elements of the labor movement into established political life, and by staving off social revolution through expansion of the welfare role of the state. In the New Deal, public officials and business leaders instituted many of the mechanisms by which the state regularizes, stabilizes, and rationalizes the economy and society for the benefit of the corporate sector—by, for example, private business planning, collective bargaining, fiscal and monetary controls, military spending, and social insurance. Seen in this light, the New Deal represents, paradoxically, a conservative expansion of state activities. While it is traditional to define state expansion as "liberal," we would argue that since expansion was directed toward the preservation and cementing of the position of private capital and the maintenance of the social class system, it must be judged "conservative." As one scholar has suggested, the New

Deal must be seen as the final maturation of capitalism into the modern welfare state.[1]

Such an interpretation may prove bothersome to many people, particularly because of what appears to have been significant business opposition to Franklin Roosevelt and the New Deal. What we shall attempt to demonstrate, however, is the existence of two wings of the business class: medium and small business represented in part by organizations like the National Association of Manufacturers (NAM); and big business, represented by men such as Gerard Swope of General Electric, Myron Taylor of U.S. Steel, and by organizations such as the National Civic Federation (NCF) and the American Association of Labor Legislation (AALL). Each wing held opposing views of the role of the state. The latter tended to be articulate and influential speakers for the positive state; the extreme vituperation toward the New Deal shown by business leaders of the NAM persuasion should not obscure their important role in the New Deal.

Nevertheless, it is also the case that some leaders of big business, encumbered by the maxims of laissez-faire capitalism and Social Darwinism, certainly failed to comprehend the real meaning of the New Deal and its benefits to business enterprise. Franklin Roosevelt was himself somewhat baffled and confused by business hostility. He saw the New Deal as a preservative, as a program to save the private property system by fusing welfare benefits to a capitalist foundation and in this way creating long-term stability.[2] His basic attitude was that for capitalism to survive, it would have to rid itself of reckless speculation and unregulated fluctuation, and that with the assistance of the state, business could regulate itself for its own benefit and for the overall benefit of society. One of his principal biographers believes that FDR, seeing himself as the main preserver of the capitalist system in its time of greatest crisis, was both hurt and confused by the attacks of some business leaders.[3]

While sophisticalted elements of big business were in full support of the New Deal, it took the Second World War to convince the business community as a whole that the expansion of state activities was in their interest. This switch in attitude is probably best demonstrated by the failure of the conservative Eisenhower administration to dismantle the positive state, and the wholesale, though temporary, defection of business leaders to the Democratic party in the 1964 election when faced with the anti-New Deal, antiwelfare state pronouncements of the Republican candidate Barry Goldwater.

THE FIRST NEW DEAL

Compared to the relatively passive administrations of the Republicans during the 1920s, the first one-hundred days of the new Roosevelt Administration seemed revolutionary indeed. In that short and exciting period in American life, legislation came forth for the regulation of business, agriculture, the stock market and banks, and for the institution of emergency relief and public works projects. Americans by and large applauded and rallied to a president who seemed to grasp the magnitude of the crisis and the extent of their misery, and who seemed willing to move against the worst depression in history. We believe, however, that these emergency measures best demonstrate the conservative thrust of the New Deal, and its goal of preserving capitalism and the class system.

What is important to comprehend, if we are to grasp the conservative proclivities of the Roosevelt administration, is the extent of the crisis that gripped American capitalism in 1933. Unemployment, as can best be determined, reached 15 million on the day of Roosevelt's inauguration in 1933, about one-third of the total work force.[4] In Pennsylvania, one-third of the population was without income of any kind. In West Virginia, many mines were closed, and miners out of work. Reports of widespread begging and hospital admissions for starvation filled the newspapers. In Chicago, 40 percent of the able-bodied were unemployed. Breadlines were commonplace in most large cities. Bank failures accelerated with their resultant depressing effects on business activity and disastrous consequences for family savings. In 1932 over 2,000 banks closed their doors, while almost 1,500 followed suit in the following year. By 1933 the crisis in banking had become national and unmanageable, with some of the major, big city banks going under. The situation was so serious that on Inauguration Day, 1933, most states had declared bank holidays. In agriculture, the depression that started in the 1920s accelerated. Between 1929 and 1932, total farm income fell from $13.6 to $6.3 billion. Farmers were faced with rapidly declining income in the face of stable mortgage costs and rising equipment costs and, not surprisingly, farm foreclosures escalated in the early 1930s. In industry, gross income in the manufacturing sector fell from $68 billion in 1929 to $28 billion in 1932, with no sign of recovery in the offing.

One response to massive joblessness, hunger, and misery was the explosive rise in mass disorder. Local relief offices were raided and seized in many localities. City councils, state legislatures, and even the national congress were faced with recurrent protest marches. In some cities, people organized to physically prevent evictions. In rural areas, farmers began to organize to physically prevent farm foreclosures. Rent riots took place in several cities, Chicago in particular.

American capitalism was clearly in grave danger, with industrial and agricultural indicators plummeting, the banking system in a state of crisis, major portions of the population without jobs or income, the local relief system in collapse, and popular anger rising against big business and finance. In such an atmosphere, it is probable although not certain, that political leadership could have moved in any direction it desired to meet the crisis. The fact that the Roosevelt administration moved to revive capitalism, to restore it to health rather than to transcend it, suggests its basically conservative orientation.

Emerging Measures

The manner in which it chose to deal with the banking crisis is a good example. Instead of moving to nationalize the banking system, as most observers suggest was conceivable, given the crisis, Roosevelt chose to restore it, but with enough alterations to ensure its health. After a series of meetings with leading bankers, Treasury Department officials, and former Hoover advisors, FDR decided to reopen sound banks in the hands of their owners and managers.[5] With the exception of a handful of banks, the remainder were allowed to reopen after Treasury Department intervention and reform of banking practices. The Emergency Banking Act of March 9 authorized the Reconstruction Finance Corporation to supply working capital to banks by buying their stock, and for the Federal Reserve banks to make loans to nonmember banks and business enterprises. Formal legislation was buttressed by the president's first "fireside chat" on March 12, in which he expressed confidence in the banking system and urged citizens to redeposit their money.

This combination of vigorous legislation and presidential leadership had, by the end of March, saved the banking system. Deposits climbed dramatically, especially in gold and gold certificates. The immediate crisis had been met. In the words of one of the participants, Raymond Moley:

> *It cannot be emphasized too strongly that the policies which vanquished the bank crisis were thoroughly conservative policies. The sole departure from convention lay in the swiftness and boldness with which they were carried out. Those who conceived and executed them were intent upon rallying the confidence, first, of the conservative business and banking leaders of the country and, then, through them of the public generally. . . . If ever there was a moment*

*when things hung in the balance, it was on March 5, 1933—when
unorthodoxy would have drained the last remaining strength of the
capitalist system. Capitalism was saved in eight days.* . . . [6]

With the short-term crisis under control, the administration turned to
the long-term rationalization and stabilization of the banking system. By
1935, banks were forced to divorce their investment affiliates from their
commercial operations, thus preventing them from participating in reckless
speculation. The use of Federal Reserve credit for speculation also was dis-
allowed for the first time. To reestablish depositor confidence and to
prevent damaging "runs" on the banks, the administration moved to ensure deposits through the Federal Deposit Insurance Corporation (FDIC).
These reforms were bolstered with extensive loans and investments by the
federal government in banks of various sizes. More power was granted to
the Federal Reserve Board to regulate credit and currency supply. Thus,
by 1935, not only had the immediate crisis been met, but the system had
been significantly stabilized and rationalized through elimination of weak
banks, the insurance of deposits, stronger monetary controls, and controls
on speculation.

The response to the farm crisis, a crisis that had been severe since at
least 1925, was also conservative in its effects. In the eight years from
1925 to 1933, farm prices fell, farm income plummeted, costs rose (equipment, taxes, etc.) and foreclosures accelerated. Out of the potential
repertory of responses to this crisis, the New Deal chose a system with
which we are saddled to this day, a system that produces for *profit* not for
use. [7] In the face of widespread hunger during the Depression, the administration decided that the solution to the farm crisis was to raise farm
prices by eliminating abundance and recreating scarcity. The original measure utilized four methods for accomplishing these goals (1) restriction of
output and removal of surpluses from the market, (2) direct payments to
farmers for reducing their output, (3) taxing primary processors to raise
revenue for these benefits, and (4) encouragement of voluntary associations among farmers, processors, and distributors to raise and to maintain
prices.

Such a program has outcomes that still hold true to this day. Since payments were made in proportion to previous and potential production, the
bulk of the benefits flowed to the biggest and most prosperous farmers.
Reduction of farm acreage, allied with the natural inclination of the
farmer to produce as much or more from the reduced acreage, and linked

to the ready availability of government benefit funds, led to the acceleration of farm mechanization. The result was the displacement of millions of tenant farmers, sharecroppers, and marginal farm owners from the land, adding fuel to the migration to cities and to the West and to the explosion in relief rolls. All of this, of course, took place in addition to escalating food costs for the consumer and amid high unemployment and destitution. And yet, the New Deal had, indeed, launched federal agricultural policy on the road toward profitability and stability for the farmers who remained, particularly the largest ones among them.

The National Industrial Recovery Act
The most interesting piece of legislation during Roosevelt's first-one-hundred days as president, given its relationship to the long history of state intervention to stabilize and rationalize capitalism, was the National Industrial Recovery Act (NIRA) which established the National Recovery Administration (NRA). In the NRA, we see an important manifestation of efforts by a wing of the business class to use the powers of the state to reduce competition, to stabilize prices, to bring industrial peace and, consequently, to render its economic environment more predictable.

As discussed above, the early part of the twentieth century saw a reaction to and a concerted attack upon laissez-faire economics by business leaders, social gospel clergy, academic sociologists and economists, and other influential intellectuals. The new positive state theorists proposed a society based on cooperation, efficiency, and science rather than on anarchistic and unstable competition, and they saw their efforts bear their first fruit in the Federal Trade Commission of the Wilson administration. This dream of a government-supported business commonwealth would be nourished by World War I industrial mobilization, the efforts of Herbert Hoover, and would reach its full flowing in the NRA of the New Deal.

Encouraged by the experience with the FTC, the movement to create voluntary industrial trade associations for the purpose of regulating competition and maintaining prices, had become a social cause by the eve of World War I.[8] This trade association movement converged with other streams of activity to encourage industrial cooperation, namely, the scientific management movement and recurrent efforts by government to create special representation relationships with business organizations. All of these movements toward cooperation merged and solidified in the experience of World War I mobilization. The War Industries Board, under the leadership of Bernard Baruch, used existing trade associations and encouraged the development of trade associations where none existed, in order to encourage cooperative relationships within industries, between industries, and between government and industry. The goal was to seek the most widespread cooperation in mobilizing production for war. It attempted to meet this goal by dividing the job of regulating commodity production into divisions headed by the representatives from the largest firms, allowing them, in effect, to set production and pricing policies for their own sectors. As one of the board's administrators said, "Conservation, priority, curtailment, price-fixing, all required such cooperation and agreement within each industry that the Government was constantly exhibited as requiring in its hour of peril the very things which had been four years denounced as criminal."[9]

While the War Industries Board was only partially successful, it being in existence scarcely more than a single year, the dream of a cooperative business system was greatly enhanced by the war experience and its advocacy was continued after the war, most particularly by then Secretary of Commerce, Herbert Hoover. While Hoover feared government coercion, he believed that a rational and scientific capitalism required a system of voluntary sectorial planning under business leadership. As Secretary of Commerce, he encouraged the formation of trade associations in a wide variety of industries, most notably in rubber, oil, and coal, under the umbrella of the FTC, all for the purpose of advancing industrial self-regulation. The codes of fair trade that were formulated were directed at price maintenance, elimination of cutthroat competition, and establishment of uniform standards.

In the crisis of the Depression, New Deal political and business leadership turned to this vision of cooperative capitalism. The result was the National Industrial Recovery Act.

The central belief among advocates of this act was that the main cause of the economic depression was traceable to overproduction and inadequate prices, a situation especially marked in coal, textiles, and agriculture.[10] The proposed remedy, which flowed naturally from the analysis, was to reduce competition, raise prices, and reestablish healthy and stable profits. The central device would be government permission for firms within each industry to form trade associations, to set production quotas and prices, and government suspension of the Sherman and Clayton Antitrust Acts. Prominent business leaders connected with the War Industries Board of World War I, impressed by that experience, advocated official recognition by the state of its role as "cooperator, adjuster and friend" of big business. Gerard Swope, president of General Electric, in his "The Stabilization of Industry" speech before the National Electrical Manufacturers Association in 1931, called for a cooperative commonwealth that would include mandatory trade association, collective bargaining, and old age, disability, and unemployment insurance. Swope's proposal was endorsed in the same year by Henry Harriman, the Chairman of the Chamber of Commerce of the United States.

In the National Industrial Recovery Act of 1933, which closely approximated the Swope plan, President Roosevelt demonstrated his agreement with such thinking. He called the NIRA the machinery for a "great cooperative movement throughout all industry . . . ," and the means to meet "a national emergency productive of widespread unemployment and disorganization of industry." The essential feature of the measure was a provision to make the previously voluntary codes of fair practice in each industry the law of the land, enforceable by the state, and to encourage and even impose codes where none existed.

In the process of actual code writing, the largest firms in each industry tended to dominate the proceedings.[11] Although the NIRA made provision for consumer and labor representation, the general opinion among NRA administrators was that the heart of the measure depended on self-government by the leaders of big business. Coupled with its highly organized nature and its access to expert opinion, this bias among administrations led to a situation in which the largest corporations were able to dominate code writing and to impose the codes on their smaller competitors with the sanction of the federal government.

It seems that big business domination of the code process was not unexpected or unwelcomed by the administration. As President Roosevelt put it to the Commonwealth Club in 1933, in urging support for NIRA:

> *The responsible heads of finance and industry, instead of acting each for himself, must work together to achieve the common end. They must, where necessary, sacrifice this or that private advantage, and in reciprocal self-denial must seek a general advantage. It is here that formal government . . . comes in.*

In government sponsorship of "codes of fair competition" which were, in fact, written by and for the major corporations so that they might restrict competition, we see an excellent example of Marx's notion that the capitalist state "parades around under the banner of universality" while it serves class ends.

General support for NIRA was relatively short-lived, and enthusiasm for it had waned well before the Supreme Court declared it unconstitutional. Once it became apparent that the codes were dominated by the industrial giants, opposition to it began to mount from agriculture, from small and medium-sized business, and from unions that had been largely excluded from the code writing. Interestingly enough, the strong public sentiment against NIRA forced the NRA to scrutinize business practices more closely, but since the codes were already written into law, the scrutiny amounted to little more than harassment, a situation that served only to antagonize big business. The growing disaffection for NRA among big business was multiplied by the surge in disorderly labor organization spurred by Section 7a of NIRA, which encouraged labor organization. While business leaders advocated collective bargaining, most of them had not expected the type of militant labor organization represented by the Congress of Industrial Organizations (CIO). Finally, and perhaps most importantly, the practices encouraged by the NRA simply did not work. In many of the industries where hopes were highest, textiles being a case in point, profits were no higher after the institutionalization of the codes than before.[12] As a result, by the time the Court struck down the NRA, almost all support for it had disintegrated, and few people mourned its passing.

Another reason for declining business support for NIRA was that businesses realized the same end results—the regulation of competition, pricing, and production—could be attained through less visible, though still state-sanctioned procedures. With the end of the immediate crisis, the need had passed for open state supervision which brought in its wake the potential for harassment and public scrutiny. Big business came to realize that private arrangements, single industry regulation, and government aids such as tariffs, subsidies, and loans, would establish the same oligopolistic practices without the need for the continual public scrutiny encouraged by NRA. In the post-NRA wreckage was established our contemporary tendency to depend on private single-industry planning, government assistance and protection, and minimal enforcement of the antitrust laws.[13]

THE SECOND NEW DEAL

In the first months of the New Deal we see, then, the largely successful efforts to save the capitalist system through reform. We have only touched on several of the many New Deal programs in this period, but we hope to have focused on those with the most long-term significance and interest. The banking laws helped complete the machinery of self-regulation for the major banks started in the progressive era and represented by the Federal Reserve Act. The Agricultural Adjustment Act constructed a framework for farm price supports and production restrictions beneficial to the largest farmers that is very much a part of farm policy today. Although the machinery fell by the wayside, the National Industrial Recovery Act was interesting for its continuity with a long history of business self-regulation, beginning with the Interstate Commerce Commission, and encompassing the welfare state theorists, the scientific management movement, the New Nationalism, the New Freedom, World War I mobilization and the volunteerism of Herbert Hoover. It is also interesting because it brought into the open, and therefore made vulnerable practices that were from the point of business leaders best kept under cloak.

We have accounted, however, for only a portion of the New Deal. Even for those historians who reluctantly admit to the conservative outcomes of the first New Deal, the claim is made for a second New Deal, represented by the passage of the Social Security and Wagner Labor Relations Acts, in which the state demonstrated its concern both for the worker and the disadvantaged. The second New Deal, it is said, saw a turning away from support of the corporate sector and a turn toward issues of social justice. Our contention, however, is that measures like Social Security and the Wagner Acts were essential concomitants to a rationalized and stabilized capitalist order, and a response to uncontrolled class conflict, and that at least one wing of the business class had long been involved in agitation for such reforms.

In 1935, the New Deal did seem to turn to the left. In that year came increases in spending for emergency relief and public works, some spending for public housing, subsidies to the arts, the Social Security Act, and the Wagner Labor Relations Act, all accompanied by some anti-big business rhetoric by the president. In several speeches, he attacked what he called the "economic royalists" and called for a "soak the rich tax" (although it is significant that he never actively supported such a measure in Congress). No doubt, much of the misperception about the "second New Deal" is derived from the rhetorical behavior of the president, because a careful scrutiny of the principal measures leaves little doubt about their nonradical, even, conservative character.

THE SOCIAL SECURITY ACT
Clearly the major impetus for the second New Deal was a serious political crisis for the president, especially the threat of widespread domestic turmoil and popular support for radical legislative measures. The year

1934 was particularly troublesome. Encouraged by Section 7a of the NIRA and embittered by employer opposition, workers organized ever more militant strikes and factory takeovers. Entire cities—Minneapolis, Toledo, and San Francisco—were closed by general strikes and subsequent police violence. Perhaps more important, a series of movements seeking economic redistribution were gaining tremendous momentum after it became apparent to most people that the initial invigorating flourish of the New Deal had not bettered the lot of the average American. Huey Long of Louisiana led a "share our wealth" movement that sought free homesteads and education, inexpensive food stuffs, severe limitations for fortunes, and a minimum guaranteed annual income of $5,000. Long was so popular, in fact, that until his assassination, FDR feared that he would split the national Democratic party and deny him the renomination. Father Coughlin, the influential "radio priest" of Depression days garnered the support of millions of listeners for his program of currency inflation, guaranteed wages, and the nationalization of banking and natural resources.

The largest and most influential movement was led by Francis Townsend of California who advocated the disarmingly simple proposal that every citizen over the age of sixty receive a pension of $200 per month with the only conditions being that they not hold a job (thus opening up employment for others) and that they spend all of their money within 30 days (thus stimulating economic recovery). By 1936 there were an estimated 7,000 Townsend clubs throughout the country and a membership of over two million people.[14] Moreover, 25 million people signed petitions in favor of the plan. To the leading students of the legislation, it was the Townsend Plan and its widespread support that led to the Social Security Act.[15] In the words of one of the leading architects of the measure, Secretary of Labor Frances Perkins ". . . there was the Townsend plan which both drove us and confused the issue. Without the Townsend plan, it is possible that the old-age insurance system would not have received the attention which it did at the hands of Congress."[16]

There were even more radical stirrings in the population to add impetus to the new priorities of the New Deal. The Unemployed Councils and the radical Unemployed Leagues, both grew rapidly in 1934, demanding greatly expanded relief efforts. While it is almost impossible to gauge their national strength, the membership of the latter exceeded 100,000 in Ohio, and 70,000 in Pensylvania.[17] In Congress, there was surprising support for the Lundeen Bill that called for unemployment compensation (with no time limitations) commensurate with local wages, financed by taxes on inheritances, gifts, and high incomes, and administered by workers' and farmers' councils.

It was clearly in response to this combined agitation and its clear threat to political and social order that the administration moved to incorporate the rhetoric of reform, though not its substance, in the Social Security Act. While the measure met the widespread demand for unemployment and old-age benefits, and thus symbolically moved to meet strongly felt grievances, in substance, the measure was highly conservative. The most important feature of the measure was to make it an insurance program rather than a program financed out of general revenues. In fact, the major internal battle in the administration was over whether to finance the measure from payroll taxes, or from taxes on upper income groups.[18] The president, who never wavered in his desire to have an actuarially sound insurance system, chose the former, and thus brought about a system in which the worker was forced to save for a rainy day by subtracting money from his current wages. As we shall suggest in a later chapter, the system that was ultimately constructed proved to be one of the most regressive in the Western world, since it features a flat tax rate, an income limit above which no taxes are taken, and the exclusion of taxes on property and securities income. To make matters worse, in the words of one of the leading supporters of the New Deal: "(It) left millions of old people uncovered, and in any case payments under old-age insurance would not begin till 1942."[19]

The essentially conservative nature of the Social Security Act is demonstrated most graphically by the support it received from many business leaders, who saw it as sound and conservative. Strong opposition by the reactionary National Association of Manufacturers ought not to detract from the fact that it was strongly endorsed by the Business Advisory Council, the representative for progressive big business. Strong public support was given the program by men like Gerard Swope of General Electric, Walter Teagle of Standard Oil, Henry Harriman, of the U.S. Chamber of Commerce, Winthrop Aldrich of the Chase Manhattan Bank, James Rand of Remington Rand, and W. A. Harriman of the important investment house of Brown Brothers, Harriman.[20]

Not only was Social Security supported by an important element of big business, there is abundant evidence that the initial groundwork for social security legislation had begun several decades before the New Deal under business sponsorship. As one of the leading students of the measure, said, "The American Association for Labor Legislation [AALL] created and sustained the organized social insurance movement in the United States."[21] The AALL efforts in the area of social insurance began in 1910 with a series of research studies and proposals on the subject that came to largely determine the terms of the debate and the central features of the old-age insurance. In fact, the direct precursor and model for the Social Security Act was the Wisconsin Plan passed in 1932, written by Professor John R. Commons and two men with close ties to the AALL, Arthur Altmeyer and Edwin Witte. It is interesting to note, given its centrality to the Social Security Act, that the AALL was an offshoot of the big-business created and dominated National Civic Federation. The goal of the AALL was to bring together reformers, economists, and business leaders for the promotion of uniform state and national labor laws, for as its motto said, "Social Justice is the Best Insurance Against Labor Unrest."

It is clear, then, that the Social Security Act did not represent a turn to the left by the New Deal. In reality, the measure was a legislative response to what has been called "The Thunder on the Left," but it responded to it in a way that was highly conservative, consistent with reforms proposed by an important element of the business class, and supported in its final form by most prominent business leaders. The measure had the effect of supplying minimal benefits to the elderly and the unemployed, thus blunting demands for more radical change. Yet at no time did it challenge the structure of inequality. The act showed a recognition, as did Bismarck's Germany, that no modern state can survive with widespread destitution and discontent.[22]

The Wagner Act

To many people the most significant legislation of the New Deal period was the Wagner Act, which lent government support and legitimacy to the right of working people to form themselves into unions. It seemingly revolutionized American political life by bringing labor into a position of parity with big business, and changed forever their relative power positions. Strong business opposition to the Wagner Act and its implementation, from the Depression to modern times, is abundant proof that the legislation was not trivial.

While much of the above is probably true, it is by no means the whole truth, since it oversimplifies the picture. We know, for instance, that unionization has not affected the distribution of the relative shares of national income toward labor, nor have unions been able to maintain their position of parity with business. We know, moreover, that union leadership offers no basic challenges to corporate prerogatives of decision making, but confines itself largely to wage demands which are easily passed on to the consumer in the form of higher prices. More important, however, there is strong evidence to suggest that at least some elements of the business class believed collective bargaining to be an essential ingredient for industrial peace and stability, and had long lobbied for it. We shall review this issue at some length.

The Wagner Act was the immediate reaction to a situation of widespread labor turmoil sparked by Section 7a of the National Industrial Recovery Act. It required that, in return for the privilege of self-regulation through NRA codes, businesses would have to allow their employees the right to "organize and bargain collectively through representatives of their own choosing. . . . " In response to 7a, working people all over the United States flocked into unions. Under the leadership of United Mine Workers leader and future head of the militant Congress of Industrial Organizations, John L. Lewis, explosive expansion of union membership took place in the auto, rubber, mining, oil, publishing, and entertainment industries. Both the president and business leaders were surprised by the pace and scope of the movement, especially because of labor tranquility in the 1920s. Employer response to the wave of organization was both to refuse to bargain with the new organizations and to form company unions under its own control. Since the NIRA enforcement machinery was extremely weak, employers increasingly refused to appear before or to cooperate in any way with the National Labor Board (NLB), which was charged with oversight of collective bargaining. Employers easily circumvented rulings by the NLB, and used harsher and harsher means to deal with the incipient labor organizations. Employer noncompliance was made even more universal by a settlement, which the president reached with General Motors over the objection of the NLB, that seemed to sanction company unions. According to one observer: "The president's settlement of the automotive strike, . . . was accepted by many employers as a guarantee that they could avoid dealing with trade unions.[23]

When the hope that Section 7a originally generated among working people met increasing employer hostility, some of the most serious labor violence in American history exploded. In Toledo, an entire city was brought to a halt by the strike of workers at an auto parts supplier, supported by the Unemployed League and the Marxist American Workers party. The response of the organized employers and local government was increasingly violent, and was met in kind by striker counterviolence. In

Minneapolis, a general strike materialized as labor armed itself to fight the Citizens' Alliance, an employer's organization that had for years prevented widespread unionization through propaganda, violence, espionage, jury tampering, and similar means.[24] Needless to say, the results were bloody and verged at times on class war. In San Francisco, the violent response by employers and police to a waterfront strike led to a crippling strike by almost every union in the city and brought the city to a virtual halt. In the great cotton textile strike, perhaps the greatest strike in American history, the entire Eastern seacoast and one-half million workers were idled.

By the end of 1934 it seemed that with the spread of labor agitation and strike action, the nation was on the verge of class warfare. It is reported that the Secretary of State Cordell Hull worried publicly about the threat of a "general strike" that would topple the government.[25] The Wagner Act was a move to thwart the threat of escalating disorder, once labor had been unleashed, by adding compulsion to Section 7a. It was intended to force employers to abide by its provisions. In the face of industrial chaos and escalating class conflict, it was clear that something had to be done. Under the leadership of Senator Wagner of New York, legislation was written that defined unfair labor practices on the part of employers, protected the "closed shop," granted the right to organize, and created the National Labor Relations Board (NLRB) with power to enforce its decisions on employers. The Wagner Act was a perfectly understandable response to the wave of class conflict and labor militancy that had been irrevocably unleashed by Section 7a. As such, it does not need extensive examination. What does need to be explained, however, is the original inclusion of Section 7a in the National Industrial Recovery Act. How did it happen to get there? Of one thing we can be sure, it was not the product of labor union agitation.

Again, we must consider the wing of the business class that was committed to a cooperative rather than a competitive capitalism, and that realized that labor would have to be brought into cooperative arrangements to assure stability. From at least the turn of the century, some sophisticated business leaders and a handful of business organizations advocated the institution of collective bargaining as a method to regularize labor contracts, to eliminate wildcat strikes, and to imbue union leaders with a sense of responsibility for industrial peace. Department store executive and influential National Civic Federation member William Filene encouraged his employees to form themselves into unions as early as 1898.[26] The Anthracite Coal Commission, an NCF-sponsored body composed of business leaders looking into labor troubles in the coal industry, proposed in 1903 that

> *Experience shows that the more full the recognition given to a trade union, the more business-like and responsible it becomes. Through dealing with businessmen in business matters, its more intelligent, conservative and responsible members come to the front and gain general direction of its affairs.*[27]

Mark Hanna, prominent businessman, power in the national Republican party and president of the National Civic Federation, was also a voice for collective bargaining. Besides encouraging labor organization in his own enterprises, he undertook numerous efforts to convince his peers of the rationality of worker's organizations.

> *To have success in conciliation, or arbitration, there must be thorough and effective organization on both sides.*
>
> *I believe in organized labor, and I have for thirty years. I believe in it because it is a demonstrated fact that where the concerns and interests of labor are entrusted to able and honest leadership, it is much easier for those who represent the employers to come into close contact with the laborer, and, by dealing with fewer persons, to accomplish results quicker and better.*
>
> *The trusts have come to stay. Organized labor and organized capital are but forward steps in the great industrial evolution that is taking place. We would just as soon think of going back to primitive methods of manufacturing as we would to primitive methods of doing business, and it is our duty, those of us who represent the employers, from this time on to make up our minds that this question is one that must be heard.*
>
> *You are well aware that there has been a tendency in this country, from the very nature of things, to what is called socialism. Everything that is American is primarily opposed to socialism . . . . There is nothing in the organization of society in this country that can afford to permit the growth of socialistic ideas. They are un-American and unnatural to us as a people.*
>
> *In the beginning of this work I received great encouragement from an address which Samuel Gompers (President of the American Federation of Labor) made in Cooper Union Institute, in New York, about a year and a half ago, when he took the broad ground that in the interests of labor there was no room for the socialist or the anarchist, no room for men who undertook to disturb the principles of our society and government. When such words came from a man*

leading the largest labor organization in the world, a man of advanced thought and of honest intent, I know that now is the time to strike, now is the time to proclaim to the American people that in the consideration of this question, which sooner or later must be forced upon us, we must consider what is for the best interest of society as well as for our material development. [28]

The aforementioned offshoot of the NCF, the American Association of Labor Legislation (AALL), was in the first two decades of the twentieth century the major organized force for the promotion of uniform, progressive labor laws. Its extensive efforts in research, education, and the promotion of legislation extended into the fields of industrial disease and accidents, health insurance, unemployment compensation, and collective bargaining. Guiding their efforts was a concern for social justice, efficiency, and uniformity. Its general perspective was that the threat of social revolution and industrial turmoil would only be eliminated by having a healthy work force that had a stake in ongoing operations. Stability would be a product of cooperative efforts, consistent legal standards, and stable expectations by all participants.

The industrial mobilization of World War I was an opportunity to practice these cooperative arrangements on a widespread basis. Besides allowing for extensive business self-regulation, the War Industries Board required that affected industries encourage the organization of their workers and for industries to enter into collective bargaining relationships with them. While the experience was short-lived, the war provided a powerful precedent for amiable working relationships between the leaders of big labor and big business. The war mobilization experience, besides having a profound influence on Gompers and Sidney Hillman of labor, also reinforced the collective bargaining proclivities of Gerard Swope destined to be the influential president of General Electric. In the 1920s Swope became a vocal advocate of uniform labor legislation, particularly unemployment and disability insurance and collective bargaining. In 1931 he proposed the Swope Plan that included provisions for the suspension of the antitrust laws and union participation, and served as a model for the NRA legislation. In 1933 he proposed that the only legitimate basis for employee organization was free elections, not the imposition of the company union. In 1938 Swope became one of the first business executives to conclude a national collective bargaining agreement with a major industrial union and, thus set an important precedent for his fellow executives. [29]

We are not for a moment advancing the absurd contention that labor organization was the product of corporate conspiracy. Clearly, the advance of collective bargaining was built upon the efforts, bravery, and even blood of American workers. Moreover, most business leaders remained openly hostile to such organizations during the 1920s and 1930s, and this hostility was expressed brutally and frequently by antilabor violence during the Depression. The National Association of Manufacturers led vigorous antiunion campaigns throughout this period and even into the post-World War II period. We are saying, however, that not all business leaders were so intransigent: a significant number of corporate and financial leaders organized in the NCF and the AALL, affected by the welfare state theorists and social gospelers, and experienced in collective bargaining because of their war mobilization activities, clearly saw the need for labor organization and involvement in a system of stable, cooperative capitalism. These men were the leaders of some of the major corporations and financial institutions in the United States, and were men of considerable political influence—for example, Mark Hanna, J. P. Morgan, August Belmont, W. I. Harriman, Gerard Swope, Lincoln Filene, and Bernard Baruch.

Much of the misperception about the relationship between business and the New Deal can be cleared up if we comprehend that there were two wings to the business class. One encumbered with the intellectual baggage laissez-faire economics, believing in free competition and the sanctity of contract between the firm and each individual worker, opposed both government regulation of the economy and collective bargaining. The other wing, which became more influential as the implications of the industrial revolution became evident, believed in a cooperative, regulated capitalism in which big business was guaranteed a predictable and stable environment through unionization, national collective bargaining contracts, and state regulation of the economy.[30] This wing of the business class saw its perspective incorporated into policy by the landmark legislation of the progressive era, and by the National Industrial Recovery Act of 1933, including Section 7a. In the crisis of the Depression, the leaders of the New Deal accepted the analysis that the way out of economic crisis was the road of cooperative capitalism. The right of working people to bargain collectively was part and parcel of that analysis. What is important to note is that organized labor at no time lobbied for Section 7a of the NIRA. Indeed, until the 1930s, it actively opposed government intervention into labor-management relations.

There is no gainsaying the importance of the Wagner Act. By putting teeth into the guarantees of Section 7a (after widespread labor agitation and turmoil), it ensured the place of organized labor as a power in the American political system; "it promoted and validated . . . the trade unions as fully legitimate institutions on the American scene."[31] However, the Wagner Act in no way signaled a radical turn leftward by the administration in the so-called second New Deal. What the measure accomplished, in fact, was precisely that degree of labor peace and cooperation predicted by the progressive leaders of business. It did lead to uniform national contracts enforced by the unions themselves, to regularized bargaining in place of sporadic wildcat strikes, and to a general sense of "responsibility" and "statesmanship" among a union leadership that grew more and more conservative.

TWENTIETH-CENTURY REFORM

There is much confusion about reform in the twentieth century, particularly with respect to progressivism and New Deal liberalism. The confusion arises from the incorrect interpretation of the expansion of state activities. Most often, state expansion is interpreted by both liberals and conservatives as a movement to the left, as the demonstration of the commitment of the state to a more equitable society. We have argued, however, that while there were in fact scattered examples of such a commitment, the heart and the essence of reform in this century has been an attempt to rationalize and stabilize corporate capitalism. Through several devices, most of which are operative today, progressives and New Deal liberals helped to impose some order on the economic system, and helped to liberate the corporate sector from the vagueries and dangers of the business cycle. The New Deal was an advance on earlier reform not only because it honed the tools of business cycle regulation, but also because it helped to temporarily create a situation of labor peace by legitimating collective bargaining through conservative unions, and it demonstrated for the first time how turmoil might be temporarily controlled through the parsimonious and judicious use of welfare and relief expenditures.

Nevertheless, what is at base so striking about these various reforms was their inability to solve the basic structural problems of capitalist society. Despite all of its efforts, the New Deal barely touched the roots of the economic crisis. In 1938, for instance, the unemployment rate was still almost 20 percent of the work force, with few prospects in sight for its amelioration. It would, in fact, require the massive stimulus of the Second World War and the emergence of the United States as the main actor on the world stage in the postwar period to provide a powerful, if limited antidote to the permanent crisis of capitalism.

NOTES

[1] Paul Conkin; *The New Deal* (New York: Crowell, 1967).

[2] William E. Lenchtenburg, *FDR and the New Deal* (Evanston: Harper Torch Books, 1967), p. 168.

[3] James McGregor Burns, *Roosevelt: The Lion and the Fox* (New York: Harcourt, Brace & World, 1956).

[4] See Irving Bernstein, *The Turbulent Years: A History of the American Worker, 1933–1941* (Boston: Houghton-Mifflin, 1971) and Francis Fox Piven and Richard A. Cloward, *Regulating the Poor: The Functions of Public Welfare* (New York: Pantheon, 1971).

[5] Much of the discussion of the banking crisis and the administration response is based on Broadus Mitchell, *Depression Decade* (New York: Holt, Rinehart and Winston, 1947).

[6] Quoted in ibid., p. 135.

[7] Ibid., Chapter 6.

[8] See the discussion in Grant McConnell, *Private Power and American Democracy* (New York: Knopf, 1967), p. 58.

[9] General Hugh S. Johnson, quoted in Mitchell, *Depression Decade,* p. 230.

[10] Bernstein, *The Turbulent Years,* p. 19.

[11] See Ellis Hawley, *The New Deal and the Problem of Monopoly* (Princeton: Princeton University Press, 1966); Bernstein, *The Turbulent Years;* and Mitchell, *Depression Decade,* for confirmation of this point.

[12] Gabriel Kolko, *Main Currents in American History* (New York: Harper and Row, 1976), p. 130.

[13] Hawley, *The New Deal and the Problem of Monopoly.*

[14] Piven and Cloward, *Regulating the Poor,* p. 101.

[15] See Paul H. Douglas, *Social Security in the United States* (New York: McGraw-Hill, 1939); Roy C. Lubove, *The Struggle for Social Security* (Cambridge: Harvard University Press, 1968); and Edwin E. Witte, *The Development of the Social Security Act* (Madison: University of Wisconsin Press, 1962).

[16] Foreward to Witte, *The Development of the Social Security Act,* p. 6.

[17] Piven and Cloward, *Regulating the Poor,* p. 107.

[18] Reported in Douglas, *Social Security in the United States.*

[19] Arthur M. Schlesinger, Jr. *The Politics of Upheaval* (Boston: Houghton-Mifflin, 1960), p. 40.

[20] G. William Domhoff, *The Higher Circles: The Governing Class in America* (New York: Random House, Vintage Press, 1971) p. 214.

[21] Lubove, *The Struggle for Social Security,* p. 29. Confirmed by Douglas, *Social Security in the United States,* p. 12.

[22] The first extensive practice of the welfare state concept on a national scale was in authoritarian Bismarckian Germany. Bismarck had introduced in Germany most of the social services that are by now familiar parts of the landscape in western nations, most particularly provisions for illness, accidents, old age, and disability, financed through a system of compulsory insurance.

Central to any explanation of Bismarck's behavior in Germany was his fear of class conflict and mass movements of the left. The introduction of social service and state protection against the contingencies of industrial life were seen by him as a means by which the working class would be wed to the nation without seriously threatening the privilege of the class system (primarily because social services were financed out of compulsory insurance paid by the workers themselves). In his own words, "The thronging to them [the Social Democratic Party] will cease as soon as working men see that the government and legislative bodies are earnestly concerned for their welfare."

[23] Quoted in Bernstein, *The Turbulent Years,* p. 218.

[24] Ibid., p. 231.

[25] Burns, *Roosevelt: The Lion and the Fox.*

[26] See the discussion in Philip Taft, *Organized Labor in American History* (New York: Harper & Row, 1964).

[27] Domhoff, *The Higher Circles,* p. 227.

[28] From Marcus A. Hanna, "Industrial Conciliation and Arbitration," *Annals of the American Academy of Political and Social Science,* Vol. 20 (1920), pp. 21, 24–26.

[29] In a confidential poll of industrialists in 1937 to pick the "best brains in American management," Swope ranked first. Bernstein, *The Turbulent Years,* p. 611.

[30] These two wings are seen most dramatically within the steel industry. The largest firm in the industry, U.S. Steel Corporation, under the leadership of investment banker Myron Taylor, rather easily reached a collective bargaining agreement with CIO head John L. Lewis. The smaller companies known as "little steel," on the other hand, fiercely resisted unionization and sponsored some of the worst antilabor violence in American history.

5
THE STRUCTURE OF MATURE CAPITALISM

The end of the Second World War ushered in a period in American history which seemed so boundless in its potential that several commentators were moved to announce the commencement of the "American Century." Out of the destruction of the war there emerged, in this view, an American economic and political system that had transcended the problems of capitalist development, a system in which basic antagonisms and contradictions had fallen before the juggernaut of economic abundance and technical virtuosity. We are now beginning to learn that this period stretching from about 1945 to the early 1970s, in which fundamental problems had seemingly been solved, and in which the "end of ideology" had been declared, was but a phase in the history of the capitalist mode of production in the United States. It was a phase, in fact, that might be represented at its beginning by the mushroom cloud over Hiroshima announcing America's new hegemony, and at its end, by images of Americans clamoring aboard evacuation helecopters for the undignified exit of the United States from Saigon and all of Indochina.

One cannot, of course, realistically assign precise dates to such a complex history as we have tentatively done above. It is only in hindsight that one can discern the merging of the many streams of development which represent the early phase of a particular historic period, and the disintegrative, disruptive, and contradictory developments which signal the transformation of one historical period into another. In the course of the past two chapters, we have examined the elements of the slow transformation of laissez-faire capitalism into a more concentrated form, and the various means by which the state attempted to come to grips with it during the progressive and New Deal reform periods. We demonstrated how, in the course of this complex interaction, most of the building blocks of the modern positive state were assembled by the end of the 1930s, though they had not yet been constructed into a finished edifice. In the last chapter of this book, we shall turn our attention to what we believe is the slow disintegration of the configuration of forces that comprise our present historical phase, and signs of the emergence of a new one. In this chapter and the one that follows, however, we shall devote our attention to the analysis of the structure, dynamics, and implications of mature corporate capitalism, and its political expression in the modern positive state, the social formation which most Americans have directly experienced, and the one with which they are necessarily most familiar.[1]

Consistent with our theoretical position throughout this book, we shall structure our analysis around the consideration of the contradictions posed by developments in the capitalist mode of production, in the struggle of social classes, and in the position of the United States in the world capitalist system. With respect to these issues and to anticipate the materials to follow, we might point out that all of the trends at work in the four or five decades before the Second World War come to full flower, and assume their contemporary form in the years during and immediately after that terrible conflagration. More specifically, by the late 1940s and early 1950s there emerges in the United States a social formation characterized by a corporation dominated dual economy, by a deeply divided working class analogous to the dual economy, and by the absolute supremacy of the United States in the world capitalist system. Each of these developments brings in its wake a set of contradictions which only the state can briefly bring under control, but which, in the process, creates a new and more deadly configuration of contradictions. In the pages that follow, we shall turn our attention to the detailed analysis of these developments.

THE CORPORATION AND THE DUAL ECONOMY

The key to understanding the modern American economy is an appreciation for the extreme concentration of economic activity into the hands of a relatively small number of giant industrial, commercial, and financial firms, and the relegation of the vast majority of remaining business firms to the netherlands of economic life. This development is of such a magnitude, we would argue, that the practices of the positive state are best explained by the needs and requirements of these large-scale business enterprises, as well as the problems which are created by their activities.[2]

The Structure of the Corporate Economy

What is most obvious is the growth and concentration of economic activity among America's corporations. It is not easy, however, to really grasp the magnitude of these modern institutions, to comprehend their size, concentration, and power, though Richard J. Barber helps us with the following description:

> *General Motor's yearly operating revenues exceed those of all but a dozen or so countries. Its sales receipts are greater than the combined general revenues of New York, New Jersey, Pennsylvania, Ohio, Delaware, and the six New England states. Its 1,300,000 stockholders are equal to the population of Washington, Baltimore or Houston. G.M. employees number well over 700,000 and work in 127 plants in the United States and forty-five countries spanning Europe, South Africa, North America, and Australia. The total cash wages are more than twice the personal income of Ireland. G.M.'s federal corporate tax payments approach $2 billion, or enough to pay for all federal grants in fiscal year 1970 in the field of health research. The enormity of General Motors . . . should not be thought of as unique. Some 175 other manufacturing, merchandising and transportation companies now have annual sales of at least a billion dollars. One rivaling G.M. — is Standard Oil of New Jersey. With more than a hundred thousand employees around the world . . . , a six-million ton tanker fleet . . . , and $17 billion in assets . . . , it can more easily be thought of as a nation than a commercial enterprise.* [3]

This leads us to another observation about the modern corporate system, and that pertains to the existence of a giant sector within the corporate sector; an economy within an economy if you will. Students of the subject agree that concentration is not merely the story of the dominance of the corporation over other forms of business enterprise, but also the dominance of a relatively few corporations over all others. In 1962, for instance, out of 180,000 manufacturing corporations, the *one-hundred* largest accounted for 55 percent of all net capital assets, and 58 percent of all after-tax profits. [4] In 1969, after-tax profits remained at 58 percent for the top one-hundred firms and almost 25 percent for the top ten. [5] Moreover, on most indicators, concentration has been increasing steadily for the past several decades. [6] " . . . The 100 largest firms in 1968 held a larger share of manufacturing assets than the 200 largest in 1950; the 200 largest in 1968 controlled as large a share as the 1,000 largest in 1941." [7]

We gain a similar picture of concentration if we look at particular industries. Thus, in 1966, the *top four* firms in each industry accounted for the following percentages of all output.[8]

Aerospace	67%
Motor vehicles	79
Computers	63
Tires	71
Cigarettes	81
Soap detergent	72
Photographic equipment	67

In several sectors, concentration is even more striking. In aircraft engines, for instance, two firms account for almost 100 percent of production. In heavy electrical equipment, two firms produce 80 percent of the industry total. In computers, a single firm, IBM, accounts for about 90 percent of all production.[9]

The engine of this consolidation is the continuing process of mergers between firms, a process in which, over the past twenty years, the top one-hundred firms have accounted for 35 percent of all merged assets. Or to take another view of the same subject, the share of total assets enjoyed by the top 500 mining and manufacturing corporations nearly doubled in the years between 1955 and 1970.[10]

Although we have focused on manufacturing, similar patterns of concentration and consolidation hold for banking, insurance, merchandising, transportation, and utilities.[11] As of 1964, for instance, *one-tenth* of *one percent* of all commercial banks in the United States held 24 percent of all deposits. Concentration is even more dramatic in the field of trust management (and more important, because the power to invest trust accounts leads to influence in corporate decision making) where but twenty-five banks accounted for almost two-thirds of all trust assets. Finally, as few as twenty banks manage half of all private pension fund assets.[12]

Concentration is enhanced by the heavily interlocked nature of large business firms. Nominal competitors, for instance, usually have directors sitting on each other's boards of directors, raising the suspicion that competition is not the essence of their relationship. Interlock is further enhanced by the trust activities of banks, by trade associations, by the practice of price leadership and, occasionally, by outright collusion and conspiracy.

This description of corporate concentration would be incomplete without an appreciation of its worldwide scope. The American tourist soon learns that he can easily purchase a Coke, Kodak film, Standard gasoline, a Singer sewing machine, Tide detergent, and Ivory soap in almost any country in the nonsocialist world. American and foreign businesspersons can purchase American computers, machine tools, heavy road equipment, tractors, and an infinite variety of other goods directly from American-owned subsidiaries in Europe, Latin America, Canada, or Asia. These mundane examples merely highlight the undisputed fact that American corporations control a good deal of the world's economy and that the expansion has not yet abated. As the French journalist J. J. Servan-Schreiber has so graphically put it: "Fifteen years from now the world's third greatest industrial power, just after the United States and Russia, may not be Europe, but American industry in Europe."[13]

The worldwide scope of the American corporation is a phenomenon characteristic primarily of the largest firms. Only 16 percent of all American companies, for instance, owned almost 60 percent of total U.S. foreign investments in 1957. The top one-hundred firms, moreover, accounted for approximately 75 percent of all earnings on foreign investment.[14] Concentration in the foreign market, then, is even more extreme than in the United States.

Concentrated economic power in a relative handful of business enterprises has enormous implications for American economic life and, as we shall see, for social and political life as well. Most obviously, these giant corporations have amassed sufficient power to allow them, in general, to tame and transcend the marketplace. Instead of the market system envisioned by Adam Smith, a system characterized by vigorous competition between many small firms, a new system has emerged on the American scene, one that economists term *oligopoly*. Oligopoly leads to private control of prices and profits, and thus wide discretion in the decision-making power of corporate executives.[15] Oligopolistic power means that a few firms are able to control the marketplace, to deny entry to new firms, to control sources of raw materials, and to generate their own internal sources of capital for investment and expansion.

What has emerged is the fully integrated firm.[16] As described by economist John Kenneth Galbraith, the primary goal of the modern giant corporation is predictability, stability, and the avoidance of risk, results neither automatically nor ordinarily forthcoming in the marketplace. In order to reach predictability and stability in an industrial process that requires the mobilization of enormous resources of capital, equipment, technological talent, and manpower, the corporation attempts to stabilize its environment by controlling the availability and prices of its raw materials, by securing long-term labor agreements, by setting its price levels and production targets through administrative and intercorporate cooperative practices, and by convincing consumers to part with their dollars through massive advertising campaigns. Through such mechanisms, the mature corporation attempts to stabilize its economic environment and to guarantee to itself a substantial profit and steady growth. When it finds itself unable to accomplish such goals by itself, or in cooperation with other business enterprises, it turns to government for assistance.

This is not to say that all competition has disappeared from the corporate sector. Since capital always seeks to expand, there are times when one or more firms are tempted to break the agreed upon rules of the game for short term advantages. The costs of such strategies in the long run, however, are too high, and are widely recognized as such, and most of the giants are willing to forego vigorous price competition in the interests of stability and guaranteed profitability.

> *With price competition banned, sellers of a given commodity or of close substitutes have an interest in seeing that the price or prices established are such as to maximize the profits of the group as a whole. They may fight over the division of these profits . . . but none can wish that the total to be fought over should be smaller rather than larger. This is the decisive fact in determining the price policies and strategies of the typical large corporation . . . .*[17]

With the banning of price competition in the monopoly sector, the remaining field of competition is defined by the sales effort (advertising, planned obsolescence, model changes, etc.) and the fight over fractions of market shares.

The Impact of the Corporate Giants

Being institutions of such concentrated economic might, the giant corporations cannot help but profoundly affect the lives of all Americans. It is through the expenditure of funds made possible by the engine of accumulation (i.e., through the investment decision) that the corporations most clearly demonstrate both their power and their impact on our lives. It is corporate management, acting as the instrument of large stockholders, that determines the relative distribution of funds to research, to technological innovation, to executive compensation, to stockholders, to philanthropy, to advertising, and to political campaigns, for example. These decisions by corporate executives deeply affect, even shape our entire society; yet it must be emphasized that they remain *private* decisions. In socialist economies, for instance, such momentous investment calculations take place in national planning agencies, subject to political control. In the United States, however, the corporate sector performs this critical function. In sum, the management of the giant corporation makes *private decisions* designed for *private gain* with *public consequences.* Some of these public consequences are obvious to most observers; others remain obscure. Yet all of the consequences, since they shape our lives, are important and must be examined.[18]

Take the power of corporate managers to decide plant and office location, a decision that superficially may not appear to have important social effects, but one that in reality helps to decide which communities will flourish and which will perish; in which locales people will live and work; and which locales will be barren and empty. The decision, for instance, to locate the principal factories of American industry in a handful of northern cities, added to the near insatiable demand for labor in these expanding industries and, finally, the desire for a source of labor that would keep the emerging working class fragmented, caused corporate leaders to turn to the destitute black population of the southern states. The result, of course, was the greatest migration in American history—the flight of Southern blacks from failed farms to the teeming cities of the north. In but half a century, the typical American black was transformed from a Southern farmer to a non-Southern urbanite. Census figures demonstrate the magnitude of the change.[19]

Table 5-1 Negro Out-Migration from the South

Period	Net Out-Migration	Annual Average Rate
1910–1920	454,000	45,400
1920–1930	749,000	74,900
1930–1940	348,000	34,800
1940–1950	1,597,000	159,700
1960–1966	613,000	102,000

In fact, while only 10 percent of the American black population was urbanized in 1910, 70 percent were fully urbanized by the late 1960s, a startling demographic change in so short a time.[20]

It should be added that the net out-migration rate of blacks has slowed down considerably in the past twenty years, but this too can largely be traced to the decisions of corporate leaders. To escape the wage demands of strong unions and to take advantage of a readily available cheap labor supply, an ever increasing number of prominent corporations are transferring their plants and offices to the South, and attracting potential northern-bound blacks to southern cities.

One might add numerous cases of location decisions and their impact. The decline of New England as an economic region, for instance, is closely tied to the movement of the shoe-making and textile industries to regions of low labor costs, first in the South, and then overseas to locales as diverse as Singapore, Taiwan, and Korea. Location decisions are so important to local communities, in fact, that they will often go to extraordinary lengths to attract or keep an industry. Thus, special tax breaks and cost-free services such as water and electricity are rather common. Some locations go even farther. South Carolina advertises, "We'll train your workers free," while Ohio claims "... we believe that the greatest contribution that anyone can make to the people of the state is to create an economic climate and attitude toward industry that will, in the end, provide more and better jobs. That is why 'Profit is not a Dirty Word in Ohio.'"[21] Localities go to these lengths because it means jobs and a measure of prosperity.

Location decisions are neither the only decisions made by corporate managers nor the most important. Private corporation decisions, when considered in the aggregate, determine primarily the kinds of work that Americans do. Since capitalism is an economic system devoted to exchange and profit and since it is little concerned with the development of human potential, it demands that people shape themselves to the available jobs. Little concern is evident for creating jobs suited to individual attributes and talents. The industrial revolution and the concomitant rise of the giant corporation, for example, forced most Americans to abandon their farms, their crafts, and their small businesses in favor of tending machinery in large plants and offices. Americans were forced to alter their very means of livelihood in response to the demands of the industrial system.

Needless to say, Americans must still alter their lives to meet the demands of the industrial system. In fact, the process of vocational reshaping may well be accelerated by what is called the cybernetic revolution, the increasing use of computers and automated processes in material production. Cybernation has had and will continue to have many familiar consequences. Production-line workers are being laid off as simple repetitive process becomes automated. In the chemical industry, for instance, output has soared 27 percent since 1956, while at the same time, the number of jobs has fallen by three percent.[22] Nor may nonproduction line workers remain unconcerned, for cybernation is encroaching into the more routine white-collar and clerical occupations.[23] This does not mean that cybernation is devoid of benefits. It does mean, however, that both the direction of cybernated processes and the pace of their introduction are largely determined by the private decisions of corporate managers. Americans will be required, as in the past, to shape their vocational preparation accordingly.

It follows from the above discussion that private corporate decisions concerning the occupational structure profoundly affect and shape American education. This is true because American education, with some notable exceptions, has been largely vocational in nature, geared to training people for available jobs in the marketplace. Thus, the forces that determine the structure of jobs and work determine also the shape of job preparatory education. There is no reason to believe that the relationship between jobs and education will diminish in importance in the future. In fact, with the encroachment of cybernation, and the sets of advanced, intellectual, and nonmanual skills required, the formal educational system will certainly bear an even heavier load in the future.

Actually there is an extremely tight relationship between American education and the needs of private business enterprise.[24] In pre-Civil war America, prior to the industrial revolution, people gained their livelihoods through farming, trading, or in small businesses, none of which required exotic training. Vocational education was part of family education. One learned a trade or a vocational role either within the family group or within a small, close-knit community. However, with the emergence of large-scale industrialization, the training in skills necessary for getting available jobs, mainly repetitive factory labor, was unobtainable in the family. The skills, values, and behaviors appropriate to farming, trading, or business were inappropriate for factory work. To fill the training vacuum, business and educational leaders helped to introduce in the late nineteenth century universal, mass education through high school, with an explicit emphasis on education for punctuality, obedience to authority, loyalty, minimal reading and calculating skills, and other job-related skills and orientations. It appears also that the explosion in mass higher education in the United States after World War II was and remains a response to the needs of the industrial system. That is, the vast increase in the number of persons in some contact with higher education is primarily a response to the need for a more highly trained and self-directed work force that much of the American economy requires today and will need in the future.

It is clear that corporate enterprise shapes the curriculum of higher education (to say nothing of research priorities) to adapt occupational training to its own resource needs. It does so, if for no other reason, than it shapes the job structure in the economy, and American students, given no other rationale for learning, naturally demand that colleges prepare them for occupational survival. In addition to these student pressures, the needs of corporate enterprise are translated into university policy through their general domination of university boards of trustees. Almost without exception, the boards of trustees of the leading universities in America, the bodies that usually make the decisions on the general direction and purposes of the educational enterprise, are composed of prominent leaders from big business and high finance.

There remain several additional avenues by which corporate needs are tied to university functions. Most directly, business quite often makes large financial contributions to colleges and universities to institute specific programs either in research or training, particularly in various business fields, law, and engineering. The money is usually so attractive that it is a rare university that will refuse to begin the desired curriculum. The direct contribution from an individual business enterprise is supplemented by the educational activities of the great foundations, organizations initially created to serve as tax dodges for wealthy stockholders. Given the vast economic resources at their disposal and the willingness of their directors to use those resources, foundations like Carnegie, Mellon, Ford, and Rockefeller have had an enormous impact on the shape of American higher education. Observers have reported, for instance, that the foundations are largely responsible for everything from the current shape of medical education, to team research, to the behavioral orientation in the modern social sciences,[25] to the introduction of the concept of the Ph.D. from Germany.[26]

Nor should we overlook the ways in which private corporate decision makers affect the lives of Americans through the ubiquitous institution of advertising. "By and large, most of the products we use to dress, transport, and amuse ourselves are created by large corporations that have done a good job of convincing us that our status or our sex appeal depend on which of the very similar autos, televisions, or deodorants we choose."[27] Now it must be granted that there remains much debate about the actual impact of advertising, with much of the fundamental research still to be done. Evidence, for instance, of the ability of advertising to compel the consumer to buy one brand name over another remains inconclusive. If there is any agreement at all about the impact of advertising, and from our point of view it is much more important than brand differentiation, it is advertising's ability to raise the general level of consumption, to convince the consumer that he or she needs deodorants, second cars, vacation homes, snowmobiles, electric toothbrushes, and the like. If we are a consumer society as universally claimed, then advertising is probably the key factor in making us so.

To John Kenneth Galbraith, it is the creation of these consumption needs that represents one of the pillars of our economic system. Recall his thesis that the modern industrial system is a gigantic exercise to reduce risk, to control all aspects of production: prices, sources of raw material, and employee behavior. A critical element in risk reduction is the assurance that consumers will buy all or a significant proportion of the goods that are produced. Growth requires the production of more and more goods, and to prevent stagnation, the consumer must be convinced that he needs to consume more. As each need is met, new needs must be created or else the consumer would cease buying, thereby throwing a wrench into the economic works.

A significant proportion of the content of advertising is directed toward the legitimation and "cosmeticization" of the industrial system itself. Thus, we are reminded that at General Electric, "Progress is our most important Product," or that DuPont makes "Better things, for Better Living through Chemistry." We are told that oil companies are deeply concerned about the environment and that they have bettered the lives of the Eskimos from whose land they extract oil. Private utilities extol the virtues of private enterprise, and warn of the dangers of public ownership. Auto companies treat us to long dissertations on their endless efforts to improve the safety of their product, while land development corporations sing to us of their concern for the beauty of the wilderness that they have "preserved." Advertising, then, is not only directed at the consumption effort but also at convincing us that our abundance is due to the corporate system, and that any injustices and inequities in the system are being tackled with benevolent enthusiasm by big business.

The dominant sector of our economy, then, is controlled by a relative handful of giant enterprises that have largely transcended the pricing discipline of the marketplace, and whose every action has important implications for social life in general. These are enterprises characterized, in the main, by large-scale production, capital intensive technologies, substantial and stable profits, relatively fixed market shares, and formal processes of collective bargaining. At the other end of the dichotomy, and incorporating by far the largest *number* of business enterprises in the United States, is what might be called the *competitive* sector.[28] In this sector, firms are subject to the cruel discipline of the marketplace, being too weak to control their environments. They are the pure price *takers* of traditional economic theory. These firms are characterized, in the main, by low productivity, limited, local, and unstable markets, intense competition, poor wages and working conditions, and high incidences of business failure. Not only do the vast majority of American businesses fall toward this end of the spectrum (small manufacturers, restaurants, grocery stores, service stations, etc.), but a majority of the blue-collar work force inhabits its regions as well. The following figures suggest the dimensions of the two sectors:

Table 5-2 The Dual Economy, 1974

	Percentage of National Income	Percentage of Total Work Force
Monopolistic industries	40	33
Competitive industries	32	39
Other (unclassified, government)	28	22[a]

[a]Includes 6 percent unemployed

Source: Richard C. Edwards, *et al., The Capitalist System* (Englewood Cliffs, N.J.: Prentice-Hall) 1977, p. 119. Based on William D. Shepard, *Market Power and Economic Welfare* (New York: Random House, 1970) and *Statistical Abstracts of the United States* (Washington, D.C.: U.S. Government Printing Office 1975).

THE ORGANIZATION OF THE WORKING CLASS

The dual economy finds its reflection in the organization of the working class. The concentration, organization, and sectoral planning characteristic of the monopoly portion of the economy finds almost perfect articulation in the organization of labor. As we discovered in the last chapter, the largest and most far-sighted corporations discovered during the Great Depression that collective bargaining with stable and nationally structured labor organizations was a necessary part of any system of regulated corporate capitalism. Further convinced by the strongly positive experience of union-management collaboration during the Second World War, pushed by labor militancy after the war, and mollified by the legislative diminution of union power through the provisions of the Taft-Hartley Act, monopoly sector firms all came to terms with collective bargaining as a permanent and useful feature of the industrial order by the early 1950s.

As predicted for a long time by many business leaders, unionization in the monopoly sector has been of considerable benefit to the corporate planning function. Collective bargaining adds to the environment's stability and predictability by standardizing wage costs between industrial firms, by sanctioning strikes only at the expiration of a contract (thus ending wildcat strikes), and by establishing contracts that are binding on all union members. Union leaders, embraced in the high councils of government and business, tend increasingly to restrain their own membership and to negotiate "realistic and responsible" agreements with business leaders. The logical conclusion of such a process is in sight. With the announcement in May 1973 of a no-strike, no-lockout agreement between labor and management in the steel industry, government, corporate, and labor representations pointed to a new era of industrial peace in the United States.

Such an outcome has been enhanced from the labor side by the strong commitment by the leaders of organized labor to the corporate domination of the American economy. Unions like the International Workers of the World, the longshoremen, and the CIO were once a significant force for change and reform in American society. Its leaders often articulated a vision of a better society and the role of labor in its creation. Today unions are concerned with little more than wage-and-benefit increases, increases that are easily absorbed by oligopolistic firms that pass along wage concessions to the consumer in the form of higher prices.

Unions have accepted the battleground defined and dominated by the corporations. Unionism is no longer a movement concerned with the totality of American society. Unions have not, except for the expenditure of a little money on Democratic candidates, entered the political arena with a program. They have confined their energies to the corporate theater.[29] Within that arena, as confined as it is, it rarely challenges management prerogatives, but devotes its energies almost purely to compensation. In short, labor unions are well integrated into American society, and offer no basic challenges to the status quo. They are, in other words, conservative institutions. There has been a lack of vision and purpose in the unions, and this helps explain the apathy of the ordinary worker. Unions do not question the worker's subordinate position in the work place, the purposes of production, or the role of corporations in society and economy.

The failure of an alternative vision, and therefore of countervailing power, lies in the basic acceptance of business values by union members and leaders. National opinion polls conducted to ascertain attitudes toward business show little significant differences between union and non-union members.[30] Historically, the mainstream of American unionism, articulated by and personified in Samuel Gompers, has basically accepted the American business system and has struggled to secure a place within it.[31]

The commitment to business values is also demonstrated by the fact that unions have themselves begun to invest in big business. As the pension and welfare funds of unions began to accumulate, and lacking any anti-business class consciousness, leaders naturally turned to big business as the "soundest" investment. The possibility of big labor acting as a significant countervailing force is called into question when its own financial position as a set of organizations is based on the health of the corporate sector of the economy.

One section of the working class, less than 25 percent of the work force (mostly in mining, manufacturing, transportation, and construction) finds itself organized into powerful unions able to negotiate wages and working conditions which, relative to the remainder of the working class, are quite substantial. Negotiation is possible, it is important to reemphasize, because collective bargaining takes place with those enterprises which, because of their size, complexity, and capital intensive character, require an environment of stability conducive to long-term planning; and which, because of their market position, are able to pass increased labor costs on to the consumer. Nevertheless, it is important to add that the organization of labor in this sector seems to have reached a plateau, for the proportion of workers in the economy who are in unions has been, for years, in serious decline. The major reason for the decline is that in those industries where unions have traditionally been strongest, automation and changed market demand have led to a sharply reduced need for blue-collar workers. Industry employment between 1947 and 1959, for instance, fell 60 percent in mining, 40 percent in railroads, 33 percent in telegraph, 30 percent in textiles, 24 percent in lumber, 15 percent in metals, and 10 percent in rubber. Census data through 1977 show that the trends in this direction have continued apace. Between 1960 and 1977, for instance, the percentage of the workforce engaged in manufacturing fell from 31 percent to 24 percent.[32]

Unions have been severely crippled by two other factors. First, there is a major movement of industry to the South where unionism is weak and antiunion sentiment is substantial. Second, and probably much more important in the long run, is the changing nature of employment in advanced industrial societies. From 1947 to 1977, white-collar employment —that is, professional, technical, clerical, and sales workers—rose by over 12 million, while blue-collar workers fell by four and one half million.[33] By the late 1950s, in fact, there were more white-collar workers in the economy than blue-collar workers. This is significant because unions historically have not been very successful among the white-collar working class, possibly because of the perceived status differences between them and manual workers. While there are growing trends toward unionization of some white-collar groups such as teachers and other government workers, the pace of unionization lags far behind the rate of creation of white-collar jobs.

If monopoly sector workers have been able to stabilize their employment, improve their working conditions, and negotiate a living wage, the same cannot be said for competitive sector workers.[34] Since firms in this sector are, by definition, caught in situations of intense competition, and are, by and large, unable to generate the funds requisite to significant increases in productivity (e.g. increasing the capital: labor ratio), surplus value is generated in the most primitive forms. While surplus value extraction in the monopoly sector takes a *relative* form, being dependent on improvements in the general skill and educational levels of the labor force and improvements in the technological infrastructure, surplus value extraction assumes an *absolute* character in the competitive sector (for example, low wages, long hours, unimproved working conditions). It is in this sector that one finds low paid, casual, and seasonal labor as the predominant form, and a heavy concentration of minority group members, women, and the elderly, all without the protection of unions. Needless to say, the tremendous heightening of the differences in interest between monopoly and competitive sector workers caused by racial and sexual divisions helps contribute to the political ineffectuality of the American working class.

AMERICA IN THE WORLD CAPITALIST SYSTEM
Finally, one must come to grips with the implications of the transformation in the world role of American capitalism. The end of the Second

World War ushered in a thirty-year period in which the United States assumed the position as the preeminent power in the world capitalist system, a conclusion that is possible to draw from observing the scale of its military might, the size of its industrial capacity, the power of its finance, and the scale of its use of world raw materials. A few of the following figures help to suggest the degree of that preeminence. In the year 1960, for instance, net foreign investment by the United States was almost twice as great as the combined net foreign investments of Britain, France, Germany, and Japan combined.[35] Or to take another example, of the fifteen largest multinational corporations in the world in 1976, a total of eleven were predominantly American owned and controlled. Additionally, American owned and operated firms accounted for 60 percent of sales, 56 percent of assets, and 71 percent of aggregate net income among the top fifty industrial enterprises in the capitalist world.[36] Finally, it has been estimated that the United States alone consumed at least 40 percent of the entire world's output of nonrenewable resources during the period under consideration.[37] Other dramatic figures could be added to the list but the point, we hope, is unambiguously established: America's preeminent position as an industrial, financial, and military power relative to the other capitalist countries, developed and less developed alike. As we shall learn in the next chapter, this new world position of American capitalism has generated a number of opportunities, problems, and contradictions that have required vigorous and sustained governmental activity.

The U.S. position of preeminence is the product of a long evolutionary history involving the transformations of its own mode of production and interactions with the economics and politics of the other capitalist powers. It is the story of gradual supremacy over European and Japanese capital, penetration into the Third World, and eventually, conflict with the socialist world.

The United States first emerged as an influential world power in the late nineteenth and early twentieth centuries supported by the incredible growth of its economic power, a power constructed out of the raw materials of the industrial revolution, the rise of the giant corporations, an explosively growing population and internal market, and unmatched agricultural and raw material resources. The years 1871–1899, in fact, "saw the most rapid expansion of capital and industry over any long period of American history ...."[38] The growing economic power of the United States provided the muscular base for the initial and often tentative probes into the world economic system during the late nineteenth and early twentieth centuries. However, in order to fully explain the world economic system, we must add other considerations.

First, while the health of the American economic system did not as yet require massive overseas transactions (as it would later), particular sectors were significantly involved in export trade. By the 1880s, in fact, a significant portion of total American agricultural production was directed towards overseas markets, as was the production of particular industrial firms like International Harvester. Second, with the filling in of the frontier by the end of the late nineteenth century, a frontier that had been perceived from James Madison to Frederick Jackson Turner as the safety valve for the mass discontents generated by market society, various business, political, and intellectual leaders began to see economic and political expansion beyond the continental United States as an important goal. The viewpoints of observers like James Bryce who saw the filling in of the continental United States as "a time of trial for democratic institutions"[39] was buttressed by the outbreak of serious labor turmoil, radical unionization drives, and socialist and anarchosyndicalist appeals already alluded to in previous chapters. Rapid growth, concentration of capital, proletarianization of labor, and economic fluctuations (the depressions of 1873, 1883, and 1893, and the financial panic of 1907, etc.) attendant to the rise of monopoly capitalism created a set of problems whose solution, in the eyes of many, lay in overseas economic and political expansion. It is to this period, then, that are attached America's first ventures in colonialism (Puerto Rico, Hawaii, the Philippines), tentative steps into Asia (China and Japan), and the consolidation of its economic domination of Latin America.

It is to war, however, that we must turn as the main catalyst for the growth of the world role of American capitalism, given war's positive effects on the United States itself and its adverse effects on its principal capitalist rivals. It is within the context of war that the relative positions of various capitalist powers were transformed in the first half of the twentieth century. In the First World War, the United States did not enter the active fighting until the last year of conflict. In the years preceding its entry, America's factories supplied the industrial goods and war materials required by the Entente, the agricultural commodities no longer forthcoming from the ravaged fields of Europe, and, most important, the loans which enabled Britain, France, and its allies to finance the years of struggle and suffering. The war had the effect of enormously expanding the industrial capacity of the United States, its financial participation in European capitals, and the penetration of the normal export markets of the distracted combatants (particularly in Latin America and Asia).

The First World War rendered asunder the economic, political, and psychological stability of the European old order and world capitalism . . . . The prewar world had been economically centered in Great Britain, with sterling the standard of world trading and London the capital of world banking. The war seriously shook the value of the pound, greatly diminished the French franc, at least temporarily destroyed the German and Austro-Hungarian economies and their roles, and opened the door to the accession of the United States to its principal, though not wholly dominant, role in world finance to match the industrial preeminence it had attained before the war. The new United States control of world trade markets reflected this reality. [40]

It is the Second World War that puts the finishing touches on this history of ascendency, for that war not only left the principal capitalist rivals of the United States temporarily but profoundly prostrate (Britain, Germany, and Japan) but demonstrated the expansionary possibilities of massive deficit military spending, a lesson that is etched into the perspectives of American business and political leadership to this day. The immediate affect of the war, however, was to jolt the United States out of the Depression which the New Deal had failed to dent. By July 1940, more than a year before America's entry into the war, Congress had appropriated the hithertofore unprecedented sum of $12 billion for defense (annual average defense expenditures during the 1930s were under $2 billion). This stimulus to the economy, added to the war orders from Europe, had an immediate and galvanizing effect on the sick economy of the Depression. In but a single year (1940), employment jumped 10 percent, payrolls rose 16 percent, industrial production increased 25 percent over the 1935–1939 average, farm incomes rose, and production of consumer goods rose 25 percent. American exports jumped 28 percent in the same year. [41] Needless to say, the process of economic advance that occurred during this initial year of the war, steadily escalated with each succeeding year of the war.

While entry into the war after December 7, 1941, obviously had serious negative consequences for many Americans—namely massive battlefield casualties—the overall impact on the world position of the United States was decisively positive. The war, which was fought in areas far distant from the continental United States, stimulated the exponential expansion of the entire industrial base and infrastructure of the economy (particularly of the largest corporations),[42] while the financial and productive bases of Britain, France, Germany, and Japan were being devastated. The European dependence on U.S. loans, both during and after the war and most clearly seen in lend-lease arrangements, helped pave the way for the postwar financial domination of the dollar and the decline of all other capitalist currencies. This development was concretized in the 1944 Bretton Woods Conference which set the dollar as the principal reserve currency in the capitalist world. Furthermore, the weakened position of rival capitalist nations allowed the United States a relatively free hand in the economic and political penetration of the former colonial domains of its rivals: namely, in the Pacific (Japan), Indochina (Japan, France), the Middle East (Britain), and Latin America (Britain, Germany). That this was not an entirely innocent process can be seen in the inclusion of a clause in the Atlantic Charter of 1941 guaranteeing free and equal trade access to Britain's Commonwealth territories after the war for American business in exchange for America's wartime assistance.[43] Finally, given their weakened position and the absence of alternative sources of support, the European economies themselves became subject to a massive invasion of American investment capital. In Europe U.S. investment increased from $1.7 billion in 1950 to $44.5 billion in 1974.[44]

Within a decade of the end of the Second World War, given full development of all of the above trends, the United States stood as the unchallenged economic, political, and military power among the capitalist nations, a position which formed the basis of the so-called "American Century." It was to remain in this position, in fact, for no more than a quarter of a century.

IMPERIALISM

To be the preeminent capitalist country, however, means more than being simply the most important nation within a group of highly developed peer nations. It is also to be in position at the head of a world system which lives off of the surplus extracted from less developed and underdeveloped countries. As we have pointed out elsewhere in this volume, capitalism is a system that preses outward from national boundaries in the never ending search for sources of profit, raw materials and markets, and over the centuries it has managed to tie together, through an elaborate system of unequal market relations, all of the nonsocialist world. This elaborate system, one which we shall call *imperialism,* ties together *core* capitalist states (the centers of accumulation) and less developed *periphery* states (the centers from which economic surplus is extracted), and adopts the latter to fit the needs of the former through economic, political, and military methods. As the leading capitalist power during the three decades after the Second World War, the United States has both led and benefited disproportionately from this international and unequal system.

Early Forms of Imperialism

Imperialism is not the first example in world history of the subordination of one nation by another. Nor is it the first example of expansionism or militarism. Nevertheless, unequal relations, expansionism, and militarism take on particular forms under modern capitalism which distinguish it from previous forms, and which heighten its impact on subject societies. James O'Connor has offered a succinct yet persuasive description of the capitalist form of domination we term imperialism.

> *Precapitalist and capitalist societies differ in the following ways: first, in precapitalist societies, economic expansion was irregular, unsystematic, not integral to normal economic activity. In capitalist societies, foreign trade and investment rightly are considered to be the "engines of economic growth." Expansion is necessary to maintain the rhythm of economic activity in the home or metropolitan economy and has an orderly, methodical, permanent character. Second, in precapitalist societies, the economic gains from expansion were windfall goals, frequently taking the form of merely sporadic plunder. In capitalist societies, profits from overseas trade and investment are an integral part of national income, and considered in a matter-of-fact manner. Third, in precapitalist societies, plunder acquired in the course of expansion often was consumed in the field by the conquering armies, leaving the home economy unaffected. In capitalist societies, exploited territories are fragmented and integrated into the structure of the metropolitan economy. Fourth, in precapitalist societies debate within the ruling classes ordinarily revolved around the question whether or not to expand. In capitalist societies, ruling class debates normally turn on the issue, what is the best way to expand.*[45]

In the earlier stages of capitalism, imperialism took a form very much different from the contemporary one. While modern imperialism maintains its system of domination through elaborate, indirect, and barely visible methods, early capitalism extracted surplus in rather crude ways. Direct plunder, for instance, formed the basis for the earliest capitalist accumulation process and provided the motive force for capitalist development. The plunder generated by the wave of crusades from the eleventh through the fifteenth centuries, to take a case, provided the capital for the rise of the Italian city states.[46] In the fifteenth and sixteenth centuries, plunder from the New World (transferred from Spain because of its horrendously adverse balance of trade) formed the basis for capitalist development in England, Holland, and Germany.[47] The naked theft and sale of human beings (slave trade) was an important factor in England and Holland's rise as important merchant and financial powers. Marx described these processes as follows:

> The discovery of gold and silver in America, the extirpation, enslavement and entombment in mines of the aboriginal population, the beginning of the conquest and looting of the East Indies, the turning of Africa into a warren for the commercial hunting of blackskins, signalized the rosy dawn of the era of capitalist production. These idyllic proceedings are the chief momenta of primitive accumulation.
>
> The treasures captured outside Europe by undisguised looting, enslavement, and murder, floated back to the mother country and were there turned into capital.[48]

After the era of primitive accumulation through plunder had sparked the industrial development of the core capitalist states (England, Holland, Germany, and France), the relationship between these states and the subordinate periphery underwent an important transformation. The need for direct and brutal plunder gave way to the necessity for assured supplies of raw materials for factories and markets for finished products. The need for regularized if unequal trade, a more benign form of plunder, if you will, led to the fashioning of more stable and predictable linkages between core and periphery. We thus see in the late nineteenth and twentieth centuries the development of a worldwide system of colonialism, a system in which the core capitalist states established direct political/military rule over less developed societies.[49] Each colonial power attempted to establish areas of privileged trade and investment closed to other core capitalist states. This period witnessed, then, an intense competition between the major European powers to carve Africa, Asia, and the Pacific into colonial spheres of influence.

Except in a very minor way, the United States never became seriously involved in colonialism. As strange as it may seem, if we discount the short-lived formation of colonial outposts in the Carribean after the Spanish-American War, American imperialism has always taken anticolonial forms. That is to say, its own unequal relations with the less developed world, its own extraction of surplus from the periphery, has not depended upon direct political rule and administration of these areas, but upon more indirect and, we must add, more efficient methods. There has been much speculation about why American imperialism has taken anticolonial forms. Some have argued that America's own colonial past made it ideologically difficult to impose such relations on other peoples. Others have suggested that America had no need of external colonial expansion because of its own internal empire, the vast areas stretching to the Pacific Ocean available to it after the extermination of the Indians and the victory in the Mexican War. Still others have suggested that by the time the United States was overcome with the expansionary impulse after the turn of the century, the known world had already been carved up and parceled out among the major European powers, and little remained for the nourishment of the American appetite. Finally, others point out that the emergence of the United States as the industrial (but not financial) leader of the capitalist world after 1900 gave it an economic power in world trade that would allow it to become predominant if it were allowed to trade freely with all parts of the world. Such an objective position in the world required less its own colonies than the right to penetrate the colonies of the European states. The famous "Open Door" policy articulated by Secretary of State John Hay is the best single example of this world posture (calling for the opening of the China market to all capitalist countries, irrespective of already established European spheres of influence), and it became the hallmark of American policy in general. As historian William Appelman Williams puts it, "the policy of the open door was designed to clear the way and establish the conditions under which America's preponderant economic power would extend the American system throughout the world without the embarrassment and inefficiency of traditional colonialism."[50]

Contemporary Imperialism

Whatever reason one chooses to explain the phenomenon, the fact remains unarguable that American imperialism has been and remains anticolonial. Nevertheless, it remains imperialism. That is to say, it continues to be a system in which the well-being of the core capitalist state, in this case, the United States, is dependent upon the extraction of wealth from less developed areas. In modern capitalism, this extraction is accomplished through a complex international economic network of trade, finance, and direct investment under the direction of American multinational corporations. The level of extraction is not insignificant. In direct investment, for instance, the difference between total dollars invested overseas and total dollars realized by multinational firms in 1974 was $13.2 billion, up from $1.7 billion in 1965.[51]

Increasingly, the capitalist world is tied together into relationships of superordination and subordination by the direct investment activities of the multinationals, the outright purchase and establishment of mines, factories, communications systems, and transportation, and their integration into a worldwide division of labor. In most of the less developed world, as a result, the control of domestic mineral, agricultural, and manufacturing assets is lodged in the hands of the multinationals. In this division of labor, periphery countries are becoming the suppliers of some single component (whether raw materials like copper or bauxite, or an industrial product like auto engines or frames) that is processed or assembled into a finished product elsewhere on the globe under the managerial direction of corporate headquarters, normally in the United States. The inherent weakness of the periphery societies in such a system in which each performs some specialized economic task under core capitalist managerial and financial direction should be more than obvious. The hegemony of the American multinationals in this world division of labor is suggested by the fact that in 1971 they accounted for more than 50 percent of total world direct foreign investment. Great Britain was next closest at 15 percent of the total, while no other single country accounted for more than 6 percent.[52] There is also every indication that American direct foreign investment is expanding significantly, if not precipitously (see Table 5-3).

The rapid expansion of these investment figures are accounted for primarily in the expansion of the Canadian and European markets. Thus, of total investment in 1967, about 60 percent was in those two markets, up about 10 percent since 1957. Now it may be argued that the heavy investment in Western economies disproves the contention that American corporations are involved or interested in the exploitation of Third World natural resources. It is important to point out, therefore, that much of the investment in Western Europe, Canada, and Japan is in firms that are themselves heavily involved in the Third World.[53] Moreover, the 40 per-

Table 5-3   U.S. Foreign Investment, by Year (in billions)

1929	1946	1950	1955	1960	1965	1970	1974
7.5	7.2	19.0	29.1	49.4	81.5	116.4	196.6

Source: Richard C. Edwards, et al., *The Capitalist System,* (Englewood Cliffs, N.J.: Prentice Hall), 1977, p. 476, based on U.S. Department of Commerce, *Survey of Current Business.* (Washington, D.C.; U.S. Government Printing office), 1975.

cent of direct investment in the less developed parts of the world is important. Forty percent is not an insignificant figure. It is a major portion of all overseas U.S. economic activities by corporations, and accounts for a very high percentage of its profits. *In fact, the rate of earnings on American foreign investment was more than twice as high in underdeveloped nations (18.7 percent) as in developed (8.3 percent).*[54] Moreover, important firms such as Exxon (60 percent of its profits), Mobil (52 percent), and Gulf Oil (29 percent) are almost entirely dependent on their earnings in the less developed countries.[55] Finally, the investment in the Third World is related to strategic sectors of our economy, as we shall demonstrate below.

Imperialism is also tied together by the financial networks of the core capitalist countries. The conduct of international business requires an infrastructure of finance, currency transaction, and credit, so it is not surprising that a world capitalist banking structure, mainly under the direction of the United States, has grown enormously over the past three decades. This world banking structure enhances the capacity of multinational companies to float short-term loans to convert currencies almost instantaneously, and to gain access to international bond and equity capital, and also enables the United States in particular to dominate domestic banking in the less developed countries. The size of such operations is impressive. Fully 28 percent of net earnings for the seven largest banks in the United States were from foreign operations or to take other figures, the total foreign assets of U.S. banks increased *seventeen* times between 1966 and 1974.[56] Such domination not only gives operational control of local currencies and credit policies to an outside nation, but makes local savings (in U.S. branch banks) available to international companies. To the extent that these local savings are siphoned off, it follows that they become unavailable for domestic development.

Theories of Imperialism

As the leading capitalist country, the United States thus stands at the head of a system of world imperialism which ties together core capitalist states and peripheral less developed states through the mechanisms of financial domination, unequal exchange, and the direct ownership of resource and industrial capacities, and which transfers wealth from the periphery to the core as a matter of course. What needs to be further explored, at this point in the analysis, are the reasons why imperialism is "a way of life" for capitalist society, why the United States, in particular, is locked in to such a world system.

Convincing theories of imperialism all begin with a consideration of the inner logic of mature capitalism and the requirements of its major component part, the corporate sector. One theoretical position holds that concentrated capitalism, as its firms continuously increase productivity and productive capacity in the race with other firms for profits, is always pushed toward the abyss of overproduction (since consumers, in a system of highly unequal income distribution are never able to purchase all that the system is capable of producing), and the concurrent problem of unused capacity, unemployment, and unrealized profits. In the United States, the overcapacity problem becomes increasingly more serious. The Federal Reserve Board has reported, for instance, that the manufacturing utilization rate was only 77.2 percent in the 1970–1975 period as compared to a 91.9 percent rate in the 1950–1954 period.[57] As historian Gabriel Kolko has pointed out, "the capitalist economy's traditional nemisis of inadequate demand and over-expansion [has] reappeared in almost classic form despite all the vast means that [have] been employed to counteract them."[58] The search for loci for the use of surplus capacity becomes ever more imperative as core capitalist countries have accelerated their development into concentrated, corporate forms. Imperialism, in this view, is an inevitable phase in the development of the capitalist mode of production, a way to temporarily escape some of the basic contradictions in the capitalist mode of production.[59]

In fact, business leaders and politicians in the United States have long looked to expansion in overseas markets as the key to the problem of overproduction and its attendant adverse effects on American life.

John D. Rockefeller, 1898: *Dependent solely upon local business we should have failed years ago. We are forced to extend our markets and to seek for export trade.*[60]

Woodrow Wilson, 1912: *Our industries have expanded to such a point that they will burst their jackets if they cannot find a free outlet to the markets of the world . . . . Our domestic markets no longer suffice. We need foreign markets.*

Woodrow Wilson, 1913: *We must establish a government in Mexico under which all contracts and business and concessions will be safer than they have been.*

John L. Lewis, CIO 1940: *Unless substantial economic offsets are provided to prevent this nation from being wholly dependent upon the war expenditures we will sooner or later come to the dilemma which require either war or depression.*

Fortune magazine (1944): *A new emphasis on enlarged consumer sales at home would have to be paralleled by a tremendous expansion of foreign trade and foreign investment.*

Dean Acheson, 1944: *If we do not do that [expand], it seems clear that we are in for a very bad time, so far as the economic and social position of the country is concerned. We cannot go through another ten years like the ten years at the end of the twenties and the beginning of the thirties, without having the most far-reaching consequences upon our economic and social system . . . .*

When we look at the problem, we may say it is a problem of markets . . . . The important thing is markets. We have got to see that what the country produces is used and sold under financial arrangements which makes its production possible . . . . You must look to foreign markets.

We cannot have full employment and prosperity in the United States without the foreign markets.

We are thus treated to a rather strange convergence of opinion concerning the roots of American policy between radical thinkers and business and political leadership: "that the continued health of the American economy and the maintenance of American society in its current form requires expansion. This requirement means that foreign countries must be kept *open* to American corporate penetration through investment, that raw material supplies be readily and cheaply available and that socialist movements which might serve to threaten these objectives be opposed."[61]

Fortune Magazine, 1940: *What interests us primarily is the longer-range question of whether the American capitalist system could continue to function if most of Europe and Asia should abolish free enterprise.*

Added to the problem of overproduction as a motive force for overseas expansion is the dependency of the United States on raw materials sources in the less developed world.[62] While the fact of petroleum dependency is by now obvious, what would no doubt surprise most Americans is the degree to which the United States has become, in general, a dependent society in terms of most of its resource requirements; the degree to which it is a raw material *have-not* nation. Almost every raw material needed to keep the industrial system in operation depends on raw materials found only in the Third World. We have become a net importer of such materials.

Imports of certain materials are even more marked. Almost all of our supply of bauxite, used to make aluminum, is imported. Oil is also imported in this respect, as is iron ore. Dependence on these areas will become even greater in the future. It has been estimated, for instance, that by the year 2000, 75 percent of our supply of iron ore will have to be imported.[63]

Perhaps the most startling indication of our dependence on foreign sources of raw materials is that almost all raw materials considered critical to national defense are imported, three-quarters from Third World Countries (Table 5-4).

Table 5-4 Classification of Strategic Industrial Materials[64] by Degree of Dependence on Imports

Number of Materials	Rate of Imports to New Supply (Percentage)
38	80–100
6	60–79
8	40–59
3	20–39
7	20–39
62	Less than 20

The above discussion has dwelled solely at the *macro* level, examining how developments in mature capitalism as a whole have compelled the system toward imperial expansion into every corner of the globe. One could make an equally persuasive case for the inherently expansionary nature of mature capitalism by taking a *micro* view, that is, by examining the business practices of individual giant corporations. Most importantly and most simply, overseas operations translate into higher profits, and the rational firm with the resources to make it possible (mainly giant corporations) invariably focus escalating proportions of their operations beyond the constricted business boundaries of the United States. The data, much of which we have supplied earlier, demonstrate two points quite conclusively. First, profits from overseas operations are at least twice as high as those from domestic operations.[65] Second, overseas investment, production, and profit taking are concentrated among the largest firms in the American economy.[66] The bases for the generation of super profits by the largest firms are not too difficult to discern. With high costs in fixed capital already in place at home, and market saturation a recurrent problem, the easiest way to increase sales without the necessity of cutting prices is to find new markets. Overseas markets remain the only loci where saturation is not yet a reality, and therefore, open to the sales effort. Profitability is also the outcome of conducting most foreign operations in environments characterized by minimal taxation, and scant consumer and/or environmental requirements. Finally, in those increasingly common operations where production and assembly is being transferred overseas so as to cut tariff and transportation costs, multinational enterprises are blessed with an abundance of cheap labor in places like Korea, Taiwan, and Singapore, labor that works for wages often less than one-tenth that paid to American workers. The temptations of shifting operations overseas are great indeed.

The multinational firms are also expansionary because of their dependency on unsubstitutable raw materials for their operations. Expansion into overseas areas, that is, direct ownership and control of raw material supplies is one way that the giant corporation attempts to add stability and predictability to its operations. Steel companies, therefore, seek not only additional markets but control of assured supplies of iron ore. Aluminum companies seek dependable supplies of bauxite. To have such supplies in the hands of either industrial competitors or hostile social systems are situations to be avoided at all costs. It must be added that the effort to control raw materials is not simply one of supplying needed materials for the industrial machine, but to ensure the stability of market shares by denying resources to potential new rivals. The major oil companies, to take a case in point, traditionally searched for new oil reserves even during those periods characterized by a world oil glut so as to keep the "independents" from challenging their domination of the industry.

Whichever theoretical explanation one chooses, and we are of the opinion that all of them must be taken together, it is abundantly clear that mature capitalism requires expansion into the far corners of the globe and the subordination of the less developed countries to its needs as an economic system. No other set of theoretical explanations has yet been able to adequately describe the inexorable drive of mature capitalism toward expansion, and a world structure of unequal relations between core and periphery.

TOWARD THE POSITIVE STATE

In this chapter, we have attempted to describe the principal structural features of mature capitalism in the United States, focusing primarily upon the corporate dominated dual economy, the division in the working class between monopoly and competitive sector workers, and the preeminent position of the United States in the world capitalist system. While we have occasionally alluded to some of the problems and implications that attend to these structural developments, that has not been our primary purpose in the present discussion. In the next chapter, however, we shall focus our attention upon the problems and contradictions which arise from the main structural features of mature capitalism, and the degree to which government has become the single institution temporarily capable of dealing with them. In our analysis of this symbiotic interaction, we shall, in fact, be constructing a description and a theoretical explanation of the modern positive state.

NOTES

[1] In the course of this and the next chapter, we shall speak of mature capitalism and the positive state in the *present* tense. We shall do so because, although forces are now visible which portend the end of an era and the beginning of a new one, we remain today largely within the midst of the configuration of forces that have characterized the postwar period.

[2] The relationship between the giant corporations and the state is examined in the next chapter.

[3] Richard J. Barber, *The American Corporation* (New York: Dutton, 1970), p. 20.

[4] Walter F. Mueller, "Recent Changes in Industrial Concentration, and the Current Merger Movement," in *Hearings: Subcommittee on Antitrust and Monopoly of the Committee on the Judiciary, U.S. Senate, 88th Congress, 2d Session* (Washington, D.C.: U.S. Government Printing Office, July 1964). Reprinted in Maurice Zeitlin, Ed., *American Society, Inc.: Studies of the Social Structure and Political Economy of the United States* (Chicago: Markham, 1970), p. 24. Note that the assets of the top 500

corporations almost doubled from 1965 to 1972. See *Statistical Abstracts of the United States, 1973* (Washington, D.C.: U.S. Census Bureau, 1973), Table 777.

[5] U.S. Department of Commerce. *Survey of Current Business July 1970,* Table 6-15.

[6] Gardiner C. Means "Economic Concentration" in *Hearings: Subcommittee on Antitrust and Monopoly of the Committee on the Judiciary, U.S. Senate, 88th Congress, 2nd Session* (Washington, D.C.: U.S. Government Printing Office, July 1964), pp. 8–19. Reprinted in Zeitlin, *American Society, Inc.*

[7] Daniel R. Fusfield, "The Rise of the Corporate State in America," *Journal of Economic Issues,* Vol. 6, No. 1 (March 1972) pp. 1-22.

[8] Harry M. Trebing, Ed, *The Corporation in the American Economy* (Chicago: Quadrangle, 1974), p. 4.

[9] William D. Shepard, *Market Power and Economic Welfare* (New York: Random House, 1970), pp. 152-154.

[10] Richard Barnet and Ronald Müller, *Global Research: The Power of the Multinational Corporations* (New York: Simon and Schuster, 1974), p. 230.

[11] See Robert L. Heilbroner, *The Limits of American Capitalism* (New York: Harper Torchbooks, 1966), p. 11.

[12] See the Patman Committee Staff Report for the Domestic Finance Subcommittee of the House Committee on Banking and Currency, 90th Congress, 2d Session, *Commercial Banks and Their Trust Activities: Emerging Influence on the American Economy* (Washington, D.C.: U.S. Government Printing Office, July 1968). Reprinted in Zeitlin, *American Society, Inc.* Out of approximately 14,000 banks in the United States, the top ten controlled more than one-fourth of all assets and deposits in 1972. See *Statistical Abstracts of the United States, 1973,* Table 708.

[13] J. J. Servan-Schreiber, *The American Challenge* (New York: Avon Books, 1968), p. 3.

[14] Howard J. Sherman, *Profits in the United States* (Ithaca: Cornell University Press, 1968) Reprinted in Zeitlin, *American Society, Inc.,* p. 44.

[15] Gardiner Means, "The Administered Price Theory Reconfirmed," *American Economic Review* (June, 1972), pp. 292-306.

[16] See John Kenneth Galbraith, *The New Industrial State* (New York: Houghton-Mifflin, 1968), for a more complete description of the integrated, mature corporation.

[17] Paul Baran and Paul M. Sweezy, *Monopoly Capital* (New York: Monthly Review Press, 1966), p. 59.

[18] On the need to study the public effects of the corporation see the pioneering but largely ignored work of Andrew Hacker, *The Corporation Take Over* (New York: Harper & Row, 1964); "Power to Do What," in Irving Louis Horowitz, *The New Sociology* (New York: Oxford University Press, 1965); and "A Country Called Corporate America," in Trebing, *The Corporation in the American Economy.*

[19] Quoted in the *Report of the President's Advisory Commission on Civil Disorders* (New York: Bantam, 1967), p. 240.

[20] Ibid., p. 243.

[21] Quoted in Edwin M. Epstein, *The Corporation in American Politics* (Englewood Cliffs, N.J.: Prentice-Hall, 1969), p. 106.

[22] Michael D. Reagan, *The Managed Economy* (New York: Oxford University Press, 1963), p. 196.

[23] For the details of these developments, see the pioneering work of Harry Braverman, *Labor and Monopoly Capital* (New York: Monthly Review Press, 1974).

[24] See Samuel Bowles and Herbert Bintis, *Schooling in Capitalist America* (New York: Basic, 1976); Samuel Bowles, "Unequal Education and the Reproduction of the Social Division of Labor," in Martin Carnoy, ed., *Schooling in a Corporate Society* (New York: David McKay, 1972); and Michael Katz, *The Irony of Early School Reform* (Cambridge: Harvard University Press, 1968).

[25] See Robert Dahl, "The Behavioral Approach in Political Science," *American Political Science Review,* Vol. 55 (December 1961), pp. 763-772.

[26] For a discussion of this history see Ferdinand Lundberg, *The Rich and*

the Super-Rich (New York: Bantam, 1968), Chapter 10, "Philanthropic Vistas."

[27] Edward S. Greenberg, "The Corporate State," in Edward S. Greenberg and Richard Young, *American Politics Reconsidered* (Belmont, Cal.: Wadsworth Publishing, The Duxbury Press, 1973), p. 61.

[28] For a full discussion of these concepts see James O'Connor, *The Fiscal Crisis of the State* (New York: St. Martin's Press, 1973).

[29] Neil Chamberlain, "The Corporation and the Trade Union," in Edward S. Mason, ed., *The Corporation in Modern Society* (Cambridge: Harvard University Press, 1960).

[30] See the important data collected by Epstein, in *The Corporation and American Politics.*

[31] See Ronald Radosh, "The Corporate Ideology of American Labor Leaders from Gompers to Hillman," *Studies on the Left,* Vol. 6 (November–December 1966), pp. 66–68. It is also clear that unions have been strong supporters of American foreign policy, a foreign policy that is designed to serve the needs of giant corporations. From at least the 1930s, union leadership has echoed corporate desires for market expansion and control of supplies of raw materials. Moreover, organized labor has long been staunchly anticommunist and was an enthusiastic junior partner in the fabrication of the cold war hysteria.

[32] The first set of figures are from Solomon Barkin, "The Decline of the Labor Movement," in Hacker, *The Corporation Takeover,* p. 225. The last figures are from Table #654, *Statistical Abstracts of the United States* (Washington, D.C.: U.S. Department of Commerce, 1977), p. 400.

[33] Table #654, *Statistical Abstracts of The United States* (Washington, D.C.: U.S. Department of Commerce, 1977), p. 400.

[34] There is a growing and significant third-labor sector which we have not mentioned; namely, government employment. Quite naturally, the expansion of state activities in the era of mature capitalism leads to analogous expansion in governmental employment. We shall have more to say about this in the next chapter.

[35] Ernest Mandel, *Marxist Economic Theory Vol. II* (New York: Monthly Review Press, 1970), p. 450.

[36] Barnet and Müller, *Global Research,* p. 184.

[37] Gabriel Kolko, *Main Currents in American History* (New York: Harper & Row, 1976), p. 386.

[38] Ibid., p. 35.

[39] Quoted in Alan Wolfe, *The Limits of Legitimacy* (New York: Free Press, 1977), p. 89.

[40] Kolko, *Main Currents,* p. 195.

[41] Broadus Mitchell, *Depression Decade* (New York: Harper Torchbooks, 1969), Chapter 11.

[42] Of $175 billion in war contracts between 1940 and 1944, the top ten companies received 33 percent of the total, while only thirty-three companies received around 50 percent. Kolko, *Main Currents,* p. 312.

[43] Great Britain accounted for 47 percent of private investment in Latin America prior to the First World War. By the mid-1950s, direct investment by *all* countries other than the United States was almost negligible. Arthur MacEwan, "Changes in World Capitalism," *Radical America,* Vol. 9, No. 1 (January, 1975), pp. 1–23.

[44] Richard C. Edwards, et al., *The Capitalist System,* (Englewood Cliffs, N.J.: Prentice-Hall, 1977), p. 456.

[45] O'Connor, *The Fiscal Crisis of the State,* p. 170.

[46] Mandel, *Marxist Economic Theory Vol. II,* p. 103.

[47] Ibid., p. 107.

[48] *Capital,* Vol. 1, Part VIII, Chapter 31.

[49] Alan Wolfe makes the important point that colonialism was simply the most popular form of imperialism during this period, and that capitalism was quite flexible with respect to the tools of domination. See Wolfe, *The Limits of Legitimacy,* Chapter 3.

[50] William Appleman Williams, *The Tragedy of American Diplomacy* (New York: Delta, 1959), p. 43.

[51] Edwards, et al., *The Capitalist System,* p. 476.

[52] Ibid., p. 474.

[53] A distinction best pointed out in Harry Magdoff, "The Logic of Imperialism," *Social Policy* (September–October 1970).

[54] U.S. Department of Commerce, *Survey of Current Business* (October 1970).

[55] U.S. Department of Commerce, *Survey of Current Business* (September 1966).

[56] Kolko, *Main Currents,* p. 382.

[57] Ibid., p. 339.

[58] Ibid.

[59] These views are best seen in Baran and Sweezy, *Monopoly Capital;* Lenin, *Imperialism: The Highest Stage of Capitalism;* Harry Magdoff, *The Age of Imperialism* (New York: Monthly Review Press, 1966); James O'Connor, "The Meaning of Economic Imperialism," in James O'Connor, *The Corporations and the State* (New York: Harper-Colophon Books, 1974); and Kolko, *Main Currents,* Chapter 9.

[60] All quotes in this section are from Williams, *The Tragedy of American Diplomacy.*

[61] Greenberg, "The Corporate State," p. 63.

[62] Much of what follows is based on Magdoff, *The Age of Imperialism.*

[63] Ibid., p. 49.

[64] Ibid., p. 50.

[65] For many companies, profit proportions from overseas operations are even more striking. In 1971, Standard Oil (NJ) enjoyed 52 percent of its total profits from abroad; GM, 19 percent; Ford, 24 percent; IBM, 54 percent; Mobil, 51 percent; ITT, 35 percent; and so on. See Edwards, *The Capitalist System,* p. 480.

[66] In 1970, 30 percent of *all* income derived from the foreign operations of U.S. firms were accounted for by the top ten U.S. industrials. The top fifty accounted for 50 percent of the total. See Thomas Weisskopf, "American Economic Interests in Foreign Countries," Center for Research on Economic Development, University of Michigan (April 1974), mimeo, p. 16.

6
THE MODERN POSITIVE STATE

By most indications, it would seem that the United States has transcended the problems that have historically plagued capitalism. Giant corporations are blessed with the productive, financial, and technical capacity to produce goods and services in quantities hithertofore never even imagined. Significant and strategically located elements of the work force are directly represented by labor unions in regularized and stable collective bargaining arrangements, transposing the classic labor-management confrontation from the factory floor and the streets to the negotiating table and regulatory agency office. America's position as the preeminent power in the world capitalist system gives it access to cheap raw materials in the Third World and favorable access to markets for its finished goods and agricultural products all over the nonsocialist world, in developed and less developed nations alike.

Such a confluence of favorable structural developments, it is safe to say, has never before occurred. It is not surprising, therefore, to find many social thinkers making the claim that the endemic problems of capitalism, which both the friends and foes of capitalism have always acknowledged, have been decisively and irrevocably erased, opening up a new era of growth and promise. The "American century," in this view, is no mere flight of the imagination or a publicist's construction, but a budding reality, soon to reach full flower.[1]

The reality of mature capitalism in the United States, however, is another matter entirely. In fact, there is a cruel paradox at work in the very processes of growth and concentration that its major economic actors pursue so assiduously. Capitalism's economic success leads to a number of disturbing and potentially disruptive contradictions. Success at one level of the system creates a new set of severe problems at another level that the major corporations are unable to solve by their own devices, and in consequence of that dilemma, they generally turn to the government for assistance. Some of these new difficulties involve, among a host of others, excess productive capacity, technological unemployment, excessive research and development costs, insufficient investment outlets, and poverty and social instability among competitive sector workers. However, state intervention introduces an additional dilemma into the equation. While it helps to lessen the impact of some of the problems, the act of intervention itself creates new problems; namely, bloated governmental budgets, bureaucratization, inefficiency, and the inevitable outcomes of permanent inflation and fiscal crisis.[2] In the remainder of this chapter, we shall examine this complex set of processes.

THE STATE AND THE CORPORATE SECTOR

The dynamic processes of economic growth and concentration among the largest corporations create certain difficulties for both society in general, and the corporations in particular. As firms in the corporate sector take over and absorb increasing numbers of small businesses from the competitive sector, for instance, society is faced with the problem of surplus capitalists, people who become dispossessed as small property holders are transformed into wage and salary employees. We can see this at work primarily in agriculture (though it remains a more general phenomenon), where deposed small and medium-sized farmers are continually transformed into farm laborers or urban migrants. More importantly, the inescapable tendency for corporate sector firms to attempt to increase their profits through technological innovation, and plant relocation to areas of cheap labor (mainly overseas), inevitably contributes to problems of permanent unemployment. Or to take another example, as economic concentration and technological innovation advance among the giant firms, firms in the competitive sector are less able to remain economically viable, a situation which further exacerbates their problems of low wages, poor working conditions, and business failures. All of these difficulties, difficulties which arise, it must be repeatedly emphasized, from the very success of corporate enterprise, requires that the modern capitalist state be actively involved in programs of welfare, job retraining, and insurance against sickness, old age, and economic insecurity. We shall touch on these issues in the course of our discussion.

Regulating the Business Cycle

The problems endemic to the largest corporations that call for state intervention are not inconsiderable. Most importantly, the implications of business failure and economic instability become increasingly serious for investors and society in general as the size of industrial enterprises continually expands. The dissolution of a major firm has serious adverse consequences for employment, the business health of subcontractors, the stock portfolios of individual and institutional investors, and the fiscal solvency of local communities. As for the corporations themselves, overall economic stability and assured business activity remain central concerns because of their need to rationally plan the utilization of their vast financial, technical, and manpower assets. The state has, with varying degrees of success, taken on this problem of economic stability by attempting to smooth out the dips and peaks of the business cycle through use of its powerful monetary and fiscal tools.

The starting point for grasping this set of state activities is the realization that capitalism, whether laissez-faire or monopoly, is inherently unstable, prone to periods of excess capacity and unemployment, as well as inflation.[3] From the beginning of the industrial revolution to its final worldwide collapse in the 1930s, world capitalism suffered a recurrent series of ever more serious convulsions, characterized by high unemployment, business bankruptcies, and the erosion of investment. Between 1870 and 1929 the National Bureau of Economic Research recorded sixteem depressions in the United States alone. To the economists who believed that capitalism was self-correcting, the tenacity and persistence of the Great Depression was sobering. It remained for the great economist John Maynard Keyes to explain that tenacity and to demonstrate how unguided, undirected capitalism had fully as many forces working to maintain economic depression as forces leading to recovery.

The key element in the instability of the capitalist economy, according to Keynes, is the *unpredictability of private investment.* Production and employment and thus the level of economic activity under capitalism is dependent upon the willingness of business leaders to invest out of their profits. Since a business usually only invests when there is likelihood for further profit, investment always fluctuates with changes in the prospects for profit; at times more than savings; at other times less than savings. Given these often severe fluctuations between investment and savings, the level of economic activity also tends to fluctuate wildly. Keynes' solution, and it is one that all Western capitalist nations have now adopted, is for government to act as a control device on spending and investment through its power to tax and to spend. In this way, government can theoretically stabilize the economy by controlling the level of total or aggregate spending According to one leading economist, modern capitalism probably owes its survival to this set of spending and taxing strategies.[4]

Capitalism always faces the problem of using profits, of not allowing profits to lay idle, of what Marxist economists Paul Baran and Paul Sweezy call "the problem of surplus absorption." According to Baran and Sweezy, under the American system of monopoly capitalism, a system in which giant corporations are relatively free to set their own prices, to control their sources and costs of raw materials, and to induce consumption, there is an inevitable tendency of aggregate profits (the surplus) to rise (see Table 6-1).[5] Since the surplus tends to rise both absolutely and in com-

Table 6-1 The Size of the Economic Surplus

	Surplus (Aggregate Profits)	Surplus as a Percentage of GNP
1929	$ 48.9 billion	46.9
1939	43.5	47.8
1949	133.6	51.7
1959	264.2	54.7
1963	327.7	56.1

Source: Joseph D. Phillips, "Appendix: Estimating the Economic Surplus," Table 22 in Paul A. Baran and Paul M. Sweezy *Monopoly Capital* (New York: Monthly Review Press, 1966).

parison to the gross national product (GNP), capitalism faces an increasingly severe problem of using that surplus, of not allowing it to remain idle. To utilize this surplus capital, government attempts to encourage demand. Since aggregate demand or the total level of spending is composed of the sum of private consumption spending, private investment, and government expenditures, government can maintain high demand through expenditures when consumption and investment lag, or it can cut expenditures (or raise taxes) when there is too much demand leading to inflation. Since the New Deal and the government-induced economic expansion of the Second World War, the governments of the United States and of other Western capitalist nations have recognized the need for the state to expand aggregate demand so that it will match the ever growing productive capacity of the monopoly capitalist economy. It is primarily in relation to the need to use this ever increasing surplus that we find the best explanation for the explosion in public spending in the United States and other Western nations. *The state spends because it must!*

While Keynesian economics tells governments to *spend,* it offers no advice as to the *object* of spending. The principal axiom is that government maintain aggregate demand at a level sufficient to match productive capacity. Government can do so by spending money on literally anything it desires—tanks, housing, medicine, transportation, and medical care, for example. Why is it, then, that the United States chooses to spend nearly one-half of its treasury on military materials? Why is it that little of the public treasury is directed toward the enhancement of the qualities of life of the average American? Why is there, in the words of John Kenneth Galbraith, public squalor amid private affluence?

While it is theoretically possible for the state to spend more on social and human needs than on military hardware, the imperatives of capitalism as a system make it highly unlikely. First, central to capitalism as an economic system is the private ownership of the means of production (e.g., factories, machinery, finance capital), and the use of that productive apparatus to generate private profits. Whatever else the state chooses to do under capitalism it must operate within the constraints of private ownership and private profit. Nothing that it does can significantly challenge these two values.

Second, advanced capitalism is built upon a class system in which a few own capital, and the remainder sell their labor for wages and salaries. Ownership of capital leads to enhanced life chances in all areas of social life—health, housing, security, life expectancy, legal justice, and so on—whereas the sale of labor power leads to diminished opportunity for life benefits, especially as one descends the skill ladder within the wage and salary group. Access to income is tied directly to the productive process; the only legitimate claim to income arises from the value of one's labor power or the ownership of the means of production. Inherent in capitalism, in short, is a situation of severe class inequality. The people who own capital have every reason to want to stay on top of the benefit structure, and since they have the political power to influence the direction of state policy, it is highly unlikely that public policy would ever significantly challenge inequality.

Class inequality serves many useful functions for the people at the top of the social structure. Most important, it stacks probabilities so that those on top are given a head start in the maintenance of their positions. Because the owners of capital and their heirs enjoy good health, the best in education, and abundant financial resources, they start the competitive race several leagues ahead of the rest of the population. Inequality also ensures that the dirty work of society will get done—that cotton will get picked, that homes will get cleaned, that produce will be harvested, that steel will be poured, and that coal will get mined. Severe inequality ensures that since so many people have so little, they will be willing, no matter how demeaning, dangerous, or dirty the work, to sell their labor in exchange for the wherewithal to maintain life. Equality would, moreover, destroy the work incentive under an economic system such as ours, where workers, having no control over either the process or product of their work, have no intrinsic motivation to work. Inequality is, in the absence of gratifying labor, the major incentive for productive effort under capitalism.

If we understand that the central values of advanced capitalism are private ownership, private profit, and inequality, then the pattern of public sector spending in the United States begins to make a great deal of sense. If spending were shifted in a major way from the defense sector to the fulfillment of human needs and the enhancement of life quality, the central values would come under direct attack. Massive spending on decent and aesthetically pleasing public housing for low- and medium-income families would represent a direct challenge to the interests that benefit from the private housing market: builders, realtors, lending institutions, and so on. As a result, we have a situation in which public housing is inadequate measured against housing needs. Rather than spend money for decent public housing, we spend public funds for urban renewal projects that benefit only downtown real estate and financial interests, for loans to subsidize middle- and upper-income suburbs, and for highway systems designed to link these suburbs to downtown offices and department stores. Public policy is thus channeled away from activities that would threaten profits and inequality and toward activities that enhance them.

What is true of housing policy in the United States holds for other public policy areas as well: policy is directed toward the maintenance of private ownership, private profit, and inequality. Public funds in transportation, as a result, are not directed toward the construction of massive and inexpensive public transportation systems, but toward subsidization of highways (and thus the auto, rubber, and oil industries) and airports (used primarily by those at the upper end of the social scale). Public monies are not directed toward massive efforts to equalize educational opportunities, because that would challenge the educational advantages of the affluent. Public provision of universal, inexpensive medical care would not only challenge the health advantages of the affluent but would also undermine the profit positions of medical professionals and hospitals. Successful experiments in the generation of cheap electrical power by public authorities like TVA are prevented from moving beyond the single case, since this would challenge the private ownership of power resources and, consequently, private profit from the sale of these resources. We could multiply the examples, but the point has been made. Public sector spending cannot, under advanced capitalism, fundamentally challenge private ownership, profit, and inequality.

Defense spending is the perfect solution for capitalism because it allows spending sufficient to fuel the economy without at the same time threatening the private sector. The attractiveness of defense spending derives from several different perspectives. Most important, spending for military purposes poses no threat to the private ownership system. It provides no goods or services (such as housing, food, and transportation) to the general population that would eliminate the profits of private producers. Spending is generally for items that have no civilian counterpart—tanks, bullets, missiles, and counterinsurgency training, for example. Military spending also takes place within a manufactured climate of fear, which helps prevent careful scrutiny of the defense budget. This explains partly why defense budgets are both large and expandable. Nor surprisingly, this system of high expenditures and minimal accountability leads to the generation of healthy profits for a relatively few giant corporations. Another interesting characteristic of defense spending is that the sophisticated, complex, and expensive weapons systems that comprise much of the budget are almost always obsolete before they become operational, so that there is an ever recurring need for new weapons systems and, given the military contracting system, ever recurring private profits. Complex weapons systems also allow giant corporations to utilize their highly skilled, scientists, computer specialists, and systems analysts. Finally, construction and maintenance of a giant military establishment is a necessary concomitant to the protection of the worldwide interests of American business, the protection of markets and sources of raw materials, and the prevention of socialist expansion.

It is no mystery, then, that public sector spending has increased in the United States since the 1930s, that the defense sector accounts for such a large proportion of public spending or, finally, that nonmilitary public spending is usually not a force to balance such spending. If we keep in mind the values of private ownership, private profit, and inequality, the pattern makes a great deal of sense. In particular, military expenditure is a rather brilliant solution to the problem of finding a way to generate aggregate demand sufficient to fuel economic expansion without threatening the power and prerogatives of big business and finance.

Infrastructure

Besides regulation of the business cycle, the corporate sector is dependent upon the state for providing the conditions favorable to the appropriation of relative surplus value. The extraction of surplus value in early capitalism assumed an "absolute" character—meaning that extra surplus value was generated by increasing the amount of work extracted from existing workers through such methods as longer hours, the speed-up, closer supervision, and the like. In the monopoly capital stage, the characteristic form of capitalist social relations becomes what Marxists call "relative surplus value." That is to say, surplus value is generated at this stage by the reorganization of work, the improvement of tools and technology, the increase of skill and educational levels of the work force, and so on.[6]

This transition in the form of surplus extraction intimately involves the state. Increasing absolute surplus value requires nothing more than ownership of productive machinery and, perhaps, a private factory police force. With the stage of relative surplus value, however, the means of improvement lie primarily outside the financial and managerial capacity of any single firm or alliance of firms. The operative factors in profit advancement become the health of the work force, the education and skill of the worker, and the state of technological development. Rather than pay for such improvements out of profits, monopoly capital has managed, through the state, to *"socialize the costs* of retirement pensions, health plans, manpower training, research and development, and other outlays . . . ." that it cannot profitably absorb.[7] As a case in point, almost all research and development costs in the United States are covered by government, even those research activities that firms later exploit for the production of private profits. Moreover, almost all costs for manpower training in the United States are absorbed by government primarily through systems of public education. It should be noted that prior to monopoly capitalism, most training was done by the firm, usually on the job. The state thus assumes most of the costs for the development of what is called *human capital.*

The generation of private corporate profits also requires an elaborate *physical capital* infrastructure—projects such as transportation systems (airports, roads, ports), industrial development projects (electric, gas, water), land use controls and water improvement projects, and the like—which benefit capital as a whole but which are too expensive for any single corporation to finance. It is government that pays the full cost of such services, either directly or through indirect subsidy.

The most important area of physical capital development in the United

States in dollar terms has been the subsidization of the infrastructure of the automobile and trucking industry. On the average, about 60 percent of total federal outlays for transportation have been directed toward the construction of highways, with 90 percent of the costs of the Interstate Highway System and 50 percent of the costs of other primary needs absorbed by the federal government. While such governmental support has served as a central prop for what may be our most important economic sector, the costs of such a skewed transportation commitment have recently become evident to everybody: worsening air pollution, inefficient energy usage, clogged cities, highway-destroyed neighborhoods, and the like. Ironically, as the diseconomies of this heavily government-subsidized sector mount, the state is forced to pay the costs for not only the treatment of their effects (cancer and safety research, medical costs, etc.), but the subsidization of the costs of research and development of alternative systems of transportation like urban mass transit and interurban rail lines.

Much the same can be said about other areas of governmental activity. The very processes of growth and accumulation that normally are considered the most positive attributes of corporate activity generate a set of problems that require governmental intervention. As we have already said, as one set of problems is solved, a new set is generated by the act of intervention itself. In the meanwhile, the only outcome that remains relatively certain is the steady expansion of the state budget.

Diseconomies

This discussion leads us to a further consideration of what economists term *diseconomies*. While production in the United States is almost totally in private hands, much of the production of private business has serious adverse side effects that private owners do not expect to rectify. The overdependence on the automobile has the now familiar effect of making the air in many parts of the United States both unpalatable and unhealthy. Many industrial processes produce toxic chemicals that pollute rivers and streams. Other processes act to deplete precious natural resources. In almost no case, however, are business enterprises expected by political leaders to bear the costs of these adverse costs of production. A significant portion of the state expenditure is directed toward minimizing these social costs of private production through public funding (or are passed on to the consumer in the form of higher prices). It is for that reason that increasing subsidies and tax breaks are directed toward the corporations to encourage them to rectify sets of problems for which they themselves are responsible (e.g., pollution, auto safety, and industrial safety). To do otherwise would be to jeopardize the profitability of private business.

The adverse effects of economic development are not confined to the mass public, however, but often seriously affect other important industries, or, in a supreme irony, the long-term health of the very industries creating the diseconomies. The operations of one industry may increase the problem of profit extraction for another industry, and the state is often called upon to ease the impact. The very poor performance of the auto industry in the field of safety, for instance, is a matter of serious concern to the major insurance companies who must pay ever increasing costs as a result of court judgments in auto accident litigations. The insurance industry has been a leader, not surprisingly, in the effort to convince the state to push the auto firms on the safety issue, to finance research in that area, and to place a ceiling on insurance payments.

There are also cases in which the operations of a corporation not only create problems for third parties, but threaten its very own resource base. The traditional practice in mature capitalism is to increase government regulation in affected areas, but it is also to subsidize, either directly or through tax incentives, the efforts of corporations to maintain their *own* resource base. To take a case in point, it is the federal government that, in the main, pays for the reforestation of timber lands that private corporations have denuded.

Some Caveats about General and Specific Interests

The state in the era of mature capitalism must, if mature capitalism is to survive, become involved in the regulation of those contradictions which threaten the stability of the system as a whole. However, it does not necessarily do this in a unitary and logical manner because of the nature of capitalism itself. Capitalism, being deeply competitive between its units, is always in a state of tension between general class interests and particularistic ones. This tension can take on at least two generally observable forms. First, there may be a direct conflict between the needs of mature capitalism taken as a whole and some specific industry within it. An obvious recent example is the case of rapidly escalating petroleum prices, a situation which was encouraged by the oil companies, much to the benefit of their profit position, and which adversely affected the health of the remainder of the capitalist class. It is within this context that the leaders of major nonoil corporations and financial institutions began to talk about the possibility of breaking up the heavily integrated oil companies into competing units, as well as the growing need for national energy and resource planning.[8]

Second, within the context of fulfilling a class necessary function, the state may have to choose between the interests of competing industries or specific companies. We have suggested already, to take only one case, that massive military spending is a necessary part of the regulation and stabilization of mature capitalism. Yet in meeting that task, state officials are often called upon to choose between companies that are competing fiercely for military contracts. A contract involving the development of a fighter-bomber or a missile system will customarily extend over a period of many years and involve billions of dollars, and the competition for that contract will normally pit the major companies like North American-Rockwell, General Dynamics, and Boeing Aircraft against one another. This problem is customarily met by parceling out contracts in such a way that each of the major companies has an opportunity to be the prime contractor on some weapons system, and a major subcontractor on others. Such a solution is not always possible, however, and the competition for government favor is always intense. In fact, one might argue that much of the substance of contemporary politics, consuming the bulk of the energy and activity of House and Senate members, bureaucratic agencies, local officials, and lobbyists of all kinds, is organized around the question of which particular interest shall be rewarded in the process of fulfilling some overall class function. As paradoxical as it seems, then, the state can and often must serve class interests within a context of fierce *intra*class conflict.

It is only within such a framework that the extreme fragmentation of governmental power is explicable. Political analysts have pointed out for years that governmental sovereignty in the United States has been parceled out to organized interest groups, usually the most powerful groups within some economic sector, so that they might regulate, under government inprimatur, their own economic affairs. Trade associations regulate their joint affairs under the kind eye of the Commerce Department. The National Association of Real Estate Boards helps set standards and operating rules in the Federal Housing Administration. The National Petroleum Institute helps formulate national oil policy within the Interior Department. The major regulatory commissions like the ICC, FCC, etc., are dominated by the companies they are charged with regulating. The cases could be multiplied, but the phenomenon is one known to most observers and the subject of any number of learned treatises. We shall return to this theme later in the chapter. For now, suffice it to say, centers of economic power, primarily the major corporations in each economic sector, are not content that government be the guarantor of the class as a whole, but turn to it to enhance their narrow, particularistic interests as well. Not surprisingly, class and particularistic interests are often in conflict, complicating the mission of the positive state, and increasing its costs of operation.

Imperialism and American Foreign Policy

We have already pointed out at some length (see Chapter 5) how the consolidation of economic power into the hands of a relatively limited number of industrial and financial corporations has provided the imperative for America's expansion into the world as the leading imperialist power. While we have no intention of reiterating a rather lengthy argument already made, it is clear that problems of excess productive capacity and limited investment opportunities at home (resulting from the very processes of corporate growth which define its success), as well as the need to find, provide, and protect vital raw material resources for corporate productive activities and market domination, have compelled the movement of U.S. capital into nearly every corner of the globe. Needless to say, the American based multinational corporations did not and do not venture onto the world stage naked and exposed, but go with the assistance and protection of the American government. As historian Gabriel Kolko has pointed out, ". . . in the aggregate it is a fact that the final intended result of the whole course of United States foreign policy after the Civil War was to optimize the power and profit of American capitalism in the global economy, striving for the political and military preconditions essential to the attainment of that end."[9]

To attain these ends, the state has and continues to employ a wide-ranging, complex, and often contradictory set of mechanisms, only some of which require the exercise of direct military power. Nevertheless, behind many of the other mechanisms of control, and giving them force, stands the barely hidden military might of the United States. Such crude devices are rarely required, however, for in many ways, imperialism is its own regulator. That is to say, the system of superordination and subordination characteristic of imperialism as a whole is itself a mechanism of control. Direct ownership by the multinationals of the major industrial infrastructure of less developed countries gives to these firms, for instance, a powerful voice in the management of the internal affairs of the latter.

The same can be said about the role of international banking in the management of the credit, currency, and budgets of the periphery societies.

What prevents this unequal relationship from assuming the shape of perpetual crisis and disequilibrium is the formation in the peripheral societies of a *comprador* or clientele class, a network of people dependent upon and enriched by the activities of the multinationals. This class, closely tied to the export market and to the service of the multinational (as suppliers of raw materials, investment capital, services, etc.), enjoy, with American economic, political, and military support, a privileged and dominant position in their own countries. As such, they find themselves in a "dual position as junior partners of metropolitan interests, yet dominant elites within their own societies."[10] In many ways, this class remains the keystone to imperial world relations and a relatively inexpensive method to maintain unequal relations, for it becomes the main regulator of the peripheral society and the guarantor of American economic penetration. It is hardly surprising, therefore, that a very significant portion of the U.S. foreign aid program is committed to helping this class police its own societies. While they are often characterized as huge "giveaway" programs somehow detrimental to the United States, the foreign aid program is of direct benefit to the U.S. economy, to the interests of large corporations, and to those committed to the containment of socialist expansion.

How has the money been spent? If we exclude the period from 1945 to 1957 when the bulk of aid money was directed toward the rebuilding of the shattered capitalist economies of Western Europe, the bulk of aid money has flowed to those less developed countries closely tied to the American military position. From 1957 to 1967, 37 percent of all foreign aid funds were directed to only a handful of military allies: Greece, Iran, Turkey, Vietnam, Taiwan, Korea, Philippines, Thailand, Spain, Portugal, and Laos.[11] The developed nations and most of the less developed ones had to be satisfied with the leftovers. Furthermore, a recent Library of Congress report states that only "between one quarter and one third of the $115 billion that has been spent for foreign aid since the close of World War II—including "food for peace," Export-Import Bank Loans, and other categories—has been devoted to economic development, as such."[12]

The military and antisocialist purposes of the aid program can be seen in the *Alliance for Progress,* a program launched with flowery rhetoric about the humanitarian and benevolent intentions of the United States.

In testimony before the House of Foreign Affairs Committee in 1967, Secretary of Defense Robert McNamara made these observations about the alliance:

> Social tensions, unequal distribution of land and wealth, unstable economies, and the lack of broadly based political structures created a prospect of continuing instability in many parts of Latin America. The answer to these and other associated problems, if one is to be found, lies in the Alliance for Progress, to which we and our Latin American friends are devoting large resources. But the goals of the Alliance can be achieved only within a framework of law and order
> . . . .
> Our military assistance programs for Latin America thus continue to be directed to the support of internal security and civic action measures . . . .
> More specifically, the primary objective in Latin America is to aid . . . in the continued development of indigenous military and paramilitary forces capable of providing, in conjunction with police and other security forces, the needed domestic security.[13]

The chairman of this committee added:

> Every critic of foreign aid is confronted with the fact that Armed Forces of Brazil threw out the Goulart government and that U.S. military aid was a major factor in giving these forces and indoctrination in the principles of democracy and a proU.S. orientation. Many of these offices were trained in the United States under the Aid Program. They knew that democracy was better than communism.[14]

Aid programs have other intensions, as well, though all of the intentions are derived from the imperative of guaranteeing American markets, export platforms, and raw material sources. Most aid agreements, for instance, provide clauses that guarantee "[the right of U.S. capital] to enter freely into business, nondiscrimination against U.S. investors, and non-interference with ownership and management operations of U.S. investors."[15] Again, the seemingly idealistic *Alliance for Progress* committed Latin American countries to ". . . conditions that will encourage the flow of foreign investments."[16] Asked to comment on the progress of the Alliance, banker David Rockefeller said in 1965 that "the climate of investment is improving."

The major corporations not only are helped by the aid program through investment assistance, but also are helped in their export position. Aid agreements, for instance, usually stipulate that assistance funds be spent on American products and carried in U.S. flag ships. A significant proportion of American exports, which are among the most expensive in the world, are financed through superficially humanitarian programs. Thus, in one year, 24 percent of iron and steel exports, 5 percent of motor vehicles exports, 10 percent of rubber products exports, 30 percent of railroad transportation equipment export, and 30 percent of agricultural exports were all financed by aid money.[17]

There remains, then, a complex interaction between the activities of the multinational corporations, the aid programs of the U.S. government, and the native clientele classes in the protection of the structure of imperialism. One scholar has managed to closely examine these global interactions in a number of intriguing specific cases. Steven Rosen studied the transitions from the regimes of Quadro's and Goulart to the military junta in Brazil, from Sukarno to Suharto in Indonesia, from Frei to Allende to the junta in Chile, and from Papandreou to the generals in Greece—all involving regime transitions deeply affecting American economic interests in the periphery—and was able to conclude the following:[18]

> *This examination . . . has substantial implications on the relationship between right-wing governments, multinational firms and U.S. foreign policy. It's clear that, with some exceptions, high levels of activity by foreign investors and traders have been associated with anti-egalitarian regimes in other countries, and that restrictions on multinational firms have been characteristic of governments pursuing egalitarian policies. In this pattern, the interests of American business are associated with oligarchical groups even when these governments violate professed ideals of American democracy and capitalism. It isn't uncommon to see a right-wing military coup in a developing country deplored on the editorial page of an American newspaper while in the business section a host of new opportunities for American firms are described. . . . business has, overall, a "natural" preference for the right-wing and a counterrevolutionary foreign policy of its own.*
>
> *If there is a clear (but not unvarying) pattern of association between U.S. trade and investment and right-wing governments in other countries, we are led back to the question of the relative priority of economic interests in official U.S. foreign policy. The overall consistency of the aid curves with the trade and investment curves in this study suggests a harmony of policies between private traders and investors and public dispensers of foreign assistance.*

The foreign policy arsenal of the United States, in its fight to keep periphery areas open to U.S. economic activities, is not confined to the manipulation of aid programs. Note the variety of tools used in the destruction of the popularly elected Allende regime in Chile. As I have written elsewhere about these events:[19]

> When Allende expropriated the copper companies with the un-animous vote of the opposition-dominated Congress, arguing that the level of profits enjoyed by the companies over the previous sixty years had more than adequately compensated the companies, American corporate and political officials launched a campaign of economic warfare designed to wreck the Chilean economy, generate internal opposition to Allende, and prepare the ground for military coup. As Secretary of State William Rogers told a group of business leaders in October 1971, who had substantial interests in Chile, "The Nixon Administration is a business administration. Its mission is to protect American business."[20]
>
> The operative "game plan," while less direct than the military interventions ("gun-boat diplomacy") characteristic of the early decades of the twentieth century, was nevertheless deadly effective. American corporations cooperated in the effort to bring down Allende by refusing to sell spare parts to Chile; by cutting back production in non-nationalized plants, thereby increasing unemployment; by cutting private loans from American-dominated banks operating in Chile; by speculating against Chilean currency in international markets; and by subsidizing dissident groups and newspapers within Chile. The U.S. government did its part by cutting off Export-Import Bank credits; by pressuring the American-dominated international financial agencies (the International Monetary Fund, the World Bank) to end all loans to Chile; by organizing a world capitalist boycott of Chilean copper; by ending all foreign aid assistance (with the notable exception of military aid which jumped from $800,000 in the year before Allende's election to $12 million two years later!); by covertly financing opposition parties, unions, and newspapers; and by producing the funds necessary to sustain the middle-class dominated antigovernment strikes.

The remarks of the American Ambassador to Chile (Edward Kerry) addressed to outgoing Chilean President Edwardo Frei (in an effort to try to convince Frei to join an anti-Allende coup) are instructive for they give the flavor of American policy lurking unseen behind the benign public relations front: "Not a nut or a bolt will be allowed to reach Chile under

Allende . . . . We shall do all within our power to condemn Chile and the Chileans to utmost deprivation and poverty. . . ."

Other mechanisms by which the interests of the American-based multinationals are advanced by the American foreign policy machinery abound. Indeed, the means are never fixed, but are limited only by the ingenuity of American policy makers. Behind all of the machinery, however, and to be used only in the last resort, stands the military might of the United States, embodied in the uniformed and covert services [mainly the Central Intelligence Agency (CIA)]. While it has only been used occasionally, its use stands as an object lesson to those peripheral societies contemplating moves against U.S. capital. If we discount the long era of "gunboat diplomacy" in Latin America prior to the Second World War when Marine intervention was so common as to be considered a normal state of international relations, American military power (including the CIA) has been actively engaged in the years since the war in attempts to overthrow regimes hostile to American economic interests in Greece, Guatamala, Iran, Cuba, the Dominican Republic, the Congo, Laos, Cambodia, and Vietnam.

PROBLEMS OF THE UNDERCLASS AND SOCIAL CONTROL

The laws of motion of mature capitalism, the unmistakable trends toward concentration and heightened productivity, the transfer of operations to overseas locations, and the delimitation of areas of the economy open to small and medium-sized businesses, lead inexorably to the problems of surplus and exploited labor. The set of relationships inherent in the capitalist mode of production are, in fact, given a particular and heightened expression in the mature phase of its development.

In its normal course of development, capitalism is always in the process of discarding unwanted labor power, a "rhythm of social disruption,"[21] made possible by the commodity nature of labor. Driven by competition, capitalist sponsored technological advance and work reorganization have always resulted in decreases in the amount of labor required to produce a given output of goods and services. To look at it from another angle, ever fewer workers are needed to produce a given quantity of output. Capitalism is always in a race, then, to expand production fast enough to keep pace with productivity gains, the alternative being serious unemployment and underconsumption crises. The problems are heightened in mature capitalism because of the staggering increase in the rate of scientific discovery and technological development which exacerbates the productivity-unemployment problem.

Unemployment becomes, then, one of the most striking features of mature capitalism, a problem that is made even graver by the flight of corporate business overseas, as well as the incredible rate of small business failure in the economy. The trends in this process are unmistakable. In the early 1960s, for instance, economists generally considered the nation to be at "full employment" when about 3 percent of the work force was out of work. Today, economists generally consider 5 percent to 6 percent to be normal full employment, while the American economy seems stuck between the 7 percent and 8 percent figures. If one counts *hidden* unemployment, that is, people who either work parttime but want full-time work, and people who are so discouraged that they have quit seeking work, then real unemployment is probably about double the official figure.

Mature capitalism is also characterized by the intense exploitation of competitive sector workers who find themselves in a part of the economy where wages are low, benefits are almost nonexistent, job security is a distant hope, and union protection is not to be found. An explanation for this state of affairs is quite straightforward. It is a part of the economy, comprised of small and medium-sized businesses, that are so competitive and marginal, that the effort to keep costs to a minimum, particularly labor costs, is a requirement for survival. Jobs in this sector, in retail trade, services, and the like, are filled primarily by women and minorities who are unable to penetrate into the unionized bastions of the monopoly sector, as well as former monopoly sector workers displaced by technological advance and work rationalization.

The outcomes of massive unemployment and endemic labor power exploitation are not difficult to discern: inequality, marginality, and poverty. While there still remain a handful of myopic celebrators of the inherent progress of the American standard of living, most of the available evidence suggests the existence of the following:[22]

1. An extreme and stable inequality in the distribution of income, with the bottom 20 percent of the population enjoying about 5 percent of national income since 1947, and the top 5 percent taking more than 40 percent.
2. An even more extreme and stable inequality in the distribution of wealth, with less than 1 percent of the population holding over 65 percent of all income-producing property.
3. A persistance of poverty (between 13 percent and 20 percent depending on the measure used) despite a massive assault on poverty by the government during the middle 1960s.

4. An extreme and stable maldistribution of the conditions of decency, measured most pointedly by maldistributions in housing, nutrition, safety, and health.

Such a massive pool of unemployed, underemployed, and exploited labor represents a potentially disruptive and explosive mixture. The problem of social control and management that is inherent in any social organization is heightened by the laws of motion of the capitalist mode of production since it constantly adds to that pool, while it at the same time raises the expectations for mass consumption so necessary for further economic advance. Control and management of this troublesome problem can take many forms ranging from the benign to the repressive. Modern capitalism is most likely to utilize options toward the benign end of the scale, though one should not for a moment ignore the frequent use of repressive methods: police, courts, and prisons. In fact, these repressive means represent one of the fastest growing areas of the budgets of all levels of government in the United States.[23] The principal instrument for the treatment of this explosive mixture under modern capitalism, however, is the system of welfare.

The welfare commitment of the federal government began in a serious way with the Social Security Act of 1935. Under one provision of the act, the federal government agreed to contribute to state and locally administered programs of aid to the aged, the blind, the disabled, and dependent children.[24] It was thought, at the time, that these welfare measures were a response to a specific and temporary emergency, and that especially with the old-age insurance provisions of that same Social Security Act coming into effect, the welfare program would gradually wither away.[25]

Since that time two things have happened that have lead to the widespread contemporary concern with the "welfare problem." First, the average welfare recipient is no longer an elderly, white person, but a young, black mother and her children. Fully 25 percent of the nation's black population receive some form of welfare, whereas only 4 percent of the white population do so.[26] The deep-seated racism of American society alone, given no other changes in the welfare systen, would have helped to generate hostility to welfare spending. In addition, however, a second change has occurred over the past two decades—a rapid and significant increase in the relief rolls, a phenomenon most often called the "welfare explosion." In cities such as Baltimore, New York, St. Louis, and San Francisco, one in seven residents is on welfare. In Boston, one in six is on welfare, while in Detroit, Los Angeles, and Philadelphia, the proportion is one in eight.[27] The expansion since 1965 has been especially significant, with aid to families of dependent children (AFDC) the most prominent component. In the decade of the 1960s, AFDC expanded 107 percent with most of that increase taking place in the later half (71 percent) of the decade.[28]

While there has been an enormous increase in the number of people receiving welfare benefits, such programs in no way threaten the structure of inequality. Most pointedly, neither the total amount of money involved nor the average payment per recipient is anywhere near a level that would have *significant* redistributive effects. Since 1950, for instance, total welfare expenditures by all levels of government have not exceeded 4 percent of total personal income. Moreover, total welfare expenditures as a percentage of total personal income has actually *declined* since the Great Depression. Finally, despite the increase in the number of recipients, an expansion in the number of people served and an increase in the size of payments, the average payment to each recipient has actually declined over the past two decades when compared to the median income of employed males. In 1950, the average welfare payment was almost 20 percent of the median income, whereas in 1974 it had fallen to under 16 percent.[29]

Any redistributive impact of welfare spending is also diminished by the fact that recipients pay some taxes and thereby help finance their own benefits. While the poor largely escape federal taxes, they are subject to highly regressive state and local taxes that finance over one-half of welfare expenditures. While there is no way to calculate accurately how much they contributed to the $32.6 billion welfare bill in 1976, it certainly amounts to several billions.

This is not to deny that many poor people benefit from welfare expenditures. What we are pointing out, however, is that despite the "welfare explosion," the level of expenditures compared to the overall economy does not amount to much and, as a result, redistribution is only minimally affected. More important, however, welfare recipients pay a heavy price for the miniscule assistance they receive from the public treasury, a price so severe that it may negate any beneficent effects. That price is attached to the issue of social control.

The social control aspects of the welfare system primarily are embodied in the demoralizing effects of its organization and implementation, to say nothing of its intentions, which in the aggregate pointedly announce the general contempt with which welfare recipients are held. That the welfare poor are treated with contempt should not be surprising in light of American society's historic antiblack attitudes and its deeply entrenched liberal-materialist individualism. The latter set of beliefs has been the dominant political philosophy since the American Revolution. The emphasis of classic economic liberalism was on the freedom of individuals and of enterprises to pursue their own self-interest free of state controls and interference. It was believed that out of this competition would come both the enhancement of the individual and the public good. Classic liberal social thought reached its most extreme expression from 1865 to 1901, when liberal economic theory was joined to Darwinian biology by Herbert Spencer and William Graham Sumner. The Social Darwinists, as they were called, believed that through competition, especially in the economy, society was generally benefited, because out of competition the "fit" survived and the "unfit" fell by the wayside. Any interference by the state was an interference with these natural processes and, therefore, by definition, counter to the public good. Without such interference, those individuals practicing industry, frugality, and temperance would be successful in the economic struggle, and those devoid or deficient in these attributes would suffer poverty. Social Darwinism thus lent scientific legitimacy to the traditional Calvinist idea that poverty was the reward for sin and impropriety, and that material possession was proof of moral worth. As the noted churchman Henry Ward Beecher sermonized, ". . . no man in this land suffers from poverty unless it be more than his fault—unless it be his sin." Another respected Protestant clergyman during the period of Social Darwinism wrote, "I say that you ought to get rich, and it is your duty to get rich . . . it is wrong to be poor."[30]

While attitudes about the role of the state have changed dramatically since the 1930s, the general attitudes about the poor still persist. Opinion survey after opinion survey shows that most Americans tend to blame the poor rather than more general economic and social forces for their poverty. One becomes poor, it is generally assumed, because one is too lazy to work, too stupid to take advantage of opportunities, or too sinful to cease procreation. The attitudes toward the poor, not unnaturally, are reflected in the administration of welfare programs.

By far the most important respect in which welfare programs reflect the general societal hostility toward the poor is in the meagerness of their benefits. Without exception, benefits are so minimal that a recipient family totally dependent on them cannot hope to escape even the government's own definition of poverty. In 1973, for instance, the average national monthly welfare payment to a family of four was only $195.00 per person. A year's payments thus equaled $2,348 or less than one-half of the official poverty line for a family of four. The state is itself, therefore, a prime contributor to the perpetuation of poverty. There is no way, despite widespread thinking to the contrary, that people can live in any fashion approaching decency while on public welfare.[31]

For those who are forced by their situations to accept welfare benefits, further attacks on their esteem and dignity are forthcoming in the administration of welfare.[32] Some of the methods are subtle; some are blatant. Application procedures are often accompanied by harsh and disrespectful treatment by officials, demands for extensive documentary proof of poverty, long waits in crowded offices, demands for repeated filing of application forms, long delays in application investigations, and arbitrary rejections of applicants who meet all formal requirements of eligibility. The welfare system has also been rampant with arbitrary terminations from welfare rolls, even though technical requirements of eligibility are met.

> *Mr. G, a single man on Home Relief, received a letter telling him to report to Welfare the following morning to discuss his housing accommodation. When he arrived an hour late, he was severely chastised by his worker. Mr. G answered back and was then disqualified from further benefits for "obnoxious behavior."*[33]

Another method both to keep welfare costs down and to chastise the welfare poor is to give to the recipient less aid than that to which the law entitles him. In many states, for instance, recipients are eligible for "special grants" for furniture, children's clothes, food, and so on, but it is common practice for case workers either to deny information to their clients about the grants, or to discourage them from making application. Deductions are often made from monthly benefits for items such as child support payments from an absent husband or clothing and furniture from relatives, with no evidence that such resources ever reach the welfare family. Further contempt is daily shown to recipients by requiring them to relinquish certain rights in return for benefits: questioning children about parents; inspection of the home; interrogation concerning personal sexual practices; and "midnight raids" to check on the presence of able-bodied males. Agencies often threaten termination for participation in political or protest activities. Finally, newspapers, elected officials, and the public constantly demand investiations of welfare in efforts to reduce the number of recipients. Welfare agencies, as a matter of record, spent more money for welfare fraud investigations over the past decade than for the Headstart program.

It is not necessary to add other examples to show that in a society whose central values include individualism, materialism, and competition, the poor are held in contempt. It should occasion no surprise, therefore, to learn that governmental programs to assist and deal with the poor reflect this general attitude. However, one might respond that despite low benefits and harsh treatment, the welfare system is better than no system at all, and that the rise of governmental welfare activities in the 1930s and their continued expansion for four decades demonstrates the emergence of a mature positive state, concerned with accepting the responsibility for the well-being of all of its citizens, and the progressive humanization of the social and economic environment.

There is strong reason to suspect this description of the welfare state as inexorably more humane and generous, because it fails to make sense of the fact that welfare programs experience alternating periods of expansion and contraction, not perpetual growth. The best effort to explain this accordion-like pattern of welfare expenditures is the groundbreaking study of social welfare in the United States by Francis Fox Piven and Richard A. Cloward, *Regulating the Poor*. They claim that welfare spending is not so much a reflection of concern about the quality of the lives of the poor as an effort to maintain civil order, low wage labor, and inequality.

In their study they demonstrate that welfare rolls have always expanded in response to massive disruptions of civil order, and not to the widespread economic distress of the poor. They show, for instance, that from 1928 to 1933, despite serious unemployment (15 million by 1933), precipitious diminution of wages, spiraling farm failure, and drops in farm income (the latter fell 80 percent between 1929 and 1932), and resultant widespread poverty and economic distress, government did not respond to the crisis until serious threats to public order were evident. In the early 1930s there were increasing cases of the seizure of relief offices by the poor, organized resistance in both rural and urban areas to evictions, and rent riots. In 1931 there were two national hunger marches on Washington, including encampment by the "Bonus Army" of veterans. In Detroit there were massive marches by auto workers under the red banner of communism. In 1932, of course, there was also the revolutionary alteration in the electorate and the emergence of the national Democrats as the dominant party. It was in response to all of these cumulative events that the state moved in 1933 to expand welfare (through emergency relief, public works, and the Civilian Conservation Corps) and head off civil turmoil. In 1934 and 1935 additional turmoil and threats of civil disorder in the form of labor union unrest, and the combined onslaught of Huey Long, Francis Townsend, and Father Coughlin on the New Deal led to both expansions in direct relief, public works, and the passage of the Social Security Act. Most interesting, however, when the threat of turmoil was past in 1936, there was a massive trimming of the welfare rolls. After the 1936 election came the termination of emergency relief and massive cuts in public works. With the end of the threat to civil order (but not, it should be pointed out, an end to widespread economic distress) came a massive contraction of relief rolls.

The same phenomenon was at work in the explosion of the welfare rolls in the 1960s. Piven and Cloward demonstrate persuasively that the expansion of rolls was not a response to the economic distress and poverty, but to turmoil in the black ghettoes. Poverty was a severe problem in the 1950s and the early 1960s, but welfare rolls did *not* expand in response. With the technological modernization of southern agriculture came widespread rural unemployment in the 1950s, running as high as 37 percent among farm workers. With unemployment came poverty and hunger, but there is no evidence whatever that either state or federal government acted as a result. In fact, the 1950s witnessed quite the reverse in the South— the imposition of rigid restrictions and requirements and the paring of rolls.

The principal response to rural poverty has usually been urban migration, and the pattern was repeated in this case. The migration of southern blacks to urban areas, particularly outside of the South, was overwhelming. Literally millions left the farms during this period and became urban dwellers. Most of them found urban life every bit as severe as life in the rural South. In the late 1950s and early 1960s the national nonwhite unemployment rate fluctuated between 10 and 13 percent (about twice the white unemployment rate), and the subemployment rate (those only sporadically employed) in urban ghettoes reached 33 percent in the mid-1960s. And yet, even in the face of massive economic distress, severe restrictions remained on welfare eligibility. If welfare spending is, in fact, a response to distress, rolls should have rapidly expanded between 1950 and 1964, but that was generally not the case. From 1950 to 1965, total welfare recipients in all categories increased by only 1.8 million from 6.0 million to 7.8 million. From 1965 to 1971, however, the number of recipients shot up by almost 6 million to 13.5 million.

How are we to explain such an explosive expansion? To Piven and Cloward the answer is quite simple. The expansion was a political response to the widespread urban violence of the middle sixties and the growing power of black political, civil rights, and welfare groups and the perceived threat to both civil order and entrenched political power. The state commitment to the welfare of the poor which failed to be mobilized by need, was mobilized by trouble. With the decline of troubles, with the threat of civil disorder receding, we once again hear widespread demands that the welfare rolls be pared and that welfare recipients take jobs. From state to state we are beginning to see a significant contraction in the number of welfare recipients now that turmoil no longer threatens, although economic distress is every bit as severe for millions of families. We can expect such a state of affairs to continue if Piven and Cloward are correct, until the outbreak of the next round of civil conflict and political disruption.

Public welfare serves another important function, according to Piven and Cloward: it helps to maintain a pool of low wage labor to meet the personnel requirements of the private industrial and economic system. In nondisruptive times, the welfare system operates to persuade, even to force many people to take low-paying, demeaning, and even dangerous jobs. The system uses several devices to accomplish this goal. First, relief in nonthreatening times is restricted to persons who are of little immediate use to the economy—the elderly, the disabled, children, and mothers of young children.[34] Welfare payments have generally been denied to able-bodied males no matter what their state of poverty. As long as the potential existed for some present or future employment, benefits were not forthcoming. Fully 25 percent of the poor in the United States live in families headed by employed males, yet welfare benefits are usually denied to them. Welfare agencies have also traditionally attempted to deny benefits to mothers in any way involved with a man. If we see one of the functions of welfare as keeping people in the low wage labor pool. then these behaviors are no longer perplexing. The goal is to prevent benefits from reaching employable men. The commitment of the welfare system to the alleviation of poverty is, consequently, highly suspect relative to its other objectives.

Another method to accomplish the same goal is to tie relief payments to local economies. By turning over most of the administration of welfare to state and local governments, the state ensures that relief payments will in no area exceed the lowest wages paid in the local economy. If relief payments were to exceed the lowest rungs of the wage scale, there would be no incentive for people to take such low-paying jobs. In the South, it has been traditional to deny welfare to blacks in order to force them to take work as menials. It was and still is common practice to cut welfare during periods of "full employment" (e.g., cotton picking time) to ensure the availability of low wage labor.

Finally, Piven and Cloward claim that the demeaning and contemptous treatment of welfare recipients also serves a personnel function by making welfare so unattractive and oppressive that most people would take *any* work rather than face the indignities of the welfare recipient. The system creates an outcast class that no rational person, given a choice, would join. The constant ritual-like degradation of the welfare recipient, whether at the hands of the welfare workers, elected officials, or newspaper editorials, is aimed not at the recipient alone, but at any able-bodied, potentially employable worker.

Public welfare, therefore, which looks at first glance to be proof of the commitment of the modern American state to social justice, to the alleviation of widespread economic distress, and to the attenuation of severe inequalities, looks quite different upon careful examination. While no one can deny that the state is more involved in these areas than it was prior to the New Deal, or that it is slightly redistributive, it still remains true that public welfare hardly dents inequality, does little to alleviate poverty, and does much to assault the self-esteem of its beneficiaries. There is strong reason to believe, if we accept Piven and Cloward's intriguing analysis, that the welfare system mainly serves the dual functions of maintaining both civil order and a pool of cheap labor for the private sector.

A SUMMARY AND A LOOK AHEAD

In this book, we set the task for ourselves of describing and making sense of the major trends in twentieth-century government policy in the United States and of explaining the emergence of an active, interventionist state in a society that had traditionally favored a passive, noninterventionist one. We began our analysis by raising for consideration what we considered to be the most pressing and troubling problems in understanding the modern American state; namely, its size, growth, bias, and seeming ineffectiveness. We attempted to illuminate these questions by examining the genesis and development of the positive state through the analytical lens of the Marxist theory of the State, a theory that, we hope, provides a mode of analysis that does justice to the complexity and dynamism of American capitalism itself. Most central to our discussion of these issues, of course, was a description of the close interpenetration of government policy and dominant (capitalist) class interests, a symbiotic relationship that while ever present, is never fixed in final form. The dynamic nature of this class-state nexus was explained, in a theoretical sense, by reference to dynamic changes in the capitalist mode of production, in the overall configuration of the class struggle, and in America's position within the world capitalist system.

As we argued earlier, there exists no scientific way to absolutely "prove" or "disprove" the validity of the theoretical perspective we have used, nor for that matter, any other theoretical perspective. All one can reasonably expect from such a theory is that it helps the reader to more easily grasp the complexities of the modern state, the implications of its activities, and the dynamics of its development. It is entirely up to the reader to judge the degree to which our analysis in these pages has made the American "positive state" a more understandable set of social institutions.

As to alternative explanations of the modern positive state raised in the first chapter, it is our view that they remain poverty stricken, incapable of coming to grips with the history of twentieth-century governmental activities in the United States. We posited three principal perspectives other than the Marxist one that have tried to explain the nature of modern government, perspectives we have labelled reform liberal, pluralist, and free-market conservative. Recall that reform liberals see Western governments as democratic instruments of the whole people dedicated to the advancement of the general welfare. As such, western governments, it is claimed, are not the instrument of any particular class but rather transcend classes. They act to humanize the capitalist economic order through the general regulation of the market and through assistance to individuals unable to cope with industrialization and urbanization—that is, the poor, the aged, the disabled, and the unemployed.

Pluralist theorists hold a perspective that while disagreeing in many particulars with that of reform liberal theorists, agrees in essentials. Indeed, one way to look at pluralism is to see it as the operational political component of reform liberalism: as the process through which the humane state is constructed. To pluralists, as with reform liberals, western governments are, in the long run, divorced from any particular class. State policy, in their view, is at any particular time the product of temporary, majority coalitions that arise out of the welter of groups that make up modern society. However, although state policy is biased in the immediate sense toward the desires of the winning coalition, pluralists tend to argue that this is not true in the long run. Such a conclusion follows from their claim that western capitalist societies are both open and noncoercive and allow all legitimate groups to become a member of some winning coalition. In the long run, governments take into account the interests of all groups and are thus neutral and democratic at the same time. Pluralists claim that western capitalists states are likely to distribute their benefits fairly evenly throughout the whole population. Thus, we have approximated in the pluralist interpretation of the American system the reform liberal claim of government as the democratic instrument of the whole people, only this time the whole people is conceptualized as an aggregate of social groups.

Free-market conservatives explain modern government as the inevitable outcome of the interplay of selfish interests, an outcome that should cause them little surprise, of course, in light of the basic conception of human nature that informs their perspective. That is to say, to free-market conservatives, the bloated condition of modern government is the direct result of a population that expects too much, of politicians pandering to popular tastes and aspirations, to bureaucrats tenaciously guarding and expanding their territory, to various private interests seeking government support and protection for their own aggrandizement, ad infinitum. All of these built-in tendencies toward governmental growth are given further impetus, in this view, by the efforts of misguided intellectuals, irresponsible judges, and "bleeding-heart" liberals who have turned to government as the main instrument for the aid and assistance of the most disadvantaged sections of American life.

It is our view, that while each sheds some light on the issues raised in this volume, none of these non-Marxist perspectives are able, within the bounds of their theoretical structure, to account for and to explain the marked and historically consistent bias of the state toward the interests of large-scale capital; the rise of large-scale concentrated economic enterprise in the United States and the nature of its impact; or for the dynamically changing relationships between polity, economy, and society. None of the other perspectives is capable of rendering an understanding of the political economy taken as a whole, its growth, transformations, and general implications.

In particular, it is only the Marxist perspective that correctly assesses the nature of the relationship between large-scale business enterprise and the state. The other perspectives fail completely to either predict or explain this relationship. While reform liberals generally acknowledge the reality and importance of corporate enterprise, they wrongly assume that government intervention serves to distribute corporate largesse to the general population and advance the social welfare. What they fail to predict or explain is the abundant evidence that the major part of state intervention serves to advance not the general welfare, but rather the central corporate goals of private appropriation and domination of the total society. The pluralist perspective fails to an even greater extent. Within the confines of its theory, it cannot account for and deal with the implications of corporate power. Nor can it predict or explain, given its notion that public policy is the end result of constantly shifting majority coalitions, the fact that state policy consistently and over the long run has tended to favor the corporate sector over all others. Pluralism collapses as a theory when one group, the corporate sector, is the dominant force in almost every winning coalition. Free-market conservatism fails as an explanation because it totally misconstrues the relative weight of the forces demanding government intervention and thereby misses the most important point about twentieth-century American economic and political history.

Irrespective of the shortcomings of competing theoretical formulations, we hope to have convincingly demonstrated the continued usefulness of the Marxist perspective in the comprehension of American capitalism and the role of government within it. It is only from such a perspective that the ongoing reality of poverty, social class inequality, corporate concentration, foreign interventions, and state bias toward property makes sense in an interconnected and coherent manner. Furthermore, it is only from the Marxist perspective that the underlying unity of the relationship between property and state through historical changes in capitalist society remains comprehensible; it saves us from the delusion that capitalism has transcended itself into a new social form free from the drawbacks of its predecessor. As Christopher Lasch has pointed out, ". . . post-industrial [capitalism] . . . is distinguishable from earlier stages in important respects but is still capitalist in its essential features. Post-industrial society is still capitalist in the sense that the industrial system produces commodities rather than objects for use and that the important decisions concerning production remain in private hands rather than being socially determined."[35]

If we but keep constantly in mind that all modern societies require coordination and direction, and that the giants of American capitalism especially require stability, predictability, and order, then we will not misinterpret government coordination, guidance, and regulation of the economy, or its management of the working class through collective bargaining, or its welfare programs to keep the lower orders quiescent, or public spending on corporate infrastructural needs (roads, mass transit, research and development, educated manpower, etc.) as significant changes in the fundamental relationship of state and corporation under capitalism. We can rightly see such activities of the modern positive state, although an occasional enterprise is hurt in the process, as the instrument for the continued health and survival of the owning class taken as a whole. As Marx and Engels pointed out in *The German Ideology*, with new developments in capitalist enterprise ". . . the bourgeoise is forced to organize itself no longer locally but nationally and to give a general form to its mean average interest. . . . This general form is the state . . . [which is] the form of organization which the bourgeoise necessarily adopt . . . for the mutual guarantee of their property and interest. ."[36] Through the positive state, the system of property relationships is temporarily protected and preserved from the very forces let loose by capitalist development itself: a proletarianized work force, urban decay, unemployment, and the destruction of supportive institutions like the extended family and local welfare associations.The logic of the positive state, in the final analysis, ". . . is not the realization of some intrinsically valuable humane goal but rather the prevention of a potentially disasterous social problem."[37] It is precisely the inability of the state to prevent the expression of these disastrous social problems that signals the entrance of the American system into a new and threatening phase of capitalist development. We turn to this story in the next chapter.

NOTES

[1] For leading statements in this vein, see the work of Daniel Bell, *The Coming of Post-Industrial Society* (New York: Basic Books, 1973) and *The End of Ideology* (New York: Free Press, 1960).

[2] James O'Connor, *The Fiscal Crisis of the State* (New York: St. Martin's Press, 1973).

[3] See Sidney Ulmer, *The Welfare State* (Boston: Houghton-Mifflin, 1969) for the figures on unemployment and inflation.

[4] Ibid., p. 27. These tools, however, are becoming *decreasingly* potent in the regulation of the business cycle. We shall consider this issue in the last chapter.

[5] See Paul Baran and Paul Sweezy, *Monopoly Capital* (New York: Monthly Review Press, 1966) for a discussion of the problem of surplus absorption.

[6] See James O'Connor, "Surplus Value," in his *The Corporations and the State.* (New York: Harper-Colophon, 1974). For the most important discussion of this issue in recent years see Harry Braverman, *Labor and Monopoly Capital* (New York: Monthly Review Press, 1975).

[7] O'Connor, *The Corporations and the State,* p. 40.

[8] This is another general theme to which we shall turn our attention in the last chapter.

[9] Gabriel Kolko, *Main Currents in American History* (New York: Harper & Row, 1976), pp. 49–50.

[10] Susanne Bodenheimer, "Dependency and Imperialism: The Roots of Latin American Underdevelopment," in K. T. Fann and D. C. Hodges, eds., *Readings in U.S. Imperialism* (Boston: Porter Sargent Publisher, 1971), p. 163.

[11] Harry Magdoff, *The Age of Imperialism* (New York: Monthly Review Press, 1969), p. 124.

[12] Cited in ibid., p. 123.

[13] Cited in ibid., p. 121.

[14] Cited in ibid., p. 122.

[15] Ibid., p. 127.

[16] James Petras, "U.S. Business and Foreign Policy," *New Politics,* Vol. 6, No. 4, (Dec., 1968), p. 75.

[17] Charles D. Hyson and Alan M. Strout, "Impact of Foreign Aid on U.S. Exports," *Harvard Business Review* (January–February 1968), p. 71.

[18] Steven Rosen, "Rightest Regimes and American Interests," *Society* (September–October 1974), Vol. 2, No. 6, pp. 60–61.

[19] Edward S. Greenberg, *The American Political System: A Radical Approach* (Cambridge: Winthrop Publishing Co., 1977), p. 228.

[20] Quoted in Richard J. Barnet and Ronald E. Müller, *Global Reach* (New York: Simon and Schuster, 1974).

[21] A term coined by historian Eric Hobsbawn, quoted in O'Conner, *The Fiscal Crisis of the State*, p. 159.

[22] For a more extended discussion of these issues and for documentation see Greenberg, *The American Political System*. Also see Douglas Dowd, *The Twisted Dream: Capitalist Development in the United States* (Cambridge: Winthrop Publishing Co., 1977); and Richard C. Edwards, et al, *The Capitalist System* (Englewood Cliffs, N.J.: Prentice-Hall, 1977).

[23] For the best recent discussion of repression see Alan Wolfe, *The Seamy Side of Democracy* (New York: David McKay, 1973).

[24] General assistance, relief to people not eligible under these four categories, is financed entirely by state and local governments.

[25] See Gilbert Steiner, *Social Insecurity: The Politics of Welfare* (Chicago: Rand McNally, 1966).

[26] Thomas Dye, *Understanding Public Policy* (Englewood Cliffs, N.J.: Prentice-Hall, 1972), p. 90. As of 1975, moreover, over 44% of all AFDC expenditures were going to black people. Table # 550, *Statistical Abstracts of the United States* (Washington D.C.: U.S. Department of Commerce, 1977), p. 350.

[27] Ibid., p. 88.

[28] Frances Fox Piven and Richard A. Cloward, *Regulating the Poor: The Functions of Public Welfare* (New York: Pantheon, 1971), p. 186.

[29] Richard C. Edwards, "Who Fares Well in the Welfare State?" in Edwards, *The Capitalist System*, p. 311.

[30] Both cited in Sidney Fine, *Laissez-Faire and the General Welfare State* (Ann Arbor: University of Michigan Press, 1956), p. 119.

[31] It does no good, moreover, to reply that people should get off of welfare and take jobs. All available research suggests that for the most part

recipients are either aged, young children, the mothers of young children, or incapacitated males. The best estimate is that only one percent of the males in the universe of welfare recipients are employable. (See *Office of the President, 1967 Budget Report*). Given their lack of skills and an economy that thinks of a 6–7 percent unemployment rate is normal, finding work is highly problematic for most welfare recipients.

[32] Most of the remainder of the discussion of welfare is based on the brilliant analysis of the subject by Piven and Cloward, *Regulating the Poor.*

[33] Ibid., p. 159.

[34] In this respect it is similar to Social Security (in its support of persons of no immediate use to the economic system).

[35] Christopher Lasch, "Toward A Theory of Post-Industrial Society," in D. D. Hancock and Gideon Sjoberg, *Politics in the Post-Welfare State* (New York: Columbia University Press, 1972), p. 36.

[36] Karl Marx and Frederick Engel, *The German Ideology,* (New York: International Publishers, 1933), p. 59.

[37] Clause Offe, "Advanced Capitalism and the Welfare State," *Politics and Society,* Vol. 2 (Summer 1972), p. 485.

7
THE PROMISE AND THE THREAT OF LATE CAPITALISM

Capitalism as we have known it in the United States since 1945 is in the process of basic transformation into something new and ominous, and in that transformation lies both a terrible threat and an unique opportunity for the construction of a better society. Capitalism, in both its domestic and international forms, we would submit, is entering into a period in its development in which its inherent contradictions are edging it toward a system-wide crisis. That is to say, capitalism seems to be entering a period in which its most pressing problems are irresolvable" within the range of possibility that is circumscribed by the organizational principle of . . . society,"[1] in which the traditional instrumentalities are either useless or counterproductive, and in which the effort to fashion new instrumentalities to deal with multiple crises opens the possibility of system transformation.[2] As economist Ernst Mandel has posed the issue,

> *The crisis of capitalist relations of production must be seen as an overall social crisis—that is, the historical decline of an entire social system and mode of production, operative throughout the whole epoch of late capitalism . . . . The crisis of capitalist relations of production hence appears as the crisis of a system of relations between men, within and between units of production (enterprises), which corresponds less and less to the technical basis of labour in either present or potential form. We can define this crisis as a crisis not only of capitalist conditions of appropriation, valorization and accumulation, but also of commodity production, the capitalist division of labour, the capitalist structure of the enterprise, the bourgeois national state, and the subsumption of labour under capital as a whole. All these multiple crises are only different facets of a* single *reality, of one socioeconomic totality: the capitalist mode of production.*[3]

The direction we choose in meeting this system crisis will largely determine, in our view, whether we move as a society toward irrationality or rationality, inefficiency or efficiency, repression or the development of human capacities. The first step in making an intelligent choice in such matters, of course, is to understand the nature of the present crisis, as well as its potential.

THE ELEMENTS OF CAPITALIST CRISIS

It is useful to recall, as we begin to examine the contemporary crisis, the main elements in the edifice of American capitalism in its quarter-century of world economic, political, and ideological supremacy. First, we might recall that the ravages of two world wars left America's principal capitalist rivals prostrate and dependent upon her economic, financial, and military resources, and helpless to prevent her economic penetration into their former colonial empires. Out of the ravages of the war, America emerged as the single most dominant capitalist country, as well as the leading imperialist power, with all of the privileges of surplus extraction attendant to that lofty place. Additionally, the United States emerged from the war with the most powerful and productive industrial system the world had ever seen, and for a time, was able to provide its citizens with an unmatched standard of living. This industrial machine was fueled, of course, by the boost given its productive and technological infrastructure by the war itself, as well as by the general militarization of the American economy under the auspices of the "cold war." Finally, the stability of mature capitalism was constructed out of certain theoretical advances in the understanding of the experiences of the Great Depression and war mobilization which helped stimulate the formulation of governmental tools for the management of the economy as a whole, and which, for a time, safely contained the contradictions inherent in capitalism.

The dimensions of the emerging crisis are suggested by the fact that each and every one of these elements of mature capitalism in the United States are in serious and advanced states of decay and disintegration. American hegemony in the world capitalist system is giving way to the reappearance of intense intercapitalist rivalry and the revolt of important sections of the Third World. The domestic economic engine of American prosperity is beginning to sputter under the pressures of inescapable problems like endemic inflation, unemployment, fiscal crisis, and multiple externalities. Finally, the managerial tools of the state are not only becoming less able to manage system contradictions, but are themselves now beginning, in many respects, to both exacerbate ongoing contradictions and create new and dangerous ones. Let us consider each of these developments in more detail.

America and World Capitalism

In a symbolic sense, three events probably best suggest the end of American world hegemony: the hasty and ignoble retreat from Saigon, the oil boycott of the Organization of Petroleum Exporting Countries (OPEC) following the 1973 Arab-Israeli War, and the devaluation of the dollar by the Nixon administration. Each reflects in a particularly graphic way the development of trends with serious adverse consequences for America's world position. The retreat from Saigon before the advance of victorious Vietnamese liberation forces, for instance, represented America's most serious combined military, political, and ideological defeat since the end of the Second World War, and demonstrated its inability, at a reasonable cost, to keep mobilized Third World societies in a state of simple subordination. Its defeat in Vietnam had the multiple effect of emboldening antiimperialist movements at various points on the globe (Laos, Cambodia, Zimbabwa, Angola, South Africa), and undermining the confidence of American decision makers in the unbridled use of military power against less developed societies because of the potential for serious adverse political, social, and economic consequences at home. The timid response of the Ford administration to the victory of leftist forces in Angola is a particularly pointed example of this new impotence.

The protracted and eventual losing war in Vietnam was played out, moreover, within the context of the reemergence of the capitalist economies of Western Europe and Japan. Indeed, in one of history's recurring ironies, the war itself became an important contributory factor in the shifting positions of the capitalist powers as the United States saw its material and financial resources drained by the war, and the economies of its rivals fueled by massive war orders. The war, nevertheless, simply exaggerated tendencies already well advanced as Western Europe and Japan gradually emerged as powerful countervailing capitalist societies.[4] We can gain some sense of the trends at work by examining the figures in Table 7-1, all of which suggest the speed with which America's capitalist rivals have been overtaking her.

While the American economy remains the single most powerful economy in the world, it no longer stands as the unchallenged, supreme head

Table 7-1   Indicators of Economic Development (1955–1970)

	U.S.	Japan	France	West Germany	Italy
Annual percentage increase in:					
GNP at constant prices	3.4	10.4	5.5	5.9	5.6
Exports	7.4	14.4	10.8	9.7	12.6
Industrial production	4.1	14.8	5.9	6.2	7.7
Gross fixed capital formation as percentage of GNP	16.9	30.1	22.0	24.8	20.5

Source: Kelvin Rowley, "The End of the Long Boom," *Intervention,* Vol. 6 (June 1971), p. 43.

of the world capitalist system. It has found itself caught in a process of gradual yet inexorable decline relative to the other centers of capitalism. We are entering a period, in fact, which is coming to be characterized by the overall *interdependence* of the capitalist powers and the absence of a leading and guiding government among them, developments conducive to the reemergence of intense rivalry. This renewed struggle and incipient anarchy is perhaps best seen in the abandonment of the Bretton Woods arrangements (whereby, the American dollar had been made the medium of international trade) in 1971; the trade struggles with Japan involving televisions, textiles, and steel; the international struggle over guaranteed sources of oil; and the recurrent efforts of central banks to gain trade advantages through currency manipulations.

This struggle amid interdependence suggests a decreasing capability for any single country, including the United States, to unilaterally determine its own economic destiny. When the United States lowered its interest rates in 1971 so as to encourage increased economic activity, for instance, an enormous and unprecedented outflow of capital took place, seeking higher interest rates in Europe. Without coordination between them, efforts to control the business cycle in any particular country are subject to the international character of capital which determines its destination not from archaic notions of patriotism but from a calculation of likely profits. Efforts to stimulate demand in the United States, for instance, might be totally ineffective in cases, increasingly evident, where other capitalist countries are better able to attract investors because of a more inviting business climate. The United States, in short, is no longer in a position to solely shape the international flow of investment.

The decline of American international hegemony signaled by the re-appearance of intercapitalist rivalry and defeat in Southeast Asia has been given further impetus by the rise of OPEC and the termination of the era of cheap energy resources. To a very great extent, the impetus for the American postwar boom was provided by a seemingly inexhaustible supply of cheap petroleum products, a situation that no longer obtains as crude oil prices have more than quadrupled over the past decade. The results of such a transformation are obvious: decreased investment funds for the domestic American economy; enormous deficits in the American balance of payments (in the period 1960 through 1965, America averaged $5.8 billion in trade surpluses, and since 1971, trade balances have never been out of the red); and enhanced efforts by other raw material suppliers in the Third World to form cartels so as to increase the world prices for their resources.

All of these developments suggest a permanent, rather than temporary change in the position of the United States in the world capitalist system. While still the most powerful capitalist country, it is no longer in a hege-monic position relative to the others or to the Third World in general, but is, rather, locked into a situation of interdependency. This interdepend-ency is suggested by the degree to which the fates of the capitalist states are bound to each other, and particularly, how economic problems in one nation today are reflected and replayed in the others. In recent years, for instance, all of the major capitalist nations have suffered simultane-ous problems of stagnation, inflation, and fiscal crisis. Being interde-pendent with potential and actual rivals, the United States can no longer unambiguously depend upon its world position to serve as a prop to the health and vitality of its domestic economy. It can no longer count on its hegemonic position in the world to provide the breathing space for work-ing out the contradictions of its own economy. This becomes a develop-ment of serious consequence in light of the exaggeration of all of those contradictions of a capitalist economy that have lain dormant and un-expressed until recent years. It is to a discussion of the exaggeration of these contradictions in the American economy that we now turn.

Economic Crisis

It is becoming clear that the American economy is in the midst of a serious and inescapable economic crisis in which the contradictions always central to capitalist development, but kept in abeyance for several decades, are beginning to assert themselves anew. The flowering of these contradictions signals the end of an era of capitalist accumulation, expansion, and prosperity, and the beginning of an era of disaccumulation, contraction, and declining living standards. While capitalism will continue to experience the ups and downs of the business cycle, it will take place only within an overall pattern of stagnation and decline, a situation derived primarily from the decreasing ability of capitalism to extract the necessary levels of surplus value for its own expansion.[5]

We use the term "contradictions" in the sense that the very processes of development central to the capitalist mode of production generate sets of problems that are inescapable and unresolvable within the boundaries of the normal operations of the system. As paradoxical as it may seem, the emerging crisis conditions are based not on the failures of capitalism as a system but on its very success. The laws of motion of the capitalist mode of production discovered by Marx, those that pertain in particular to capitalism's inexorable expansion, concentration, technological innovation, and internationalization, lead to problems that threaten the very continuation of capitalism in its present form. While mature capitalism has been able to diffuse and deflect these problems through the activities of the state, state management is now becoming not only less effective but itself a growing problem. Thus, by doing what it does best, capitalism contributes to the creation of problems that threaten its continued successful operations.

Let us be a bit more specific about these processes. When capitalism is working at peak efficiency, it generates and is dependent upon increasing levels of capital investment, a process that forms the basis for technological innovation, plant concentration, advances in mechanization, and increased productivity. On the surface such a process would seem to be healthy and all to the good. Ponder, however, a strange paradox in which this seemingly positive process serves to increasingly undermine not only the overall quality of life, but also the successful continuation of the economic process itself. As one economist has stated the problem, "That era now draws to a close. It does so not because it failed, . . . but because it succeeded as much and for as long as it might, inexorably developing contradictions along the way. The structures and policies that made it work also finally created the conditions of its undoing."[6]

As investment and economic concentration advance in the monopoly sector, to take a case in point, the conditions for profitable operation in the competitive sector of the economy become even more desperate, with rising rates of business failure and a tighter squeeze on the low-wage, unorganized, and seasonal workers who inhabit its climes. As productivity advances in the monopoly sector, moreover, as the same amount of goods can be produced by progressively fewer workers, increasing numbers of monopoly sector workers are thrown either into the unemployment roles or into the low paid competitive sector. Similarly, as this incredible process of investment and capital development advance, the *productive capacity* of the entire system advances accordingly. While a benign process on its surface, this development makes the problem of providing adequate levels of demand increasingly difficult. That is to say, since economic decline is kept at bay only when overall levels of aggregate demand in the economy are sufficient to utilize the productive capacity of the system, capital improvement always and inescapably makes the generation of adequate demand more problematic. Demand *must* continually increase as productive capacity itself increases, a problem not easy to resolve. The Commerce Department has reported, in this respect, that the average "capacity utilization rate" in American industry fell from over 90 percent in the 1950s to under 80 percent in the early 1970s. In an economy of unequal distribution of income and wealth in which the consumption ability of a sizable part of the population is limited, the maintenance of the needed levels of demand remain problematic. In fact, all that has hithertofore kept the system from spiraling into permanent stagnation has been massive levels of government spending, primarily in the defense area, and increasingly sizable federal budget deficits. Eventually, it must be evident, the partial solution to one problem is gained only at the cost of another serious problem—namely, inflation fueled by these deficits.

Let us look at the dimensions of these closely interrelated economic problems in more detail. Central to the contemporary crisis of late capitalism is the problem of permanent unemployment generated in part, as we have suggested, by the very processes of development that define the laws of motion of capitalism. In treating labor as a commodity to be discarded when it is no longer needed, and in its requirement for a "reserve army of the unemployed" to act as a depressant on the wages of employed workers, capitalism has always required a certain level of unemployment. To these historical necessities, however, one must add the contributions to unemployment made by advances in machine technology, industrial concentration, and work rationalization. Developments along these natural lines of advance displace many workers in the monopoly sector and obliterate the many small and medium-sized businesses unable to compete with monopoly-sector firms. Additionally, as the

American economy shows increasing signs of overcapacity/undercon-
sumption, as labor costs grow, and as the squeeze on profits becomes
tighter, capitalists must search elsewhere for profitable investment outlets, thereby giving impetus to the long-run internationalization of American capital (the so-called "runaway shop") and the aggravation of unemployment with the United States.

Whatever the particular causal weight that one might give to each of
the above factors, the problem of permanent unemployment is unmistakable. As we have suggested already, unemployment is inherent and
unavoidable in a system of commodity capitalism, an observation that
is confirmed in the case of the United States by the fact that it has reached "full employment," that is to say, where no more than 4 percent of the
work force is *officially* defined as out of work, in only seven years since
1948 (1951-1953 and 1966-1969), years in which aggregate demand
was accelerated by massive war expenditures. If we include involuntary
parttime workers in the figures, unemployment has averaged 6 percent
for the last two decades. If one includes what the Bureau of Labor Statis-
tics calls "discouraged workers" (those out of work so long that they
have quit looking for work), then the average unemployment figure is
well over 7 percent.[7]

What is so striking about our contemporary situation is the significant increase in all of the unemployment figures and the resistance of the
problem to normal governmental tools, suggesting a new and more dangerous development. The official unemployment rate for 1975-1976 was
over 8 percent, the inclusion of involuntary parttime workers brought
the figure to 9.5 percent, and the addition of "discouraged workers"
pushed the figure to over 10 percent. If we include as unemployed all of
those people who experienced *some* unemployment during the previous
twelve months, unemployment touched over 20 percent of the work
force in 1975.[8] The "very long duration" unemployment (out of work
twenty-seven weeks or longer) rate rose 108 percent between the early
1950s and the early 1970s.[9] These incredible figures, the most serious
levels of unemployment since the Great Depression, have held firm despite
the most massive deficit spending and government contribution to the
generation of aggregate demand in peace-time history. In 1975, for instance, the federal deficit was $71.2 billion, while in 1976, it exceeded
$100 billion. Given idle plant and overcapacity, such a government deficit
is, theoretically, supposed to take up the slack and stimulate employment.
A measure of the contemporary crisis is the degree to which unemploy-

ment has remained relatively stable in the midst of these deficits and what is conventionally considered a period of economic recovery from the recession of the early 1970s.[10]

This situation of permanent stagnation, an economy characterized by high unemployment and idle plant, is exacerbated by what can only be called a collapse in private investment. Despite what economists term a "recovery" in the overall economy, business has not been investing in those sectors most important to long-term recovery, namely in plant and machine replacement, modernization, and capacity expansion. In 1976, such investment remained a full 13 percent below the 1974 figures. Should such a phenomenon take on a permanent character, as it seems to be doing, the ever present requirement for growing aggregate demand can only come from the stimulus of growing federal deficits.

The problem of investment stagnation is further aggrevated by the appearance of a phenomenon long thought to be a figment of the Marxist imagination, a phenomenon termed the "profit squeeze" by contemporary economists, what Marx called the "falling rate of profit."[11] For whatever reason or set of reasons, though surely the unwillingness of organized workers to fund private investment out of declining living standards, the resistance to cuts in social spending by all elements of the working class, and the slowdown in the overall rate of productivity increase are surely significant, the fact of the "profit squeeze" is unmistakable. "Net corporate profits . . . went from around 20% in the years after World War II to 15% to 16% in the early and mid-sixties, and had declined to 10% by the early 1970's,"[12] a phenomenon that is being repeated all over the advanced capitalist world. It is assuming the form, that is, of a general characteristic of late capitalism.

What is unprecedented in the history of capitalism is the existence, side-by-side with stagnation, of uncomfortably high levels of *price inflation,* a situation now popularly termed "stagflation." From the point of view of both neoclassical and Keynesian economic theory, stagnation and inflation are opposite tendencies—as one rises the other falls—and forms the famous "trade-off" problem of the "Philips curve" much discussed by economists. Another mark of the new economic crisis is the transformation in this relationship, and the tendency for the two to exist simultaneously.

We have already looked in some detail at one-half of the stagflation problem, namely stagnation, but have not given equivalent attention to its partner, inflation. Let us, therefore, examine the form and genesis of this phenomenon at greater length. There remain many candidates for the villain of this piece. The organization of the predominant sectors of the economy into monopoly forms has enabled giant corporations, as we have previously suggested, to largely transcend the disciplines of the marketplace and to become "price-setters" as opposed to "price-takers." As such they remain relatively immune in their price policies from the adverse effects of stagnation. Rather than cut prices as a means to increase their production during slack times, monopoly sector firms are more likely to cut production, lay off workers, and either maintain or *increase prices.* Such has been the case for every recessionary period since 1958. That is to say, prices in the monopoly sector have not fallen, and have characteristically grown during all recent recessions.[13] The monopoly organization of the economy provides a built-in basis, therefore, for permanent price inflation. We might add that the organization of the monopoly sector work force into labor unions (both because of the defense needs of workers and the planning needs of the corporations) remains a powerful force for the prevention of direct wage cuts in this important part of the working class, and serves as another prop to the inflationary mechanism.

Another important and long-term addition to the inflationary spiral has been the decreasingly advantageous terms of trade for primary products. That is to say, the costs of raw materials imported primarily from Third World countries has dramatically increased in recent years, led by but not confined to petroleum products. The figures in Table 7-2 give some sense of the magnitude of change. Should the producers of non-petroleum products be successful in their attempt to emulate OPEC, and there is a fair probability that some may be able to do so, the terms of trade can only become worse, and inflationary pressures increase.

Table 7-2 Terms of Trade for Primary Products

Price of Primary Products
divided by
Price of Manufactures

1966	1967	1968	1969	1970	1971	1972	1973	1974
85	82	81	82	81	81	84	105	139

Source: *UN Yearbook of International Trade,* various years.

In any discussion of inflation one cannot ignore spiraling private and public debt. Between 1955 and 1974, corporate debt quintupled until it reached well over $1 trillion. By 1974, total household debt represented 93 percent of household disposable income.[14] By far the most important contributor to this debt explosion and the general inflationary pressure, however, is the unambiguous and oft cited increase in government spending and the alarming expansion in budget deficits. This cause of inflation is widely recognized, and forms the base for the popular demand to "balance the budget." What is overlooked by those who make this demand, however, is the degree to which government has no choice in the matter. It spends, as we have already pointed out, because it must! Government spending is critical, we have suggested, for the management and control of the underclass, for the provision of a stable work force, for the provision of human and physical capital necessary for the profitable operation of the monopoly sector, for the subsidization of inefficient monopoly-sector firms, for the protection of overseas markets and raw material sources, and for the payment of the costs of the externalities of the system of capitalist market relations. Without government to service these requirements of mature and late capitalism, nothing less than chaos would reign. Most importantly, however, government is forced into massive budget deficits because it remains the single most important prop to the maintenance of aggregate demand at levels sufficient to prevent economic collapse. Without these deficits, capitalism would have surely succumbed to the system crisis predicted almost a century ago by Marx. What we are suggesting is that the crisis tendencies inherent in capitalism have been temporarily staved off only by the managerial and fiscal intervention of the national government but that the price for this massive intervention has been the reappearance of these tendencies in a more heightened form simultaneously with government-induced inflation. The result has been a steady decline in the standard of living of almost all Americans. Neither the management tools of the state nor the inner resources of capitalism as a system seems capable of reversing these secular developments.

Management or Steering Crisis[15]

Let us elaborate the last point a bit more. What we are suggesting is that the governmental tools for the management of the system, the devices for steering mature capitalism through the shoals of its own contradictions, no longer seem to work. Moreover, their very use in a time of their decreasing effectiveness has rendered the tools themselves problematic. What lends a crisis character to these development is that there have appeared no new tools with even a vague promise of rational system manage-

ment. What we are suggesting is that capitalism at this stage of its development in the United States cannot afford to discard the managerial tools it
now possesses; it cannot afford to continue to use them in the future for
reasons of their own problematic nature; and it has available to it no new
steering strategies.

The most sobering recent phenomenon is, of course, the failure of the
means by which a basically irrational system was made, it was thought,
to act rationally and efficiently. We are referring, of course, to that tool
kit of modern economic science, the monetary and fiscal devices of
Keynesian economics. As recently as 1966, the eminent economist Walter
Heller was moved to observe that "economics has come of age in the
1960s. Two presidents have recognized and drawn on modern economics
as a source of national strength and presidential power. Their willingness
to use, for the first time, the full range of modern economic tools under-
lines the unbroken U.S. expansion since early 1961 . . . ."[16] What is
increasingly self-evident is that with the monopoly organization of the
most important sectors of the economy and the resultant ability of the
major industrial and financial corporations to ignore or vitiate the prod-
ding of Keynesian managers, with endemic and permanent unemployment,
with the massive increase in the debt structure (both private and public),
with the growing government deficits necessary to avert stagnation, and
with the growing internationalization of the operations of capitalist trade,
industry and finance, the degree of managerial control available to any
single national government is ever more limited, no matter what the tools.
The promise of perpetual economic stability built upon the steering
capabilities of modern economic science was short-lived, indeed.

We are, of course, being more than a little unfair in our critique, for
in a very large sense, the anarchy of production that lies at the very heart
of capitalism makes rational, efficient, and stable economic life impossible
to attain. That is to say, while the only possible solution to the multiple
problems of late capitalism are somewhere in the direction of overall
national and even international planning for use, the competitive anarchy
at the center of capitalist life prevents both the introduction and efficient
use of such mechanisms, as each enterprise naturally seeks its own advantage, as each one attempts to carve out places of privileged operation
in the complex interstices of the government. The state in capitalism, as
we have pointed out before, is always caught between the needs and
interests of *individual capital* and *collective capital,* between the class
taken as a whole and its constituent parts. All that the state is capable of

doing, in the midst of such constraints, is to act reactively to problems, tensions, and imbalances as they arise, without rational purpose, and without the capability, in the long run, to adequately deal with the emerging contradictions.

Legitimacy Crisis

It is certainly no secret that the faith and confidence of the American people in the major institutions in our society and its leaders are at an all-time low, with no sign that the discontent is a temporary or passing phenomenon. Whether opinion polls ask about political leaders, business leaders, doctors, or teachers, whether they ask about the justice and efficacy of the political or economic system, or finally, whether they ask about personal judgments of one's present situation or faith in future prospects, the American people almost invariably respond negatively. Identification with and participation in the political life of the country is also at a historic nadir. Discontent, cynicism, and malaise, in short, today grip the vast majority of citizens in the United States. Writing in early 1977, political scientists Alan Wolfe and John Judis cogently summarized the general situation facing the new president:

> *As President Carter will face a divided people no longer united by a common vision, distrustful of politicians, government, political parties, and private corporations. He will not preside over a booming economy. There will continue to be international monetary instability, a growing urban crisis in the North, downward pressure on American worker's wages as American firms fight to maintain their competitive advantage, and a permanent unemployment problem.* [17]

At this writing, it is clear that Carter has not been able to stem the tide of the growing legitimacy crisis. In fact, Carter has already experienced in the first years of his administration, the most precipitous decline in the entire history of public opinion polling in the proportion of Americans who believe "the president is doing a good job."

We use the term crisis, for such a pervasive and a generally across the board disintegration of popular faith in the central institutions of the American social order portends serious difficulties. We say that because all stable societies are kept on an orderly, smoothly operating course by some mixture of coercion and legitimacy. While coercion is never absent (note the existence of a system of police, courts, and jails in all modern societies), the most stable societies generally are held together through the wide dissemination of notions of legitimate authority, popular beliefs that the actions of the major social institutions, processes, and leadership are right and proper, worthy of respect and support, and most important-ly, subject to willing obedience. To the extent that this sense of legitimate authority is absent, the state must unavoidably turn to more coercive methods with all of their attendant costs, inefficiencies, and potential for heightened social conflict. No society can in the long run, we are arguing, continue to function without a widely shared sense of legiti-macy among its members.

The sources of declining popular faith in the central institutions of late capitalism are many and complex, and are worth examining in some detail. At the most obvious level, of course, is the general disintegration of American economic hegemony, the implications of that disintegration for the expectations of the American people, and the apparent inability of government to reverse the tide and create hope for the future. We shall not review these materials, for to a very great extent, this entire book has been about the rise and fall of American economic, political, and ideological supremacy, and the role of the state in both the ascending and descending portions of that history. Suffice it to say, a widely shared sense of legitimacy is based, in the long run, on the ability of a society and its central institutions to meet the expectations (themselves, social system products) of its members. To the extent that the American system has continually raised the hopes and expectations of its members, a prime requirement for the construction of a steadily escalating level of demand so central to the health of capitalism, and to the extent that the system is increasingly unable to meet these hopes and expectations, to that extent does disappointment, anger, and cynicism come to replace widespread notions of legitimate authority in the population.

The problem has become increasingly salient to the dominant class in recent years. Martin Sklar has summarized the views of a new body of literature from procapitalist intellectuals and business leaders (about whom we shall have more to say later in the chapter) who are deeply worried about this developing situation in all of the major capitalist countries. They worry that:

> , , , *people in the capitalist industrial nations have put up with inequality so long as capitalism grew steadily, thereby providing sufficiently ample employment at relatively stable prices, exemplary opportunity for social mobility, and larger slices of a growing pie without changing the proportion of each slice. But the era of*

such capitalist growth, with its relatively unified national and international political purpose, is over. This is tending to nullify the legitimacy of inequality and to exhaust the people's tolerance for it, especially as the post-World War II expansion raised people's expectations and undermined the old bourgeois values of thrift, frugality, abstinence, and obedience to older authority, particularly religion. Capitalism, therefore, must operate to reconcile equalitarian yearnings with capitalist liberty, and to restore confidence in the rule of law and the guarantee of civil liberties, else it will cease to operate altogether sooner or later.[18]

While there has been little systematic work linking it to the question of legitimacy, there is very strong reason to suspect that the apparent growing *irrationalities* of capitalism as a whole[19] are coming to bring that system into general disrepute. In the search for profit that is the very lifeblood of capitalism, business is forced by the logic of the market to wastefully absorb resources, to poison the environment, and to disrupt personal lives, and communities. Where else but in capitalism are people urged to consume products that use scarce resources simply that demand might remain sufficient to prevent economic collapse? Where else but in capitalism are people urged to buy ever more cars in cities already clogged and polluted by them simply because the car is the center of capitalist production (one in six jobs is directly or indirectly tied to the auto industry, as well as 65 percent of lead production; 61 percent of synthetic rubber; 48 percent of malleable iron; 34 percent of zinc; 21 percent of steel; 12 percent of aluminum; and 8 percent of copper)?[20] Where else but in capitalism are people forced to choose between their jobs and environmental poisoning? Where else but in capitalism are efficient forms of transportation and energy usage destroyed so as to make way for more wasteful yet more profitable forms—cars for streetcars and trains, synthetic for natural fibers, detergents for soaps, etc.?[21] Where else but in capitalism is scarce natural gas burned at the wellhead because it is not profitable to collect it? Where else but in capitalism are durable goods given a built-in maximum life so as to encourage product turnover, sales and profits?

One could go on almost indefinitely with the cataloging of the inescapable irrationalities of capitalism, but it would serve no further purpose. What we are suggesting is that as times become increasingly problematic in late capitalism, the irrationalities inherent in it probably become more evident, adding to the general crisis of confidence growing from a wide variety of other sources. We suspect that Americans are beginning to sense the deep irrationalities of a system characterized by "the control of society by the relations of money, rather than the control of money relationships by society."[22]

Finally, a major factor in the development of a legitimacy crisis may well be the very visibility of the giant corporations and of the state apparatus. That is to say, in a capitalism that more closely approximates a laissez-faire form, where many small firms compete with each other in the marketplace, and where the activities of government are limited and relatively passive, the causes of economic troubles, irrationalities, and social disruption are opaque and difficult to discern. That is to say, in such a setting, results seem the outcome of relatively automatic and natural processes (the market), outside of the control of any visible set of actors or institutions. What happens, it is assumed, simply happens. The economy is something like the weather, in this view, something to worry about and talk about, but something about which little can be done, and for which no one can be blamed.

In mature capitalism, however, the main actors in economic life as well as the managers of the social steering mechanism are clearly visible. That is to say, the giant financial and nonfinancial corporations are visible for all to see as the prime movers and shakers in the economic drama. The state, for its part, carries out its role as regulator and guarantor of the economic and social order in the full light of day. With these developments, the dynamics of economic and social life are demystified; they cease to have an automatic and natural character and are reinterpreted as the outcome of human design and choice. While such a development has contributed to the strengthening of the general sense of legitimacy during times of capitalist ascendency, it has the opposite result in periods of decline. What we are saying is that with the long period of disaccumulation into which, U.S. capitalism has surely entered, blame for the emerging personal and social troubles are easily and generally apportioned to the highly visible corporations and the state apparatus, and as such, help define the terms of the current diminution in the sense of legitimacy throughout society. In that collapsing sense of support for the ongoing system and in the growing realization that human hands can and do direct the overall direction of economic and social life, lie both the dangers of an emergent authoritarian order, and the possibility for a more just and humane one organized on socialist principles. In the final section of this chapter, we turn to a consideration of these issues.

FUTURE OPTIONS

A system crisis, we have suggested following Habermas, is a state of affairs in which problems generated both exogenous and endogenous to a system become so serious in their effects on that system that they become irresolvable within the normal range of possibilities defined by its central organizational principles. In the above pages we have reviewed a range of complex and often interdependent problems which taken together add up, we have argued, to precisely such a system crisis. We are referring, of course, to a crisis comprised of basic transformations in the world position of the United States, in the operations of its economy, in its ability to manage its economic affairs, and in its support among the population in general. If we are correct in our reading of the contemporary situation in the United States, it would appear that basic transformations are on the agenda for the not too distant future. The only alternative to such basic transformations is for capitalist leadership to somehow solve the multiple problems that, taken together, are leading the system toward crisis. The direction of our analysis and, we believe, the overwhelming bulk of the evidence, suggests that the problems we have identified are intractable and unavoidable given the present structure and operation of capitalism, that the basic irrationalities, inefficiencies, and spiraling diseconomies are inescapable to the extent that they arise out of the laws of motion of capitalism itself.

If we are correct in our analysis, then the crisis can be solved only within the context of new institutional and value configurations, within a social system with different organizational and operational principles. The choices are not infinite but come down to a relative handful of alternatives. Since it is our considered judgment that the free-market alternative is nothing but a reactionary dream (in the sense that it is impossible to attain, given the political, economic, and social power of concentrated capital, that it would represent an improbable reversal of the laws of development of capitalism itself, and that the free-market is clearly irrational in its operations to almost all observers), any alternative future social organization will involve some form of planning, some conscious direction of social life through human will and intelligence. The only questions that remain, in our judgment, are those that pertain to the sources and beneficiaries of such a planned system. That is to say, who will do the planning, and whose interests will be served by that planning? What values will define the process? To perhaps oversimplify the question, we suspect that the choice will be between planning by and for capital, or planning by and for the vast majority of the population, a choice between some type of restructured authoritarian capitalism, or some form of socialism.

The Trilateral Commission and the Authoritarian Future

One likely future is that sketched out by the Trilateral Commission, a body founded by David Rockefeller (Board Chairman of the Chase Manhattan Bank) in 1973 under the direction of his long-time advisor and present National Security Advisor to the President of the United States, Zbigniew Brzezinski, and representing more than 200 of the world's most powerful banks and multinational corporations. The commission is organized around the proposition that the major capitalist centers of power (United States, Western Europe, and Japan) must jointly and cooperatively tackle the contemporary crisis of capitalism. Its leaders believe that the commission must gather together the best intellectual and business talent available to advanced capitalism so as to analyze the interrelated components of the crisis, formulate possible solutions, and press for those changes in government policy in all of the trilateral states that are required in view of the emerging crisis. The commission is comprised of an impressive collection of representatives from international finance and the multinational corporations centered in the three major regions of the trilateral world of advanced capitalism, as well as sympathetic scholars, media owners and executives, politicians, and several trade union leaders. One can gain a flavor of the commission and its not inconsiderable influence by taking note of the composition of its 1975 Executive Committee, a committee which has changed a member here and there, but remains the same in its class and institutional composition.[23]

Director, Z. Brzezinski[a]

North American Members

I. W. Abel	President, United Steelworkers
R. W. Bonner	Corporate Attorney, Vancouver
Harold Brown	President, Cal Tech (As of December 1977, Secretary of Defense)
P. E. Haggerty	Chairman, Texas Instruments
J. L. Pepin	President, Interimco, Ltd.
E. O. Reischauer	Professor, Harvard (former U.S. Ambassador to Japan)
David Rockefeller	Chairman, Chase Manhattan Bank
W. M. Roth	Roth Properties

William Scranton

Corporate Attorney (former governor of Pennsylvania)

Paul Warnke

Partner, Corporate Law Firm (as of December 1977, Director, Arms Control and Disarmament Agency)

European Members

Giovanni Agnelli

President, Fiat, Ltd.

Kurt Birfenbach

Corporation President; Member of Bundestag

Francesco Compagna

Undersecretary of State

Paul Delouvrier

Chairman, French Electricity Board

H. Ehrenberg

Member of Bundestag

Marc Eyskens

Catholic University of Louvain

Max Kohnstamm

President, European Community Institute

John Loudon

Chairman, Shell Oil

O. G. Tidemand

Shipowner, (former Norwegian Minister of Defense and of Economic Affairs)

Sir Kenneth Lounger

Former Director of Royal Institute (former Foreign Minister of United Kingdom)

Sir Philip de Zulneta

Chief Executive, Antony Gibbs Holdings, Ltd.

Japanese Members

Chujiro Fujino

Chairman, Mitsubishi Corporation

Y. Haraguchi

Chairman, Federation of Metal and Mining Unions

Y. Hayashi

Member of Diet (Japanese Parliament)

Y. Kashiwagi

Deputy President, Bank of Tokyo

K. Mushakoji

Director, Institute of International Relations

Saburo Okita

President, Overseas Economic Co-operation Fund

R. Takeuchi

Advisor to Ministry of Foreign Affairs

T. Watanabe

Chairman, Trident International Finance, Ltd.

[a]As of December 1977, National Security Advisor to the President of the United States.

The Trilateral Commission is by no means a conspiracy, a secret cabal organizing a new world order. Indeed, the composition of its membership and leadership is well known, its publications are available to the public, and its aims are openly articulated. What makes the commission of more than passing interest to us is not its secret power, but what its work tells us about the thinking, worries, hopes, and plans of the most advanced elements of the international capitalist class as well as its helpmates in intellectual and journalistic circles. An analysis of its work can give us a feel for one of the possible futures we may face, a by no means rash statement in light of the combined political, economic, social and ideological power represented in the commission membership.[24]

At the center of the thinking of the Commission is a strong sense of the impending crisis facing world capitalism. As paradoxical as it would appear to be on its surface, the commission seems to fully accept the analysis of the component parts of the crisis as presented earlier in this chapter, a crisis arising out of the reappearance of intercapitalist competition, world currency instability, discontinuities in raw material sources and markets in the Third World, endemic stagflation in all of the trilateral counties, as well as declines in the sense of legitimate authority among its domestic populations. The commission sees a world uncomfortably out of control, heading toward chaos and collapse, and it proposes a cooperative effort between the major capitalist institutions and governments to seek a stable, rationalized, and carefully managed world order able, to if not eliminate systemic problems, to as least control and attenuate them. This set of fears, aspirations, and goals should surely seem familiar to the reader, for it closely parallels the efforts of the leaders of the major domestic banks and corporations in the early part of this century within the United States (see Chapters 3 and 4), though the stage of operations, in this case, is the world rather than a single nation state. That is to say, just as some farsighted American capitalists helped construct the modern state as a way to rationalize the domestic economy in the first half of the twentieth century (histories extensively reviewed in this book), today the most sensitive and advanced thinkers among the leaders of multinational enterprises and financial institutions are attempting to grope toward institutional arrangements capable of rationalizing an international economy increasingly out of control. While there are striking parallels between the past and present reform efforts of monopoly capital, there remains an important difference: the Commission is concerned about the problems of capitalist accumulation not in a time of optimism and expansion, but in a time of scarcity and limits to growth. This altered environment suggests some of the central causes for the desperation of commission objectives, particularly within the domestic boundaries of the trilateral countries.

Before we review some of these domestic scenarios, however, let us briefly review the commission's proposals at the level of the world order. First, and most importantly, the commission seeks to stabilize world trade, to transcend intercapitalist trade wars, and to bring order to the very base of the trading system: the world monetary system broadly defined (involving banking, balance of payments, credit and investment policy, the control of inflation, etc.). The commission has tried to convince governments of the capitalist powers to coordinate their policies in all of these areas in order to avoid the disruptions that have torn the world system over the last decade and that threaten to deteriorate further unless cooperative efforts are instituted. They not only have proposed the strengthening of international institutions like the International Monetary Fund (IMF) and the Organization for Economic Cooperation and Development but also direct consultations between various governments. There has already been some movement in the latter area. Witness the series of economic summit meetings convened by the trilateral governments in Rambouillet in 1976, in Puerto Rico in the same year (at the Dorado Beach Hotel, a resort conceived, built, and owned by the Rockefeller family), in London in May 1977, and in Bonn in July 1978.

Stability in the world capitalist system also involves the stabilization of relations with the Third World, in particular, guarantees of steady supplies of necessary raw materials and prevention of default on debts owed to the principal trilateral banking institutions. The commission proposes a complex set of programs designed to increase the stake of the native *comprador* classes in the new world capitalist order, to prevent expropriations of trilateral properties, to control Third World pressures on resources through population control, and to allow regional policing by junior partners in the world system (Iran and Brazil, in particular). Most importantly, the commission proposes that international agencies (like the IMF and World Bank) provide the funds necessary to assist financially troubled nations like Zaire and Chile pay off their enormous debts owed, in the main, to American banks. This program of using tax money to help private banks collect their debts is well on the way. In March 1977, President Carter (an early Trilateral Commission member) introduced a bill proposing a healthy increase of $3.2 billion in the U.S.

contribution to the IMF, the World Bank, and the Asian Development Bank. The bill was presented to the Congress by Secretary of the Treasury Michael Blumenthal, another former commission member.

Concomitant with intercapitalist cooperation, however, several study groups within the commission have proposed a set of policies for the trilateral nations that portend a serious enhancement of domestic authoritarianism. Their proposals arise primarily out of their analysis of the causes of "troubles" in the developed capitalist nations. In this view, the steering capabilities of the state so necessary for a managed capitalism have been eroded by the decline of overall system legitimacy, by the unrealistically heightened expectations of the population, and by the growing obstacles to capital accumulation in the monopoly sector of the economy. The state has lost most of its ability to act, in view of Samuel Huntington and others in *The Crisis of Democracy,* because of the level of popular demands made upon it by a democracy run amok, a development made all the worse by oppositional intellectuals and an irresponsible press. In the words of that report:

> . . . *the operations of the democratic process do indeed appear to have generated a breakdown of traditional means of social control, a delegitimation of political and other forms of authority, and an overload of demands on government, exceeding its capacity to respond.*
>
> . . . *the advanced industrial societies have spawned a stratum of value-oriented intellectuals who often devote themselves to the derogation of leadership, the challenging of authority, and the unmasking and delegitimation of established institutions. . . .this development constitutes a challenge to democratic government which is, potentially at least, as serious as those posed in the past by the aristocratic cliques, fascist movements, and communist parties.*[25]

The most central task in the developed capitalist societies, therefore, is to stop the trend toward delegitimation, and to reinvest authorities with the stature and power necessary to the tasks that will face them. The tasks, it is important to add, are related to the institution of limited national planning so as to reestablish the grounds for capital accumulation by lowering the expectations of the population, and by altering the relative shares of national income going respectively to the capital and to labor. Again, to cite *The Crisis of Democracy:*

> *. . . a government which lacks authority and which is committed to substantial domestic programs will have little ability, short of a cataclysmic crisis, to impose on its people the sacrifices which may be necessary . . . .*[26]

Government with the requisite authority is needed to help provide the conditions for enhanced productivity, to keep wage-rate increases below the rate of inflation, to control an underclass subsisting on a much reduced level of welfare support, and to convince its population to support a program of attenuated public services. These sacrifices are necessary, it is believed by the commission, to move capitalist economics out of their position of endemic stagnation. The scope of the problem facing the commission is suggested by the following comment that appeared in *Business Week*.

> *. . . it will be a hard pill for many Americans to swallow—the idea of doing with less so that big business can have more . . . . Nothing that this nation, or any other nation, has done in modern economic history compares in difficulty with the selling job that must now be done to make people accept the new reality.*[27]

It is not at all clear what specific methods the commission has in mind for bringing about the requisite transformation, though some are beginning to come into view. Led by bankers David Rockefeller and Felix Rohatyn, there has emerged an almost universal interest among the leaders of international corporations in resource, investment, and financial planning directed, of course, to the maintenance of the health of the major corporations. Rohatyn has already proposed a resurrected Reconstruction Finance Corporation whose purpose would be the stabilization of major corporations and banks through the infusion of public funds, a proposal that has received a great deal of favorable attention.[28] There has been some speculation, as well, about imposing certain limits on the press, most notably in a stronger form of "prior restraint" and in the enhanced ability of the government to control information at its source. Some commission intellectuals have proposed a cutback in education because of its alleged inducement to the generation of unrealizable expectations. Most importantly, commission members and staff have launched an assault on the very idea that government might be the vehicle for the fulfillment of popular desires (they are careful, however, to exclude from these strictures what government might do for the corporations), holding that such government intervention is by nature inefficient, expensive, and counterproductive, a view that fits very comfortably with the general neoconservative revival centered in the pages of *Commentary* and *The Public Interest*[29] and now pervading and clogging all channels of thought and debate in America.

Whatever the particular methods and irrespective of the question of their effectiveness, the goals of the commission and the intellectuals who surround it are quite explicit: to institute national planning aimed at enhancing the accumulation capabilities of the major economic actors, to convince the population to do with less in terms of their standard of living so as to sustain the economic base, and to resuscitate governmental authority so that it can carry out these difficult tasks. Whether or not these goals can be reached remains to be seen, though definite movement in that direction is certainly evident. Most importantly, and without, we hope being unduly alarmist and conspiratorial in our view, it is of more than passing importance that the general flavor of the Carter presidency is commission derived, though he has hardly been more successful in meeting commission goals than he has been in other areas of activity. That is to say, the general tone is one of failure rather than of achievement. He himself, of course, was a member of the Trilateral Commission, as was his Vice President, Walter Mondale, and was support by campaign contributions from commission members, by speechwriters and advisors from the Commission (Brzezinski and Brown), and by timely endorsements from its members (Woodcock of the United Auto Workers, being the most important, given Carter's weakness with organized labor). It is striking, in fact, to note the degree to which Carter seemed to come out of nowhere, relying not the least on explicit support from the traditional power bases of the Democratic party, most notably, among Jews and organized labor. It is also of considerable interest that twenty-two (as of June 1977) commission-affiliated people held posts at the Assistant Secretary level and above in the Carter administration, including *every* position in the top levels of foreign and economic policy making.[30] It is also of more than passing interest that the major outlines of Carter's energy policy (drastically altered by Congress since its introduction) fit neatly into the framework of Trilateral Commission perspectives: increased energy prices, decreased consumption, subsidies and tax breaks to the energy industry, the beginnings of national energy planning, all wrapped in the rhetoric of sacrifice and nationalism, or in Carter's own words, "the moral equivalent of war."

Surely, one must not overdramatize the commission and its direct influence, yet the fact remains that it clearly represents the directions in which much of the leading opinion in advanced capitalism is moving. What is ominous about the above developments is that capitalism in the throes of crisis is perfectly capable of emphasizing the most authoritarian alternatives within the trilateral program. Some scholars, in fact, have recently become so concerned about the above potential developments in the trilateral program, as well as about developments already well under way in American life, that they have cautiously and uncomfortably begun to use the term "fascism" to describe the American future.[31] None of them, to be sure, visualizes a future with a single charismatic leader, a mass totalitarian party, or death camps. They do visualize, however, a future in which the state uses all of the tools of an advanced technological civilization to closely manage and control economic, social, and political life so as to assure and prop the position of large-scale capital, to regulate the gradual increase in the rate of surplus extraction from the mass population to assure the basis of capital accumulation, and to control discontent in the population through sophisticated police methods, repression, and scapegoating. Such a system might easily be instituted under the felt imperatives of greater efficiency, mutual sacrifice, and even national survival.

Certainly, the trilateral program already contains many ingredients of an updated version of fascism. Note its strong focus on the crisis facing the West, its call for the revitalization of central authority in capitalist governments, its views on the "distemper" of democracy, and the tendencies for democracy, unless curtailed, to overflow its legitimate boundaries, and finally, its concern about the irresponsibility of the press and the necessity of increasing controls over its activities.

The extent to which even fairly liberal, concerned, and humane social thinkers have moved in an authoritarian direction in recent years is also ominous. Note the recently stated views of economist Robert Heilbroner:

> *Given these mighty pressures and constraints, we must think of alternatives to the present order in terms of social systems that offer a necessary degree of regimentation as well as a different set of motives and objectives. I must confess I can picture only one such system. This is a social order that will blend a "religious" orientation and a "military" discipline. Such a monastic organization of society*

*may be repugnant to us, but I suspect it offers the greatest promise
for bringing about the profound and painful adaptations that the
coming generations must make. . . . I cannot find a plausible alternative to the ideal-type of a monastery—a tightly-disciplined, ascetic
religious order—as a model which the evolving societies of the world
will gradually approximate.*[32]

Developments in an authoritarian direction in American life have, unfortunately, gone well beyond theoretical propositions. During the past
decade, it is important to note, employment in law enforcement became
the fastest growing part of public employment in the United States, while
the policing function became the largest single budget item in several
major American cities. Nor can we ignore the evidence of massive and
escalating surveillance of the American population by official agencies as
diverse as local police departments, post offices, the CIA, the National
Security Agency, and the Internal Revenue Service, and the stockpiling
into dossiers and computer tapes of the information gathered in these
processes.

Finally, we must point out that the building blocks of a fascist ideology
have long existed in undeveloped but visible form in the United States,
namely, in racism and fervent anticommunism. While American racism is
primarily antiblack in character rather than antisemitic, it remains racism
and can be mobilized for the same ends. It is of some importance then to
note the increased antiblack sentiment that has reappeared as opportunities in the economy have declined. All of the hostility to "quotas" sur-
rounding the so-called "reverse discrimination" cases like Bakke have this
character.

It may seem somewhat alarmist, to be sure, to use a term like fascism,
especially in light of its normal definitions. Michael Parenti points out,
however, that the black-booted totalitarian visions central to the most
common definitions of fascism miss all of the respects in which fascism
is not too far distant from "normal" everyday life. He points out that:

*Unless one were Jewish, of active leftist persuasion or openly anti-
Nazi, Germany from 1933 until well into the war was not a night-
mare world but a fairly comfortable place. All the Germans had to
do was obey the laws, pay their taxes, give their sons to the army,
avoid any sign of political heterodoxy and look the other way when
troublesome people were disposed of.*
*Since many Americans already obey the laws, pay their taxes,
give their sons to the army, are themselves distrustful of political*

*heterodoxy and applaud when troublesome people are disposed
of, they probably could live without too much personal torment
in a fascist state—some of them certainly seem eager to do so. Or-
well's fantasies and futuristic gimmicks to the contrary, what is so
terrifying about fascism is its normality, its compatibility with the
collective sentiments of so many "normal" people.*[33]

The message of this passage, of course, is not to rest content because
of our distance from totalitarian models, but to be alert to all of those
developments in American life, both intellectual and actual, that presage
a system of corporate oriented, technologically controlled, and closely
managed systemic planning.

The Socialist Alternative

We have suggested in our analysis that the laws of motion of capitalism
first propelled the American system from something that approximated
the free market in the nineteenth century into its monopoly form under
mature capitalism, and then subsequently propelled it into a crisis phase
constructed out of the full fruition of the contradictions inherent in
mature capitalism. We have argued that this crisis of capitalism can only
be managed through a process of basic structural transformation, for
the present economic, political, and social forms are incapable of solving
the multiple and interdependent problems that together comprise the
body of that system crisis. We have also argued, uncomfortably to be
sure, that unless something is done to counter emerging developments,
most trends in the United States point to a Trilateral Commission type
authoritarianism, or even some American brand of fascism.

If the future is one of planning, as we have suggested, and if all indications point to something that looks very much like the Trilateral program—an authoritarian system by and for large-scale capital—there remains yet another alternative vision, one that may by counterposed to
that of the Trilateral Commission in its commitment to a system of planning by and for the mass of the population, an alternative vision we
would call *socialism.*

Socialism is one of those words which, because of its widespread popularity in most parts of the world, and because of the fear it evokes in some
circles, has been greatly abused and distorted. Behind all of the manipulations of propaganda, both pro and con, stands however, a set of principles
that clearly and sharply define socialism, that stand as a cogent alternative
to those principles that define capitalism, and that, finally, provide the

only humane and decent alternative to the authoritarian promise of capitalism.

At the most fundamental level, socialism is distinguished from capitalism by its commitment to a system of production for use rather than profit. That is to say, the central steering mechanism for economic life (and ultimately, it follows, for most aspects of social life) is not the pursuit of profit in the marketplace, but the rational calculation by the members of society of overall social needs and purposes. This commitment is based on the unarguable observation that all large-scale production is social in its operations and social in its effects, and to the socialist, it follows that decisions about its means and ends ought to be social as well.

Production for use has several important consequences that make it immediately attractive. In the first place, it avoids most if not all of the problems that have brought capitalism to its present crisis. That is to say, and we leave it to the reader to reach his or her own conclusion based on the examination of the general dynamics of capitalist development we have explored extensively in this book, the problems of stagnation, irrationality, waste, and inefficiency that we experience in the United States are not technologically inevitable but are largely derived from the organization of economic life around the pursuit of private profit. Despite Adam Smith's mystification about the "invisible hand," a rational and humane society cannot be constructed out of greed and the pursuit of private riches. Moreover, we would add, production for use is inherently more attractive than production for profit because it rightly places human needs and purposes back into the prominent place to which they belong. As we have said elsewhere,

> *In a just society, production can never be directed toward any other end than the betterment of the lives of human beings, to provide the means by which needs are met, and capacities cultivated. For production and accumulation to become ends themselves is to stand the world on its head, to make people the slaves of the machinery which they themselves created.* [34]

The central organizing principle of socialism, both the end purpose of production and the means for its attainment, is that of *equality*. If it means anything at all, socialism is commited to the notion that all members of a society must share in a relatively equal manner (no mathematically exact equality, of course, is ever possible) both in the material goods and services that society collectively produces and that make a life of decency, fulfillment, and self-respect possible, and in the decision-making processes by which social life is shaped and advanced. Socialists have always believed that it is only after basic human needs have been met through a procedure involving the general sharing of the social product (rather than its concentration into the hands of the wealthy few) and through a general process of democratic decision making affecting all aspects of collective life, that it becomes possible for human beings to fully develop their capacities as rational, purposeful, and caring persons.

Let us reemphasize and highlight the aspect of the commitment of socialism to a general dispersal of power in society, for to concentrate political and/or economic decision-making power in the hands of anyone but the population in general contradicts the socialist commitment to equality. To equalize the distribution of goods and services without equalizing, insofar as possible, the power to determine the directions and purposes of production, is to undermine the notions of common humanity and fellowship that are at the heart of socialism, and to block the main road to the full development of human talents and abilities, for such talents and abilities are only developed through use and practice. Rather than a system that is directed by a handful of the wealthiest members of society—as is the case in contemporary capitalism—or one that is directed by a handful of party bureaucrats—as is the case in many contemporary state socialist societies—socialism must be built upon a system of democratic participation in *all* aspects of socially relevant decision making. To be without such a practice is to be without socialism itself.

We have presented only a brief sketch of the socialist vision, but we hope that it highlights the most important elements of the kind of society that can stand as an attractive alternative to a future that is nothing less than ominous in its promise. That future, we would submit, will look very different than that to which we are accustomed, as capitalism attempts to transform itself in order to save itself. That future, unless we struggle against it with an alternative vision that is at once humane, rational, and possible, looks increasingly like an authoritarian one, whether of the benign Trilateral Commission type, or of a more harsh and repressive neofascist variety. Capital will do what it must to save itself, of that we may be sure. Only a popular movement built around a program of democratic socialism can deflect us from a path designed by others with their own interests in mind.[35] The very first step in the long struggle to get us off the path, a small step to be sure, yet a necessary one, is to generate a popular awareness of what capitalism leadership has in store for most of us, and what alternative model of the future we might pose in its stead.

NOTES

[1] Jürgen Habermas, *Legitimation Crisis* (Boston: Beacon Press, 1973), p. 7.

[2] Such a transformation, as we shall discuss later in this chapter, could be to the right or to the left, depending upon the configuration of political forces.

[3] Ernst Mandel, *Late Capitalism* (London: New Left Books, 1976), pp. 570-571.

[4] This is another historical irony. The reemergence of competing capitalist economies was greatly assisted by aid from the United States which was itself in need of healthy (though not necessarily equal) capitalist societies for trade and investment after the Second World War.

[5] See Mandel, *Late Capitalism,* for a stimulating discussion of the "long wave" of capitalist decline.

[6] Douglas Dowd, "Accumulation and Crisis in U.S. Capitalism," *Socialist Revolution,* Vol. 24 (June 1975), p. 11.

[7] All of these figures are from either the U.S. Department of Labor, the U.S. Department of Commerce, or the *Economic Report of the President.* They are collected together and cogently analyzed in Richard DuBoff, "Unemployment in the United States: An Historical Summary." *Monthly Review,* Vol, 29, No. 6 (November 1977), pp. 10-24.

[8] Ibid.

[9] *Economic Report of the President, January 1977* (Washington, D. C.: Government Printing Office, 1977), p. 221.

[10] Another indication of the steadily worsening employment situation is the dual effort to revise the meaning of "full employment" upward (from 2 percent to 3 percent in 1948 to about 6 percent today) and to rationalize, that is, make excuses for, this sluggish performance. For the history of this story see Richard Duboff, "Full Employment: History of a Receding Target," *Politics and Society,* Vol, 7, No. 1 (1977), pp. 1-26.

[11] This forms the basis of the analysis in Mandel, *Late Capitalism.* Also see Frank Ackerman and Arthur MacEwan, "Inflation, Recession, and Crisis," *Review of Radical Political Economics,* Vol. 4 (August 1972); William D. Nordhaus, "The Falling Share of Profits," in A. Okum and G. Perry eds., *Brookings Papers on Economic Activity,* No. 1, 1974; *Business Week,* December 14, 1975.

[12] David Plotke, "American Politics and Class Forces in the 1970s," *Socialist Review*, No. 37 (January-February 1978), p. 15.

[13] For the details of this story see Howard Sherman, *Radical Political Economy* (New York: Basic, 1972).

[14] Dowd, "Accumulation and Crisis."

[15] The concept of the "steering" crisis as well as the "legitimacy" crisis which forms the basis for the next section are taken from Habermas, *Legitimation Crisis.*

[16] Harvard, Godkin Lectures, March 1976.

[17] Alan Wolfe and John Judis, "American Politics at the Crossroads," *Socialist Revolution*, No. 32 (March–April 1977), p. 27.

[18] Martin Sklar, "Liberty and Equality, and Socialism," *Socialist Revolution*, No. 34 (July–August 1977), p. 95.

[19] For discussion of the general irrationality of capitalism see Barry Commoner, *The Poverty of Power* (New York: Knopf, 1976); Andre Gorz, *A Strategy for Labor* (Boston: Beacon Press, 1964); Robert Heilbroner, *Business Civilization in Decline* (New York: Norton, 1976); and Michael Harrington, *The Twilight of Capitalism* (New York: Simon and Schuster, 1976).

[20] Dowd, "Accumulation and Crisis, p. 14.

[21] See Commoner, *The Poverty of Power,* for this depressing story.

[22] A remark made by Ronald Segal, quoted in Geoffrey Barraclough, "The Great World Crisis," *New York Review of Books,* (January 23, 1975), p. 24.

[23] For general discussions of the Trilateral Commission see Kenneth Dolbeare, "The Trilateral Commission Takeover of the U.S. Government: What It Means," (Amherst: University of Massachusetts, mimeo, 1977); Judis and Wolfe, "American Politics at the Crossroads"; Lawrence U. Shoup and William Minter, *Imperial Brain Trust* (New York: Monthly Review Press, 1977); and Alan Wolfe, *The Limits of Legitimacy* (New York: Free Press, 1977).

[24] The summaries are taken from the close analysis of Trilateral Commission documents found in ibid.

[25] Michel Crozier, Samuel Huntington, and Joji Watanuki, eds., *The Crisis of Democracy* (New York: New York University Press, 1975), p. 7.

[26] Ibid., p. 105.

[27] Special issue on "The Debt Economy," *Business Week,* October 12, 1974, p. 120.

[28] *New York Times* (December 1, 1974).

[29] For analyses of this development see Lewis Coser and Irving Howe, eds., *The New Conservatives: A View from the Left* (New York: Quadrangle, 1977).

[30] Dolbeare, "The Trilateral Commission Takeover," p. 7.

[31] Most important in this regard is Bertram Gross, "Friendly Fascism: A Model for America," *Social Policy* (November/December 1970), pp. 44–52. Also see Michael Parenti, "Creeping Fascism," *Society,* Vol. 9 (June 1972); and Kenneth Dolbeare, "Alternatives to the New Fascism," (Amherst: University of Massachusetts, mimeo, 1976).

[32] Robert Heilbroner, "Second Thoughts on the Human Prospect," of *An Inquiry into the Human Prospect,* 2nd ed., (New York: Norton, 1975), p. 16.

[33] Parenti, "Creeping Fascism," p. 4.

[34] Edward S. Greenberg, *The American Political System: A Radical Approach* (Cambridge: Winthrop Publishers, 1977), p. 460.

[35] We deal extensively with the question of strategy and tactics in Greenberg, *The American Political System.*

INDEX

Accumulation of capital, 18-19, 38, 49
  under imperialism, 110-112
  in late capitalism, 163-164, 166, 174
  see also Trilateral Commission
Acheson, Dean, 117
Adams, Henry Carter, 20, 66
Advertising, 96-97, 101-102
Africa, 112
Age of Reform, 47-49, 52. *See also*
  Progressivism
Aggregate demand, 129-130, 132, 165-
  167, 169, 172
Agriculture, 6, 49, 65, 108, 149
  mechanization, 52, 55, 75
  migration from, 55-56, 75, 99, 149
  New Deal and, 72, 74-75, 78, 148
  subsidization of, 12, 74-75, 79
Aldrich, Winthrop, 81
Allende, Salvador, 140-142
Alliance for Progress, 138-139
Altmeyer, Arthur, 82
American Association of Labor Legis-
  lation (AALL), 71, 81-82, 86
"American Century," 92, 110, 126
American people:
  and corporate decisions, 97-103
  and Depression, 72, 80-81
  free-market conservatism and, 16, 21,
    153
  and legitimacy question, 171-174
  standard of living of, 143-144, 160,
    164, 167, 169
  traditional political beliefs, 5-11
  Trilateral Commission and, 180-181
  see also Expectations; Public opinion
Antistatism, 3, 6-11
Asia, 108-112, 117
Atlantic Charter, 110
Authoritarian alternative, 176-185, 187
Automotive and trucking industry, 83,
  102, 133-135, 173

Baker, Howard, 2-3
Bakke case, 184
Banking and finance, 49-50, 52, 95
  growth and mergers, 52, 54-55, 57,
    170
  and New Deal, 72-74, 78-79
  regulation, 59-61
  world structure of, 115, 138, 162
  and World War I, 108-109
  see also Trilateral Commission

Baran, Paul, 129
Barber, Richard J., 94
Baruch, Bernard, 75, 87
Beecher, Henry Ward, 146
Belmont, August, 62, 87
Bias, *see* Structural bias
Blacks, 56, 98-99
  and racism, 144, 184
  and welfare system, 144-146, 149
Blumenthal, Michael, 180
Bourgeoisie, 7, 30, 36-37, 39, 155
  as ruling class, 43
  values of, 173
Brazil, 139-140, 170
Bretton Woods Conference, 110, 162
Brzezinski, Zbigniew, 176, 182
Britain, *see* England
Brown, Harold, 176, 182
Brown, Jerry, 3
Bryan, William Jennings, 55
Bryce, James, 108
Buchanan, James, 3, 13-16
Budget deficits, 165-168, 180
Bureaucracy, 2-3, 15-16, 127, 153
Business:
  and government bias toward, 11-12
  and New Deal programs, 71-73, 75-77
  reform and role of government, 47-49,
    51-58, 66
  and unionism, 83-88
  see also Corporations; Medium and
    small business
Business cycle regulation, 128-132, 162

Cambodia, 142, 161
"Capacity utilization rate," 165
Capitalism (classic):
  contradictions in, 126-129, 164-165
  laissez-faire and free-market conserva-
    tism, 7-16
  Marxist theory, 30-42
  reform liberalism and, 18-21
  versus socialism, 186-187
  state under, 35-42, 48, 155
  transcendence of, 154
  treatment of labor, 32-33, 38, 99,
    130, 142, 165
  see also Cooperative capitalism; Late
    capitalism; Mature corporate
    capitalism; New Deal; World
    capitalism
Carnegie, Andrew, 57, 101

Carter, Jimmy, 3, 171, 179, 182-183
Central Intelligence Agency (CIA), 142, 184
Chile, 140-142, 179
China, 108, 113
Cities, 41, 52, 63-64, 66, 131
  during Depression, 80, 83-84, 148
  migration to, 55-56, 75, 98
  and welfare, 144-145, 150
Civil War, 51-52, 100, 137
Class struggle, in America, 40, 48, 84, 93, 136-137, 152-154
Class theory (Marxist), 32-36, 40-43, 77, 130. *See also* Inequality, system of
Cloward, Richard A., 148-151
Cochran, Thomas, 53
Collective bargaining, 20, 62, 70, 77-78
  business support for, 83-88, 103-105, 126, 155
Colonialism, 108, 110-113
Commerce Department, 136, 165
Common law tradition, 57-63 *passim*
Commons, John R., 62, 66, 82, 120
Communications, 49, 52, 66
Communist Manifesto, The (Marx and Engels), 30, 39
Competition, 35
  intercapitalist, 135-136, 170, 178
  in laissez-faire theory, 65-66, 142
  in mature capitalism, 95-97
  and medium and small business, 103
  regulation of, 75-78
  rise of corporations, 53, 55, 58, 61-63
  and Social Darwinism, 146, 148
Competitive sector of industry, 103, 106, 127, 143, 165
Comprador classes, 138, 140-142, 179
Congress, 60, 62, 79-80, 180
  and foreign aid, 139
  military expenses, 109, 136
Congress of Industrial Organizations (CIO), 78, 83, 104
Consumption, 35, 97, 102, 104-105, 129, 142, 165-166
  of scarce resources, 107, 173
Contradictions of capitalism, 93, 116
  endemic to growth, 127-129, 163-169
  government role, 129-151, 164, 169-171, 174
  in world system, 107, 161-163
Cooperative capitalism, 70-88 *passim*
  labor laws, 85-88
  NIRA and Social Security, 75-85
Core capitalist state, 39, 49, 110-112, 113-120
Corporations:
  beginnings and rise of, 52-55, 58

failure of and consequences, 127-128
  and government, 65, 129-132, 135-136, 155, 170, 174
  growth and concentration, 93-97, 126
  NIRA codes, 77-78
  progressive movement and, 58-62
  social impact, 97-103, 127
  work force, 56-57, 99-101, 103-106
  see also Mature corporate capitalism; Multinationals; New Deal; Trilateral Commission
Coughlin, Father, 80, 149
Crisis in American capitalism, 159-174. *See also* Trilateral Commission
Crisis of Democracy, The, 180-181
Critique of Political Economy (Marx), 31
Currency and credit, 60, 74
  and world capitalism, 110, 115, 138, 161-162, 178
Cybernation, 99-100

Dahl, Robert, 22-23
Debt, 168-169, 179
  government, 5
Defense industry, *see* Military spending
Demand, *see* Aggregate demand
Democracy, 15, 187
  excess of and American expectations, 16-17, 153, 180, 183
Democratic Party, 2, 9, 71, 104, 148-149, 182
Depressions (economic), 60-61, 108, 128. *See also* Great Depression
Dewey, John, 66
Disability and old age insurance, 77, 86, 127. *See also* Social Security system
Disaccumulation, *see* Accumulation
Diseconomies, 134-135, 175
Distribution of wealth, 52
  Depression movements, 80-81
  inequality in U.S., 143-144, 165
  see also Welfare system
Dual economy, 93, 103, 120

Economy (United States):
  domestic crisis, 163-174, 178
  dual, 93, 103
  foreign investments and government, 137-142
  imperialism and world capitalism, 106-120
  Keynesian economics, 128-131
  reforms, 47-67
  regulation of, 70-78
Education, 100-101, 131, 133, 155, 181
Eighteenth Brumaire of Louis Napoleon, The (Marx), 37

Elderly, 81-82, 106
Ely, Richard, 20, 62, 66
Employment, 18, 127, 172
  changed nature of, 105-106
  "full," 143, 166
  government, 4, 15-16
  training for, 127, 133
  related to welfare, 150-151
  vocational reshaping, 99-101
  see also Labor; Unemployment; Unions
Energy sources, 163, 173
Energy program, 182-183
Engels, Frederick, 30, 41, 155
England, 6-8, 59
  and world capitalism, 107, 109-110,
    112, 114
European countries, 56, 59, 138
  American investment in, 96, 114, 117
  colonialism, 112-113
  establishment of capitalism, 50-51
  economic rivalry, 161-162
  war effect, 107-110
  see also Trilateral Commission
Exchange value, 34, 115-116
Expectations, 16, 153, 172-173, 180-181
Export trade, 7, 108-115, 163, 168, 179
  and foreign aid, 139-140
  and market expansion, 114-120

Fascism, 183-185, 187
Federal government:
  budget deficits, 165-166
  economic intervention, 47-67
  18-19th centuries, 8, 57
  and Marxist theory, 39-42, 107, 151-
    155
  size of, 3-5
  structural bias, 11-12
  theories for understanding of, 12-25
  see also Government spending; New
    Deal
Federalist Papers, The (Madison), 22
Federal Reserve system, 59-61, 73-74,
  79, 116
Federal Trade Commission, 59-60, 61-
  62, 75-76
Filene, Lincoln, 87
Filene, William, 84
Fine, Sidney, 66
Fiscal and monetary controls, 61, 70,
  128, 160-163, 170, 179. See also
  Federal Reserve system
Foreign aid, 138-142, 154
Foreign investments, 96, 107, 110-111,
  114-115, 119, 162
Foreign policy, 137-142, 182
Forgan, James A., 60
France, 59, 107, 109-110, 112

Freedom, 5-6, 8, 66
  erosion of, 3, 10, 14-18, 47
Free-market conservatism, 13-17, 44, 47,
  70, 152
  on government bias, 21
  theory of state, 30, 153-154
Free markets/limited government ideal,
  3, 9-10, 18, 49
Frei, Edwardo, 140-141
Friedman, Milton, 3, 10-11, 13-14, 17,
  49-50
Future options, 175-187

Galbraith, John Kenneth, 96, 102, 130
Gary, Eldridge, 58
General Electric Corp., 71, 77, 86, 102
General Motors Corp., 83, 94
German Ideology, The (Marx & Engels),
  59
Germany, 59, 82, 101
  and world capitalism, 107, 109-110,
    112
Gladden, Washington, 67
Glass, Carter, 60
Goldwater, Barry, 71
Gompers, Samuel, 62, 85-86, 105
Government spending, 1-5, 128-134
  deficits and inflation, 165-166, 169
  social programs, 142-151, 154-155
  see also Foreign aid; Military spending;
    Structural bias; Subsidization
Great Depression, 61, 67, 70-79 passim,
  160, 166
  labor legislation, 82-88, 103
  riots and disorder, 72-73, 79-81, 148-149
  social legislation, 79-82, 88
  and war, 109
Greece, 138, 140, 142

Hanna, Mark, 62, 85-87
Harriman, Henry, 77, 81
Harriman, W. A., 81
Harriman, W. I., 87
Hay, John, 113
Hayek, Frederick, 3, 13-14
Health care industry, 12, 131
Heilbroner, Robert, 183-184
Heller, Walter, 170
Hillman, Sidney, 86
Holding companies, 52, 54
Hoover, Herbert, 75-76, 79
Housing industry, 11, 131, 136
Hull, Cordell, 84
Huntington, Samuel, 16, 180

Ideological domination, 34-36
Imperialism (economic), 110-116,
  116-120, 137-142

Income distribution, 80-81, 143-144, 165
Income tax, 11
Individualism, 6, 8, 35, 66, 146, 148
Indonesia, 140
Industrial revolution, 8, 51-53, 66, 99, 107, 128
Inequality, system of:
   in capitalism, 130-132, 172
   income distribution, 143, 165
   state as instrumental in, 11-12, 130, 154-155
   and welfare, 145, 148, 151
Inflation, 18, 61, 127, 129
   in late capitalism, 160, 163-165, 167-169, 181
Infrastructural spending, 133-134, 155
Insurance industry, 135
Intellectuals, 10, 75
   procapitalist, 172-173, 180
   and socialism, 14-15, 21, 153
Intraclass conflicts, 42, 135-137
Interdependency in world capitalism, 162-163
Interest groups, 136-137. *See also* Pluralism
Interest rates, 61, 162
International Monetary Fund (IMF), 179-180
Interstate Commerce Act, 55, 62, 79
Interlocking, 95
Intervention (government), *see* Government spending; Regulation
Investments:
   contradiction and collapse, 164-167
   and corporate capitalism, 97-103, 127-129
   see also Government spending
"Invisible hand" concept, 7-8, 186
Iran, 138, 142, 179
Irrationalities of capitalism, 34, 173-175, 186. *See also* Contradictions of capitalism

James, William, 66
Japan, 107-110, 114, 161-162. *See also* Trilateral Commission
Jefferson, Thomas, 3
Jews, 182, 184
Johnson, Lyndon, 20
Judiciary, 14, 16, 153
Judis, John, 171
Jungle, The (Sinclair), 58-59

Kennedy, John, 20
Kerry, Edward, 141-142
Keynes, John Maynard, 128

Keynesian economics, 128-130, 167, 170
Kolko, Gabriel, 65, 116, 137
Korea, 119, 138

Labor, 12, 20, 52, 62, 119, 127
   as commodity, 32-34, 38, 130, 142, 165
   division of and state role, 33, 35-36, 38-39
   in late capitalism, 159, 165-166
   New Deal legislation, 70, 77-78, 80, 82-88
   welfare, and low-wage, 148, 150-151, 164-165
   see also Employment; Unemployment; Unionism; Working class
LaFollette, Robert, 20
Laissez-faire capitalism, 49-52, 71, 87, 175
   versus corporate capitalism, 38
   and role of state, 57, 151, 174
Laissez-faire theory, 5-9, 13, 20, 49-50, 75
   and state intervention, 65-67
Laos, 138, 142, 161
Lasch, Christopher, 154-155
Late (or advanced) capitalism, 160-168
   and government, 169-171
   irrationalities, 173-174
   legitimacy problem, 171-174
   see also Trilateral Commission
Latin America, 108-110, 139-142
Laws of motion of capitalist mode of production, 37. *See also* Mode of production
Legitimacy, 171-174, 180
Lewis, John L., 83, 117
Local government, 63-64, 72, 83
Location of industry, 98-99, 127
Locke, John, 3, 17, 49, 607
Long, Huey, 80, 149
Low, Seth, 62
Lundeen bill, 80-81

McNamara, Robert, 139
Madison, James, 22, 108
Mandel, Ernest, 50
Marxist theory of state, 29-44
   versus non-Marxist theories, 152-154
   and profits, 167
   and surplus value, 133
   understanding of U.S. government, 42-44
Marx, Karl, 7, 112, 155, 164, 167, 169
Mature corporate capitalism:
   discussed, 92-120
   social impact, 97-103
   state role, 126-137

tensions within, 136, 170-171
and world capitalism, 106-120, 161-163
work force and unemployment, 103-106, 142-151
see also Contradictions of capitalism; Imperialism; Late capitalism
Meat-packing industry, 58-59
Medicaid and Medicare, 12
Medium and small business:
and corporations, 59-63 *passim,* 99, 165-166
failure rate, 143
and New Deal, 71, 78, 87
Mercantilism, 7, 65
Mergers, 54, 95
Military spending, 5, 70, 109, 165
need for, 130-132, 136
and strategic materials, 118
Minimal state, 50-51, 65
Minorities, 63, 106, 143
Mitchell, John, 62
Mode of production:
capitalist, 33-36, 164, 170
global concept, 31-33
and labor power, 142-144
U.S. historical development of, 48-67, 93, 152
variations in, 37-40, 42
see also Production
Moley, Raymond, 73
Mondale, Walter, 182
Monopoly, 58, 61, 97
Monopoly capitalism, *see* Mature corporate capitalism
Morgan, J. P., 54, 60, 62, 87
Multinational corporations, 107, 114-119
and U.S. foreign policy, 137-142
see also Trilateral Commission

National Association of Manufacturers, 59, 71, 81, 87
National Civic Federation (NCF), 61-62, 71, 82, 84-85
National Industrial Recovery Act (NIRA), 75-79, 84, 87
Natural law theory, 6-9
Neoconservative revival, 182
New Deal, 47-48, 67, 109, 149
First, 72-78
saving of capitalism, 70-71
Second, 78
New Freedom, 66, 79
Nixon administration, 141, 161

O'Connor, James, 111
Oil boycott, 161-163

Oil industry, 54, 102, 115, 118-119
break-up of, 135-136
Oligopoly, 96-97
Opinion polls, 3, 105, 146, 171
Organization of Petroleum Exporting Countries (OPEC), 161, 163, 168
Over-capacity/underconsumption concept, 166
Overproduction, 34, 76, 116-117, 127, 137
Ownership of means of production, 32-36, 154-155
and state role, 35-42, 130-132

Pacific area, 110, 112
Parenti, Michael, 184-185
Passive state concept, 5-11
Pennsylvania, 56-57, 72, 80
Pension and welfare funds, 95, 105
Periphery states, 39, 111-112
"comprador" classes, 138, 140-142, 179
U.S. and, 113-120
Perkins, Frances, 80
Philippines, 108, 138
"Philips curve," 167
Piven, Francis Fox, 148-151
Pluralism, 44
discussed, 21-24, 30, 152-154
Police and repression, 51, 144, 148-149, 183-184
Political theories:
antistatism, 5-11
fascism, 183-185
free-market conservatism, 13-17, 30
Marxist, 30-42
materialist individualism, 146
pluralism, 21-24, 30
reform liberalism, 17-21, 30
socialism, 185-187
Politicians, 9, 15, 21, 63-64, 153
Politics:
business, and local reform, 63-65
in pluralism, 22-24
and working class, 105-106
"Poor laws," 9. *See also* Poverty
Population control, 179
Populism, 47, 55
Positive state:
crises of, 159-175, 180
definition and terminology, 3-4, 25, 67
discussion of, 126-155
future options, 180-187
logic of, 155
see also Late capitalism; Mature corporate capitalism
Poulantzas, Nicholas, 43

Poverty, 143-144, 146
 and government bias, 11-12, 48, 154
Press, 180-181, 183
Prices, 52, 54, 58, 61-63, 75-78
 and oligopoly, 96-97, 102-103
 and stagflation, 167-168
Private property, 11, 21, 35
 in America, 6, 9, 49
 government protection of, 5, 10, 50,
  57, 71, 154-155
 rights, 10, 18, 35
Production, 78, 103, 128, 186
 adverse costs of, 134-135
 and consumption, 96-97, 102, 166
 excess capacity, 127, 137, 166
 see also Mode of production; Overproduction
Productivity, 142, 164-165, 167, 181
Profits, 33-34
 and corporations, 52-53, 55, 58, 78,
  103, 166-167
 government spending, 130-135
 and investment, 128-129
 multinationals, 116, 118-119
 versus socialist principles, 186
 of top 100 firms, 94-95
Progressivism, 47-48, 58-67, 88
Proletariat, 37, 49, 155
Protestant churches, 19-20, 66
Protestant Reformation, 6, 8
Public opinion:
 faith in authority, 11-12, 171-174
 and NIRA, 78
 on poverty and race, 144, 146, 184
 and reform, 58-59, 63
 traditional view of government, 5-11
 working class business values, 105

Racism, 144, 184
Rand, Ayn, 3
Rand, James, 81
Raw materials, 96-97, 102, 107, 112
 U.S. consumption of, 107, 117-119,
  126, 137, 139
 increasing problems with, 163, 168,
  178-179
Reconstruction Finance Corp. (RFC),
  73, 181
Reform liberalism, 14-15, 44, 47, 70
 theory discussed, 17-21, 30, 152-154
Reforms (U.S. economy), 47-52
 legislation, 55, 58-64
 local politics, 63-64
 meaning of, 64-67, 88
 see also New Deal
Regressive programs, 12, 81, 145
Regulating the Poor, 148-151
Regulation of business, 3-4, 19, 128-132, 162

beginnings, 47, 54, 59-67
 consequences, 127-151
 federal agencies, 11-12, 62, 136-137
 New Deal, 70, 72-78
Relative surplus value, 133
Republican Party, 2-3, 9
Research and development, 127, 133-
  135, 155
Rockefeller, David, 139, 176, 181
Rockefeller, John D., 54, 116
Rogers, William, 141
Rohatyn, Felix, 181
Roosevelt, Franklin, 20, 71-80
Rosen, Steven, 140
"Runaway shop," 166

Section 7a, NIRA, 78, 80, 83-84, 87
Semiperiphery state, 39, 49
Servan-Schreiber, J. J., 96
Sherman Anti-Trust Act, 55, 61-62
  176
Sinclair, Upton, 58
Size of government, 1-5
Sklar, Martin, 172
Smith, Adam, 3, 7, 17, 34, 96, 186
Smith, Al, 16
"Social Gospel," 19, 66, 75
Social Darwinism, 9, 66, 71, 146
Socialism, 14-15, 20, 67, 70, 176
 principles, 98, 185-187
 and unionism, 85, 108
 and world capitalism, 107, 117, 138
Social Security Act, 79-82
Social Security system, 12, 70, 144, 149
Society:
 authoritarian, 174-185
 control of and civil order, 50-51, 144-
  145, 148-150, 183-184
 cooperative, 66-67, 75, 82-88
 and corporate capitalism, 93, 97-103,
  137-138, 171-174
 economic theories of, 14-24
 government role, 127, 130-135, 150
 Marxist theory and, 30-42
 New Deal laws, 70, 79-88
 socialist, 186-187
 see also Welfare system
Southern states, 56, 98-99, 106, 149
Spain, 112-113, 138
Spencer, Herbert, 3, 9, 17, 67, 146
Stagflation, 167-169, 178
Stagnation, 163-165, 167, 170, 181,
  186
Standard of living, 143-144, 147, 160
 decline in, 164, 167, 169, 182
Standard Oil Company, 54, 58, 94
State governments, 4-5, 62-64, 72, 99
 and welfare, 145, 149-151

Steel industry, 58, 119
Steering capability of government, 169-171, 174, 180
Stock market, 72, 97-98
Structural bias, 11-12, 17, 21
  understanding of, 151-155
Subsidization, 12, 51, 57, 78, 169
  agriculture, 12, 74-75, 79
  and diseconomies, 134-135
Sumner, William Graham, 9, 146
Supreme Court, 61, 78
"Surplus absorption," 129
Surplus value extraction, 33, 38, 42, 56, 164
  competitive versus monopoly sectors, 106
  and imperialism, 110-114, 160
  "relative," 133
Sweezy, Paul, 129
Swope, Gerard, 71, 77, 81, 86

Taiwan, 119, 138
Taxes, 11, 79, 128-129, 145, 179
  corporations, 94-95, 134-135
Taylor, Myron, 71
Teagle, Walter, 81
Technology, 53, 127, 164-165
  and unemployment, 127, 142, 165
Textile industry, 78, 99
Third World, 107, 114-115, 118, 126
  cartels and prices, 163, 168
  revolts, 160-161
  see also Trilateral Commission
Thoreau, H. D., 6
Totalitarianism, 14, 183-185
Townsend, Francis, 80, 149
Trade associations, 62-63, 75-77, 136.
  See also Export trade
Transportation, 49, 52-53, 66, 95, 173
  government spending, 131-134, 155
Trilateral Commission, 176-185, 187
Truman, David, 22
Trusts, 52, 54, 65, 76, 95
Turner, Frederick Jackson, 108

Unemployment, 34, 116, 155
  in corporate capitalism, 127-128, 142-143, 160, 165-167, 171
  during Depression, 72, 77, 80-81, 83 148
  insurance, 62, 77, 86

Unionism, 48, 143, 148, 168
  beginnings, 56-57, 80, 82-88
  and corporations, 104-106, 126
  and NIRA, 78, 83-84
  see also Collective bargaining
United States Steel Corp., 54, 58, 71
Use value, 34

Vietnam, 138, 142, 161-163

Wages, 104, 171, 181. See also Low-wage labor
Wagner, Robert, 20, 84
Wagner Labor Relations Act, 79, 82-88
Wallace, George, 2
War, 161, 166
  first world, 65, 75-76, 79, 86, 108-109
  second world, 61, 71, 88, 92-93, 100, 106-107, 109-110, 160
Ward, Lester, 66
War Industries Board, 75-76, 86
Welfare state, 66-67, 70
Welfare system, 3, 9, 62
  Depression relief, 70, 72-75, 79, 88, 148-149
  need for, 127, 154-155
  recipients and benefits, 144-151, 181
Williams, William Appelman, 113
Wilson Woodrow, 20, 61-62, 66, 75, 117
Wisconsin Plan, 82
Witte, Edwin, 82
Wolfe, Alan, 171
Women, 106, 143
Woodcock, Leonard, 182
Working class, 42, 49, 56, 63, 167
  class inequality, 130-131
  divisions in, 93, 106, 120
  job education, 99-101, 155
  and politics, 63, 106
  see also Labor
World Bank, 179-180
World capitalist system, 39-40, 42, 48, 128, 152
  interdependency, 162-163
  U.S. foreign policy, 137-142
  U.S. supremacy, 93, 96, 106-110, 126, 160-162, 170
  see also Imperialism; Multinational corporations; Trilateral Commission